THE
UNTUTORED
EYE

THE UNTUTORED EYE

Childhood in the Films of Cocteau, Cornell, and Brakhage

Marjorie Keller

RUTHERFORD · MADISON · TEANECK
FAIRLEIGH DICKINSON UNIVERSITY PRESS
LONDON AND TORONTO:
ASSOCIATED UNIVERSITY PRESSES

Associated University Presses
440 Forsgate Drive
Cranbury, NJ 08512

Associated University Presses
25 Sicilian Avenue
London WC1A 2QH, England

Associated University Presses
2133 Royal Windsor Drive
Unit 1
Mississauga, Ontario
Canada L5J 1K5

The paper used in this publication meets the requirements of the
American National Standard for Permanence of Paper
for Printed Library Materials Z39.48-1984.

Library of Congress Cataloging-in-Publication Data

Keller, Marjorie, 1950–
  The untutored eye.

  Bibliography: p.
  Includes index.
  1. Children in motion pictures.   2. Cocteau, Jean,
1889–1963—Views on childhood.   3. Cornell, Joseph—
Views on childhood.   4. Brakhage, Stan—Views on
childhood.   I. Title.
PN1995.9.C4K4   1986   791.43'09'09352054   85-47628
ISBN 0-8386-3242-4 (alk. paper)

Printed in the United States of America

For P.A.S.

CONTENTS

ACKNOWLEDGMENTS

The writing of this book coincides with my friendship with Susan Greene. Its premises are those we have shared for fifteen years. Her interest in film and poetry, art and music fostered my own. It has been her steady encouragement that allowed me to give shape to ideas generated out of our experiences together as students. With her I met Saul Levine, who taught me how to make films, and Fred Camper, who, unknowingly, taught me how to watch them. I thank all three.

For their valuable help in researching and gathering the material that follows I thank Mrs. Elizabeth Benton, Joseph Cornell's sister; Lynda Roscoe Hartigan; Rick Stanberry and Hollis Melton at Anthology Film Archives; Robert Haller; Lauretta Harvey; and my sister, Sarah Ann Filippini. The University of Rhode Island kindly offered funds and time for my research. For sharing her insights into Cornell's *Children's Party* trilogy, I am grateful to Rebecca Sky Sitney. And for sharing his reading in the literature of psychoanalysis, I am grateful to Dr. Leon Balter. His generous bibliographic suggestions clarified and directed my work time and again.

Jay Leyda, William Simon, Stuart Liebman, Lindley Hanlon and Tony Pipolo read the manuscript in its formative stages. Each was an attentive and helpful reader. Annette Michelson, whose writing is a beacon to any hopeful critic, challenged and encouraged me to publish this book. And finally, Noël Carroll has been a guide, an enthusiast, a grammarian, a logician, and in general, more help than I ever hoped to find in preparing what follows. I thank him for his unflagging support.

THE
UNTUTORED
EYE

INTRODUCTION

So that even though my entire method were chimerical
and false, my observations could still be of profit.
J. J. Rousseau

In his 1977 volume of *Film Biographies,* Stan Brakhage makes the following comment on artistic creation in the films of Chaplin:

> For that, one must accept the haunt as real and opt, in oneself, totally for the
> world of The Child . . . which is always, in every instant, a whole world—as
> holes are, as in holy. In moments, this happens in Chaplin's work—in the
> stances, usually, of Dance . . . and/or Dream—Surrealism thru the Ballets
> Russes freeing movie-makers of the times as surely as Frued [*sic*] freed prose;
> but the Dance! . . . the Dance is The Thing!—Charlie's dance in *or* out of
> Dream.[1]

In this dense, free-associational segment, Brakhage creates a subtext for
the collected essays. The lines come at the end of a discussion of the
necessities of the art-making process, whose first criterion is to "opt . . .
totally for the world of The Child." He joins by proximity, the child
with creativity and with the figure of Freud. Misspelled, one assumes, to
make the alliteration more fluid, Freud is posited as the liberator of
twentieth-century language. An equation begins to emerge: The child is
to artistic production as Freudian psychoanalysis is to literature.

A third figure is submerged in this text, beyond the central one of
Chaplin. It is Cocteau. "Surrealism thru the Ballets Russes" invokes
Cocteau, who claimed inspiration from Diaghilev. Brakhage, like many
of the American avant-garde, confused Cocteau with the surrealists. A
great many films have been generated from that confusion. One strain
of them is the subject of this study.

This work adds Joseph Cornell to the list of filmmakers who found
childhood to be an inspiration and subject for their cinemas. Although

the influence of Cocteau on Cornell and the influence of both on Brakhage are important, my aim is to outline, in detail, the individual filmmaker's treatment of childhood. First, Cocteau's writings elaborate how childhood is represented in his films. Then, Cornell's boxes, collages, and the literary influences on them aid the analysis of the imagery and structure of his films. Finally, four Brakhage films representing different periods of his career are examined in order to show how his concept of childhood has changed. Throughout, the literature of psychoanalysis and Piaget's psychology of children helps elucidate the films.

I have deliberately chosen a thematic approach, in contradistinction to other critics of avant-garde film, such as Malcolm Le Grice. In his *Abstract Film and Beyond* he studiously denies the importance of thematic content in avant-garde film. He proposes instead the history of avant-garde film as a variation on structure, thereby minimizing the importance of the figures about whom this book is written. He does not deal with either Cocteau or Cornell. He is unwilling to analyze imagery or the content created through editing in Brakhage's films.

Other critics of avant-garde film are more useful than Le Grice, but limited by their choice of method as well. P. Adams Sitney's *Visionary Film: The American Avant-Garde, 1943–78* acknowledges a number of themes and developments from the French avant-garde to contemporary American filmmakers. His central concern, however, is in linking interpretations of films to form genres and genres to form an evolutionary history. The thematic links are sometimes lost in the grand scheme of genre. The difficulty with his proposition is that in avant-garde film, genres are more unstable than he would allow. Sheldon Renan and David Curtis have provided sketches of history. Their choice of format inhibits in-depth analysis of specific films or recurrent themes. The central contribution of both *An Introduction to the American Underground Film* and *Experimental Cinema* is to bring to light a number of filmmakers whose work would otherwise go unrecorded in film history. Annette Michelson's numerous essays on avant-garde film are primarily directed toward the relationship of the films to cultural history. Her work focuses on the central aesthetic and polemic concerns of the films and filmmakers. Finally, in his journalistic writings, Parker Tyler never had the opportunity to elaborate on the themes to which he provocatively alluded. With the exception of his case for eroticism in the cinema, his imaginative insights into the thematic content of avant-garde films were never explored in depth.

But not just any theme has been chosen as a guide through the work of these three filmmakers. Childhood is a particularly central theme in a tradition where artists have used the film medium to reflect on their own uniqueness. The confusion of the terms *personal* and *avant-garde* in reference to these films is not unfounded. A large number of the films that make up the avant-garde tradition are autobiographical, self-meditative, diaristic, or otherwise personally inflected works. One of the cornerstones of the movement has been the freedom for an individual artist to apply himself to the film medium as a self-exploratory tool. Certainly, since Cocteau, this has been the case.

There are a number of filmmakers who might easily be included in a study of childhood in the avant-garde film. The work of James Broughton, Larry Jordan, Ken Jacobs, Harry Smith, and recently Jonas Mekas touch on the theme of childhood. Each filmmaker inflects the theme in his own way, and much could be gained by studying the particularities of rendition. Cocteau, Cornell, and Brakhage were selected for study because they offer three distinct ways in which to approach the central theme of childhood. They are representative, to a great degree, of the work of the others.

A number of facts leads one to look at Cocteau's films from the point of view of his writings. In all of his creative endeavors he considered himself a poet: of theater, the novel, journalism, and film. Moreover, his work in film remains vitally close to literary sources. He relied a great deal on the Romantic tradition, especially in *Blood of a Poet* (1930). *Beauty and the Beast* (1945) was generated from the fairy tale. And he was indebted to his own theatrical Orphism in the making of the film version.

The elaborate nexus of meaning generated by Cocteau's verbal structures can be found to be mimicked by cinematic ones. Of particular importance in light of the theme of childhood is the erection of a hierarchy of seeing, simultaneously based on verbal and visual power relationships. He uses filmic structure as he uses literary form, in an obsessive reformulation of childhood perceptions of his own relationship to his parents. Psychoanalytical studies of artists have been particularly useful as an aid in understanding the mechanism underlying Cocteau's films. Freud's essay "Leonardo da Vinci" and Abraham's "Giovanni Segantini" offer insights into the recurrence of childhood trauma in the lives of artists. Their evidence comes from the journals and works of literature and art, as mine does. Finally, Cocteau had an eminence in America he did not have in Europe. His importance was felt profoundly by Cornell and Brakhage.

Cornell's films have been prefaced with a discussion of the imagery in his boxes and collages, and of his literary influences. His films are overwhelmingly made up of images from other cultural sources. They are cinematic collages made from the same impulse that inspired his other collages and boxes. The consistent use of iconography from one film to the next is conducive to thematic interpretation. He depicts birds, astrological imagery, travel, and hotels obsessively and in many different contexts.

Cornell admired Cocteau and idolized Lee Miller (Cocteau's female star in *Blood of a Poet*), and he had an intense fascination with the literature that inspired Cocteau. Romantic poetry and prose influenced many of his boxes, collages, and some of the films. He stands between the French and American avant-garde traditions. His later influence on Stan Brakhage makes him an excellent figure to mediate the treatment of childhood from Cocteau to Brakhage.

Among his repeated iconographic elements is the ambivalent figure of the androgynous child. In order to analyze this figure, the work of Freud, Abraham, and in particular, Fenichel was especially useful. Cornell's work stands on the same foundation as Cocteau's when seen with the assistance of the interpretative method of psychoanalysis. In addition to the psychoanalytic sources, I analyze passages selected by Cornell in the writings of Jean Piaget to elucidate the relationship between his editing structure and the structure of children's logic and narration.

Brakhage sees himself as a demythologizer of childhood, even though children have a privileged position in his phenomenological scrutiny of the world around him. Of the three filmmakers, he is the one who uses Freudian discourse the most in his teaching and writing in order to debunk notions of "happy" childhood. Brakhage uses Freud (and Freud's follower, Otto Rank) as a theoretical backdrop to his film aesthetics, to support his own valorization of raw perception, and to aggrandize his own creativity (in substantially the same manner as Cocteau). Although I do not emphasize the psychoanalytic methodology in Brakhage's films, it is important to note that it is intimately related to his artistic practices.

The profusion and variety of Brakhage's work permits a view of the theme of childhood over twenty years of filmmaking. In a current treatment of Brakhage's shifting child obsession, *Murder Psalm,* there is an extension of his earlier films on childhood. The optimism and idealism of the *Songs* is no longer present in his representation of children. His early vision, in which his children represented his aspirations as a filmmaker, changed into a bitter reflection on American culture and the human condition within it. The child is the barometer of the shift in Brakhage's outlook.

Brakhage acknowledges his debts to Cocteau and Cornell. He collaborated with Cornell at a formative stage of his career. Yet within the same sweeping gesture of acknowledgment, Brakhage polemicized against their idealized vision of childhood. As the father of five children and a meticulous observer of child behavior, Brakhage assumed a privileged stance as a deromanticizer of childhood.

Cocteau and Cornell bear a relatively uncritical relationship to French Romanticism and the Romantic movement in general. Wordsworth's depiction of the progressive loss of a natural sympathy with the world from childhood on in his autobiographical "Ode (Intimations of Immortality from Recollections of Early Childhood)" is the model for the filmmaker's sensibility. The *Bildungsromane* of Rousseau, Nerval, Novalis, and Goethe provide a source for imagery that can be followed in the work of Cocteau and Cornell. Both the antithetical notion of education (as seen in the schoolboy sequence of *Blood of a Poet*) and the ambivalent sexuality of youth (the hermaphrodite of *Blood of a Poet* and the boy-girl figures of Cornell's work) can be traced to European Romantic literature. The heroes of the poems and novels are on perpetual quests to avoid institutionalized education, and on their journeys encounter girls dressed like boys who inevitably become love objects. Cornell's library was replete with this literature, including such variants as Balzac's *Seraphita* and Virginia Woolf's *Orlando.* This literature affected Brakhage as well. However, his appreciation of modernist poetics, his Freudian biases, and his own experience as a father belied the effect of Romanticism to some degree—reworking the theme of childhood, casting back the period of "innocence" to the birth trauma, and including developed notions of sexuality in early childhood.

This book, then, marshals a great many resources to help elucidate some versions of childhood in avant-garde film. While the film styles of Cocteau, Cornell, and Brakhage are all very different from one another, and the personal obsessions that guide those styles are distinct, it is possible to draw the three filmmakers into the same tradition by examining the background of their films. The conclusions arrived at in close film analysis cohere as the iconography and metaphorical implications of childhood reappear in the work of each man. The uniqueness of each filmmaker *and* his contribution to the formulation of childhood in film are both set out below. The fusion of the two is the work at stake here.

1

JEAN COCTEAU
Concealed Admissions

The Literary Sources of the Concept of the Child

How does one come to understand the specific attributes of childhood according to Cocteau? Nowhere in his poems, plays, essays, novels, or films is there any thorough attempt at definition. Instead he offers hints, allusions, and maxims surrounding and approaching a definition but never elaborating one. All of these references, however, fall into three categories: memories of his own childhood, ethical precepts valorizing childhood as a superior state of being, and the representation of childhood as a mode of perception. Although Cocteau does not limit each kind of statement to a particular genre or medium, one finds a recurrence of autobiographical childhood stories in his most public works, especially in his journalism and films, while the ethic of childhood occurs most often in his poems, plays, and essays. Childhood, as a symbol of a special mode of perception, is found most clearly only in the films. There, Cocteau moves from a judgmental, aphoristic tone to a phenomenological one. He presents childhood as a stance, as a way of seeing. Particularly in *Blood of a Poet* (1930), *Orpheus* (1950), and *Beauty and the Beast* (1945), Cocteau offers an illustration of the perceptual mode that he ascribes to children. It is through the films that one comes to understand Cocteau's equation of the poet and the child. The films equate metaphor and the imaginative process with objective reality. He uses cinematography and montage to make fantasies believable. It is also through the films that one can best explore the concerns that haunted Cocteau's lifework, those themes which were rooted in an obsessive reenactment of crucial childhood experiences. In order to understand Cocteau's relationship to childhood, it is necessary to look at his intentions in the making of films. It is only by studying Cocteau's failures to do what he claims, as well as acknowledging his real achievements, that an accurate interpretation of his use of childhood can be made.

On two occasions, Cocteau was given extended access to the popular news media—once for several months in *Paris-Midi* in 1919 and again in 1935 in *Le Figaro*. Both times he chose to write autobiographically. Those two sets of articles became, in their revised form, the two sources of Cocteau's life story; from *Paris-Midi* came *The White Paper (Carte blanche)*[1] and from *Le Figaro* came *Paris Album (Portraits-Souvenirs)*. Like most good journalism, they are both sketchily written, anecdotal, and directed to the readership of the papers. One comes away from them with no continuous or thorough sense of Cocteau's childhood, only with a few small highlights and insights into the pleasures of bourgeois upbringing. But they are by far the richest source of firsthand accounts in all Cocteau's oeuvre. The *Paris-Midi* articles tend to emphasize his late youth and early poetic career;[2] *Paris Album* his childhood.

Cocteau's idea of childhood, as opposed to his childhood memories, is given a forum primarily in his other written works. The poems, plays, and such essayistic works as *The Difficulty of Being (La difficulté d'être)* (1946), *The Hand of a Stranger (Journal d'un inconnu)* (1952), and *Opium* (1929) present childhood in many lights, but never as untroubledly and optimistically as his memoirs of his own life as a child. Cocteau poses the antagonism of children to the adult world, and the knowing or unknowing rebellion of children against social forms, as the foundation for his assertion that childhood is a morally superior state of being. One finds these opinions almost autobiographical. Their point of departure is generally Cocteau's own life.

The story of a boy called Dargelos is presented and recorded throughout Cocteau's oeuvre. Cocteau asserts the story is true. However, because of the repetition of and variation on this "fact" of his childhood, the story loses itself as autobiography and becomes a moral tale, an allegory. By fictionalizing the Dargelos account, Cocteau allows himself the freedom to assert his world view over reality. This assertion underlies all Cocteau's writing about himself and is crucial to his work as a filmmaker.

The True Lie

In 1935 Cocteau was given the opportunity to memorialize the Paris of his youth in a series of articles in *Le Figaro*. He used that occasion to gather recollections that form an autobiography of sorts, later collected as *Paris Album*. Though many of the anecdotes were not new to Cocteau's readers, it was the first time that he had united them and allowed them to form a life. He had, after all, over the course of twenty years, been writing poems, plays, and essays, and he had made a film. In all of these he had interspersed autobiographical detail with fiction. Yet it was in this public forum that he chose to describe his personal history most coherently. And though he went on to make films and to write using autobiographical references, *Paris Album* remains the most informative memoir Cocteau ever produced.

He begins with a disclaimer: "I am a lie that always tells the truth."[3] This is characteristic of every work that includes "facts" about Cocteau's life. His insistence on the validity of "the true lie" *("le vrai mensonge")* permits what follows to stretch the limits of objective truth through hyperbole, interpretation, and metaphor. He posits not only his work but his life as a fiction in order to achieve a greater, more encompassing truth. He regards autobiography as useful in only one way—to elucidate the poetic vocation. To that end he relates certain key incidents that remained significant in his memory as scenes of initiation into the life of the poet. He alluded to these events in many different works and public statements and, by repetition, convinced most of his biographers of their truth. Crosland, Brosse, and Phelps repeat Cocteau's version. Steegmuller, in the most comprehensive biography, attributes Cocteau's reluctance to offer more than quips and fictions about his life to the Aristotelian principle of the greater truth of myth. Steegmuller accurately points out the loophole of such a personal mythology: "A lie, even one that tells the truth, implies a truth that is not told."[4] Frederick Brown, in *An Impersonation of Angels,* is the most skeptical of Cocteau's own version of his life. Brown provides a great deal of evidence for Cocteau's fictionalizing as an adult by comparing his stories with other sources. Cocteau's version is often very far from the truth. As Brown tells it, the crucial gap in Cocteau's report of his life is the suicide of his father. It is indicative of a great deal of calculated misrepresentation. Jacques Brosse, in *Cocteau,* also makes a valuable analysis of the importance of Cocteau's father's suicide on the life and work of the artist. The repeated imagery of suicide and Cocteau's homosexuality are attributed to this event. It will be discussed in light of the films.

There seems little hope of finding out the accuracy of stories of Cocteau's childhood. Steegmuller sought accounts from friends and relatives, but their memories ranged over very different terrain from Cocteau's. His stories will be used as a base from which to analyze their function in the substructure of his work.

The issue for Cocteau is that his childhood foretold his life as a poet/artist. In order to make the childhood conform to his demands, Cocteau edits, distorts, and even invents his personal history. In his public persona, the poet had to have an appropriately formative past in order for his life to seem a cohesive work. He resorts to truth when it is the most convincing material for a story. He sees journalism as another form of literature and allows himself the liberty of invention there as well.

In *Paris Album*, Cocteau's earliest childhood is described briefly. His suburban home of Maisons-Laffitte, was twenty kilometers outside of Paris on the border of the Saint-Germain forest. The environs were filled with busts of Roman emperors, and the social world was magnified into mythological proportions in the boy's eyes:

> Suddenly, under an implacable sky, the virtuosos arrived in an uncovered cart, without a driver, the cart of Fantomas driven by the dead. The cart of virtuosos. Melpomen or some instrumental allegory enthroned invisibly on the seat.[5]

The classical world and mythology, invoked by the presence of the busts, transformed his perception of such an arrival. What is hidden to a small child by the low angle of his perspective changed the unseen driver into an invisible one and thus changed the event from a visually obscured one to an imaginary one. And in an aside in *My Contemporaries*, the terrors of a low visual perspective were not limited to the actual world, but were extended to the imaginary reality of representation also. Cocteau was frightened of an illustration to a Jules Verne novel depicting a doctor pointing out the moon to a child.

Yet the powerlessness and terror of being small was coupled with the advantages of compactness and unobtrusiveness. Because of his size, Cocteau could find particular aural pleasure in lying in the lap of his German governess, listening to the sounds of her digestion. It is a vivid memoir of Cocteau's, one of the few of unadulterated pleasure:

> Children go through life in a state of half-asleep. Fräulein Josephine used to stretch me out on her knees as I curled up under the table napkin and digested my soup. How delightful it was, from under the napkin, in the half-sleep of childhood, to listen to her eating.[7]

Whether the half-sleep or the womblike nature of the governess's dressed lap reinforced his memory, the resultant story is told as a primal memory. The child is secure in its world, regarding the events outside it with both awe and delight. Cocteau would have been only two or three at the time when he was able to fit comfortably in someone's lap, yet the nature of memory is consistent with that of the stories of his later childhood. These all center on a rather passive self, surrounded by a world that observes him.

Two of the longest stories describe the qualities of this self-contained state that were later to be meaningful to the poet/man. In describing the Parisian apartments of his parents and grandparents, and his grandfather's passion for chamber music, Cocteau indicates the advantages of

distance, observation, and imagination over participation in the complex adult world. This alienation was enforced by adults, yet in Cocteau's telling it is willful.

> I can remember our apartment and our bedrooms and far, far away, in
> another world, in some unreal and fabulous region [*zone*], the apartment
> where my grandfather possessed a silver bath resonant as a gong and filled
> with shoes and books. He collected Greek busts, drawings by Ingres, pic-
> tures by Delacroix, Florentine coins, ministers' autographs, masks from
> Antinous, vases from Cyprus and Stradivarius violins.[7]

Cocteau continues to describe his grandfather's possessions, his
musician friends, and the secret game he played, seizing power over
adults without their knowledge:

> The great game for my cousins and myself was to crawl the entire length of
> the ceremonial staircase which linked the two floors together. The magic,
> which, I repeat, situated this apartment outside space, made this staircase a
> place unto itself, entirely self-sufficient, its supreme limit being a gate which
> my grandfather had fitted to stop us from falling down.
> The game consisted then in waiting for Sarasate to arrive, hiding behind a
> halberd standard lamp in red plush which was used in the "poor prisoner"
> game, and while later he tidied his hair in front of the mirror in the ante-
> room, seizing the opportunity of closing the gate and obtaining the picture
> "Animal Tamer in his Cage."
> While he was behind bars we thought that Sarasate, . . . looked like a lion
> dressed up as a lion tamer.[8]

The parameters of this distance of childhood from adulthood are outlined in the two parts of this story of 45, rue de la Bruyère. There is on
the one hand the terrifying and exotic "zone" that, simply by its existence outside the familiar bounds of the nuclear family, is transformed
into another world, filled with strange and forbidden objects. In the
other story, the powerlessness implied in the first is translated into
power through the game of representation. By silent and unseen trickery, the old man Sarasate is trapped in the visual field of the child who
peers through the bars of a grate, as an infant might through a crib—a
significant image for any consideration of Cocteau's scopophilia.

A second major incident that was to be important to Cocteau's future
vocation again took the form of voyeurism. The child sat and watched
his mother dress for the theater.

> I watched my mother dress. A cloud of perfume and mauve powder scented
> the room and the semi-darkness between the chintzes with their multi-
> colored designs and exotic trees and birds of paradise. Beyond the open door
> the brilliant gas-light in the dressing-room illuminated the wardrobe and the
> mirror which reflected the scene in greater beauty and depth. It was in this

mirror that I watched the preparations.[9]

The lengthy description continues as the young Cocteau associated his mother's costume, multiplied a thousandfold, with the essence of theater. The hyperbolic rendering of the pretheater rite is underlined by his imaginative removal from it. He watches her dress indirectly, reflected in the mirror. This image remained with Cocteau throughout his life. As unaware as he was of the hidden motivations for his work, he did acknowledge the influence of this childhood memory. In writing of *The Human Voice (La voix humaine)* (1929) he says:

> Perhaps the idea of having only one character on the stage came from my childhood. I used to see my mother, wearing a décolleté dress, leave for the Comédie-Française. Mounet-Sully performed *La Grève des Forgerons* and *L'Enigme* by Hervieu. He acted this monologue surrounded by extras consisting of the Sociétaires dressed as judges, members of the jury, and policemen. I used to dream about this theatre and I did not suspect that, with its gilt and its spectacle, it was so close to Guignol. I wondered how a single actor could act a play.[10]

It is significant that Cocteau did not doubt that a single actress could enact a play for a single viewer just as his mother did for him. The "play" before the play was the real influence on the form of *The Human Voice*.

The origin of a typical image in Cocteau's films also comes from this devoted attention to his mother's preparations.

> This at least is what I imagined, during the ceremonial fitting of the long gloves which were so difficult to put on; they were like dead skins which began to live, cling and take shape, as each finger was fitted in turn.[11]

His mother put on gloves. Her final gesture before going out remained for Cocteau a crucial image. Either because it was the last act before he was abandoned in favor of the theater, or because of the erotic power of the sight of flaccid gloves becoming full and shapely—erect, as it were—that he put that image, intact, into the film *Orpheus*, including even the mirror.

The childhood descriptions of framing the world, through either the bars of the gate or the rectangular mirror, are the most obvious evidence of Cocteau's early cinematic concerns. The world seen through a frame is one way of describing cinema.[12] The passivity and secretiveness involved in watching the adult world played a large part in Cocteau's attraction to film (in his equation of film and childhood). Cocteau normally uses the term *zone* to describe a purgatorial afterlife. Here the term simply denotes the unfamiliar, forbidden, and feared. To the child, any place outside the home is terrible. Yet to look at such a place, like looking through bars or into a mirror, is an exciting and long-lasting memory; even when there is no engagement with what is seen, looking itself is a potent activity. One can encounter and even transform the feared place by cleverly watching.

His relationship to that world was much more problematic than his home life, but his pattern of behavior was the same. Activities that could be watched were the most beloved. Those which required active participation, and especially discipline, were despised. He watched the shadow theater at the Théâtre Robert Houdin, and he watched movies (on the same program at the Robert Houdin, and also at the Lumière Cinématographe). He described these activities consistently with the word *spectacle,* the only word that unites his sense of children's perception of the world and the specific events that interested him.

> Good heavens, how few entertainments there were in those days! As children we were intoxicated with unending spectacles, but the poor grown-ups . . . disliked staying at home and did not possess our mysterious resources.[13]

He goes on to list a variety of entertainments and theatricals performed in Paris in the last decade of the nineteenth century. Those "unending spectacles" were all the events of home life that

> illuminate the angle from which a child glimpses grownups, on all fours, behind pantry doors and on staircases, with eyes that admit only poetic intensity.[14]

In *Paris Album,* he described the racetrack at Maisons-Laffitte as "the real spectacle, the show we most enjoyed."[15] He ended his remarks: "All this created for childhood a realm calculated to flatter its illusions of living in places unique in all the world."[16] The uniqueness of the place did not stem from the use he made of it as a child, rather, from its eclectic decoration and assembly of characters. Similarly, he describes his experience attending the Palais de Glace with his cousins. He does not mention the feeling of skating: no cold, or speed, or pain at falling, or triumph at not. Again, one reads about the decor; a childlike but aesthetic description of "the monumental mint drop covered with ice shavings."[17] And he notices high society there, well-dressed men and even celebrities: Polaire, Colette. The most cherished moments were at the end of skating, when society arrived. The children were forbidden to stay and the greatest pleasure was derived from circumventing the prohibition.

Cocteau's memorable experiences at school seem to have been primarily social rather than academic. He describes himself as a bad student, expelled for insubordination at fifteen. The boarding school he was sent to as a boy left only negative memories. Power, authority, and punishment impressed themselves on him more than anything else.

> If I close my eyes, my school memories are vacant, even sinister . . .
>   I could describe . . . tortures: dormitories at dawn, mortal terrors of being questioned, attempts to crib from one's deskmate protecting himself behind walls of dictionaries, deluges of threats, discovery of indecent caricatures, cold sweats until the deliverance of the bell.[18]

Instruction, submission to authority, and discipline in study held no charm for Cocteau. They are, therefore, rebuked as part of childhood. In his idealized autobiography, teachers and authorities in general are enemies.

> It is no use, when a head empties as fast as it is filled, when a boy, set apart for secret tasks, tries to preserve his somnambulist's sleep only to be roused with a start at the far edge of his dream by well-meaning murderers.[19]

(Later in Cocteau's writings, women will join teachers and authorities as murderers, "killers of poet's children.")[20]

The two other aspects of school Cocteau recalls are group masturbation and the class bully, Dargelos. Discussion of the former is discreetly omitted from the *Paris Album*. He describes the masturbation most concretely in *The Difficulty of Being*.

> Everyone had a hole in his pocket, a damp handkerchief. Art classes especially inspired us, concealed behind the rampart of our drawing boards. . . . The classroom reeked of gas, chalk, and sperm. This amalgam revolted me.[21]

He goes on to describe himself as knowing instinctively that he was homosexual and links masturbation with Dargelos.

Cocteau makes no distinction between the schools he attended; he includes his early adolescence as part of his childhood experience, acknowledging his own immaturity. The Lycée Condorcet, the day school that Cocteau began attending when he was thirteen, is the location of his first encounter with Dargelos. In *Paris Album*, his discussion of the horrors of school is directly followed by his description of Dargelos, whom he observed at the "deliverance of the bell."[22] The description of Dargelos is filled with attraction and repulsion, exactly parallel to his way of representing masturbation.

> He was handsome, let me add: he had the beauty of an animal, of a tree, of a stream, that insolent beauty which is only heightened by filth, which seems unaware of itself, which turns to advantage its every resource and needs merely to appear in order to persuade.[23]

Later, Cocteau becomes even more frank about the same subject:

> His presence made me ill. I avoided Dargelos, and spied on him. I dreamed of some miracle which would draw his attention to me, dissolve his pride,

reveal the meaning of my attitude, which he must have taken for absurd prudery and which was merely an insane craving to please him.[24]

Like the previous pleasures of his childhood, Dargelos is something watched and something terrifying. The supreme incident that impresses Cocteau is the well-known snowball fight in which a young boy was allegedly killed by a rock imbedded in a snowball thrown by Dargelos. He is the paradigm of Cocteau's love for one who is malevolent and unattainable. What is interesting for the moment, however, is his interpretation of the Dargelos incident in *Paris Album.* He repeats the story and makes references to it in many works, often more as fiction than as fact, but here he adds a postscript that clarifies its function in the oeuvre in general, and in *Blood of a Poet* in particular.

> I have so often read and heard that the snowball thrown by Dargelos contained a stone that finally I have almost convinced myself of it. But the stone was useless. I have always believed that mere contact with Dargelos would have been enough to change the snow into marble and harden it into murder. . . . This snowball . . . struck Paul's chest like a blow from a statue. Afterward the statue became still and nobody thought of accusing it. . . .
>
> If I dwell on this it is because this episode marvelously illuminates the forms and deformations of memory.[25]

Cocteau describes Dargelos metaphorically. Magic powers, military status, and arrogance characterize Dargelos's behavior. In much of his other work Cocteau ascribes all of these qualities to the category of childhood. Dargelos is the idealization of the child for Cocteau. What is crucial here is the last sentence, which defines memory as an important theme for Cocteau. Memory is not constant, and the act of remembering is more important than what is remembered. Memory is actively reshaped by desire and imagination, not an involuntary or automatic process.

Unending Childhood

The child appears as a metaphor for aspects of the artist in all the media in which Cocteau worked. Poems, plays,[26] novels, and mixed essayistic works are all used as a forum for a complex and shifting notion of childhood. Cocteau does not address his work to children;[27] rarely does he actually depict small children. Individual children seem not to have interested him at all. Yet the phenomenon of childhood becomes a point of reference in his work at almost every stage. Sometimes casually, sometimes with violent overtones, he construes childhood as that time of life which most resembles the lives of poets and artists. This notion requires interpretation. He speaks of people of all ages as children. He reverses the pre-seventeenth-century idea that all children are adults; for Cocteau, all adults are basically childlike. Baudelaire had taken this position before Cocteau, and Rousseau before Baudelaire. In fact, since the Enlightenment and its admission of a child's "innocence,"[28] one of the points of Romanticism has been the recovery of the qualities of childhood lost in the process of socialization.

Cocteau's tie to Romanticism is twofold. He shared the philosophical foundation that sees life as a struggle to regain innocence lost since childhood. His sense of education is Rousseauesque. He sees only the negative in institutional instruction and discipline. But it is in the later manifestations of French Romanticism, particularly the works of Nerval, that Cocteau finds the system that integrates the notion of the child with other concerns important in his work. Nerval's acceptance of dream life and his fascination with death are precursors of Cocteau's own. Nerval writes of seeing death *("sa mort")* as if it were a person.[29] Cocteau uses this device in *Orpheus*. Certain of the dreams in *Aurélia* are very like scenes from Cocteau's films. In one, the dreamer finds himself lost in a long corridor in which he encounters a giant hermaphroditic figure, hovering in the air.[30] The description is strikingly like scenes from the "Hôtel des Folies Dramatiques" sequence in *Blood of a Poet*. But even in a more general sense, Cocteau's fascination with dream and living through death are Nerval-like. The place of the child in that system is reduced from Rousseau's earlier investiture of the image of the child with innocence. For Nerval and Cocteau, the child is a mere sign of innocence, an empty vessel to be filled with significance at the author's will. The complex and meticulously studied child of Rousseau had no place in the waking dream of Nerval and, consequently, Cocteau. Nor is the autobiographical meditation on childhood of Rousseau's *Confessions* useful to the late-Romantic Nerval. He rejects both complexity and retrospection with regard to childhood in favor of the exploration of dream and death as routes to the recovery of innocence and the mystification of childhood. The child is an idealization of that goal. Its own being matters very little. (This interpretation of the importance of childhood changes with the work of Brakhage, who is much closer to Rousseau and the Wordsworth of "The Prelude" in his detailed treatment of childhood than he is to Nerval.)

The child's relationship to the unknown interests Cocteau. In Cocteau's view, children's faith in imaginary reality puts them in close touch with the phenomenon of death. The weight death carries as a psychic event for children is the result of its imaginary status. Insofar as it is imagined, the child seizes power over it and incorporates it as an event in life. Children often play dead. In children's games, death is sometimes a person, sometimes a place, and often an abstract force that functions as the ultimate (however, reversible) punishment. Death is unknown and therefore pliable as a concept. Like Nerval, Cocteau proposes that the artist emulate the child in so manipulating the unknown.

The key act in making this equation is "to believe" *(croire)*. It is a word and a concept that Cocteau strews throughout his work, often creating whole projects to explore it. Belief in the creations of one's own subjectivity is one of those coincident notions which children and artists share. "Believability," like the hallucinations of drug takers and psychotics, is that attribute of any manufactured reality which defies analysis. In Cocteau's work, when belief is raised as an issue, it is given positive value, and disbelief negative. The statue in *Blood of a Poet* ridicules the poet/artist for his lack of faith in his own work and powers. With a jeer she chides him: "I congratulate you. You wrote that one could go into mirrors and you didn't believe it." He is rewarded with passages when he believes enough to try *(essayer)*. Similarly, in *Beauty and the Beast,* Beauty's sisters are made to appear to be honking geese and cackling chickens when they do not believe Beauty's stories about the Beast's estate.

The noted child psychologist Jean Piaget discusses belief as it operates in child's play and establishes the relationship between child's play and artistic and poetic representation. According to Piaget, in symbolic play or "make-believe" the child asserts the reality of the symbol in order to satisfy his own ego.

> When the child plays, he certainly does not believe, in the sense of socialized belief, in the content of his symbolism, but precisely because symbolism is egocentric thought we have no reason to suppose that he does not believe *in his own way* anything he chooses. From this point of view the "deliberate illusion" which Lange and Groos see in play is merely the child's refusal to allow the world of adults or of ordinary reality to interfere with play, so as to enjoy a private reality of his own. But this reality is believed in spontaneously, without effort, merely because it is the universe of the ego, and the function of play is to protect this universe against forced accommodation to ordinary reality. There is no question, therefore, in the early stages of symbolic play, of consciousness of make-believe like that of drama or poetry. (It is only after the age of seven that play really becomes make-believe in contrast to "reflective belief.") The two- to four-year-old child does not consider whether his ludic symbols are real or not. He is aware in a sense that they are not so for others, and makes no serious effort to persuade the adult that they are. But for him it is a question which does not arise, because symbolic play is a direct satisfaction of the ego and has its own kind of belief, which is a subjective reality. Moreover, as the symbol-object is a substitute for the reality it signifies, there develops, during the first stages, a kind of co-operation between the two, analogous to that between the image and the object it represents.[31]

Cocteau's intention is an interesting example of Piaget's analogy. Cocteau asserts within and about his films that the viewer needs to believe in order to participate or see them. He is correct in noting the similarity of his project to that of a child at play. (In terms of ego gratification, he is perhaps more correct than he realizes.)

Both the act and the fact are important here; that is, projecting one's thought onto the real world and then pronouncing it *as* that world are both crucial. Cocteau trusts very much in the power of assertion. To project and pronounce is to believe. Though one reads with a degree of skepticism—"The poet never asks for admiration; he wants to be believed"[32]—one is forced to move to the side of the artist/poet to understand his work. In following that maxim with another—"Everything that is not believed remains background"[33]—he strengthens the move. The issue is, for whom is the poet writing? There is no overwhelming sense of the poet writing for himself; he writes to make others believe in him. Moreover, he needs to believe fully in order to convince others. He does not acknowledge it but he thus differs from children, who care very little for the conviction of their audience.

The dominance of subjectivity occurs as a theme in many of Cocteau's novels and plays. The gross metaphor that he often uses is a room, in which all of the important drama is enacted and outside of which only meddlesome and interfering forces operate. The protagonists in *The Holy Terrors (Les enfants terribles)* (1925) live most of their lives in a room. *The Holy Terrors* is a novel of the obsessive relationship of brother and sister orphans. Their intensity operates as a magnet to others, attracting and then repelling relatives, servants, and suitors. No matter what their changed circumstances, the order they establish for their lives constantly reasserts itself. They live together in one chaotic room. They exaggerate the drama of their lives, unable to acknowledge their incestuous love, and in the end die by double suicide. Their room is its own world and takes on the character of its inhabitants.

> As for the Room, the efforts of the nurses proved unavailing to subdue it. On the contrary, the wilderness spread rapidly, and before long the patient had succeeded in imposing his personal town and landscape upon chaos. Streets wound in and out among the litter; trunks flanked his broad avenues; strewn paper were his lakes; piles of discarded linen were his mountains.[34]

(In the Melville film, the presence of outside is whittled away even further.) The maddening claustrophobia, the incessant repetition of accusations and threats, and the resistance to other forces from outside (the maid, for example) remind one of the workings of a troubled mind. The game that Paul, Elisabeth, and their friends play is their life's activity. "The word 'Game' was by no means accurate, but it was the term which Paul had selected to denote the state of semi-consciousness in which children float immersed."[35] One of the adults admitted to the Room, Mariette the nurse, enters on the basis of her acceptance of their raging subjectivity, "for it was indubitably a masterpiece these children were creating; a masterpiece devoid of intellectual content, devoid—this was a miracle—of any worldly aim; the masterpiece of their own being."[36] Similarly, in *The Human Voice*, there is one room. Here the distinction between inside and out is simplified. Although there is a telephone with which to connect interior and exterior space, the only real world in the play is that which surrounds the one subjectivity that confronts us. One encounters a world of activities and emotions that are known only through a monologue. The drama is not depicted, it is spoken. By inscribing a plot (the demise of a love affair) and by offering the possibility of identification with the characters within the monologue, Cocteau asserts the reality of what is within the protagonist's mind. The central character creates all the events, motivations, and responses. For the duration of the play there is no other world but hers.

The most consistent and explicit work expounding the dominance of subjectivity is *Thomas the Impostor (Thomas, l'imposteur)* (1923). In it, Thomas's fantasy determines how he lives and dies. In his work, Cocteau allows the dangerous poet/performer, art/life metaphors to blend gracefully.[37] An impostor is, in the most benign sense, very like Cocteau's idea of artist or poet. Cocteau adds, he is also like a child.

> You will see what kind of an impostor Guillaume was. His sort are a race apart. They live half-way between reality and make believe. They are distinguished, not lowered, by the deception which they practice. Guillaume took people in without malice. The story will show that he took himself in. Like any child, cabby or horse, he forgot wht he really was.[38]

The story is of a young man who poses as the son of a noble to gain access to society and to life's opportunities. His success depends on the conviction with which he plays his part. The distinction between the part and his true self is lost. The end of the novel emphatically describes the conjunction as possible and desirable.

> "A shot," he said to himself. "I'm lost unless I play dead."
> But in him, fiction and reality were one.
> Guillaume Thomas was dead.[39]

In order not to be found out, he dies. Thomas became a hero, achieving the status for which he had lived as a fraud. In his enthusiasm for the part, Thomas loses sight of the limits of fantasy and carries on as if his role were his life. With such a character, Cocteau sets forth the proposition that if the will to believe is strong enough and the performance convincing enough, the lie will become true, the fantasy reality.

> All children possess the magic power of being able to change themselves into what they wish. Poets, in whom childhood is prolonged, suffer a great deal when they lose this power. This is undoubtedly one of the reasons which drives the poet to use opium.[40]

When Cocteau describes this as a capability of children, he speaks of their psychic reality and the power they have to convince themselves of the absolute reality of their fantasy. He extols them even further as the best audiences for others' fantasies as well. Their ability to identify with what is on stage, screen, or in a book is their primary virtue as spectators. The arena of the theater corresponds to childhood insofar as it enfolds an audience in its artificial space and time. The theater that interested Cocteau sustained the illusion of reality, even if one of a circus or sideshow (such as *Parade*). Brechtian distance, for example, would have no place in Cocteau's notion of theater. For Cocteau, the spectator was not meant to see and hear a performance critically; one should believe. In a note on film audiences, Cocteau derides sophisticated audiences for their cynicism. He sides with "the public." "The public at large does not prejudge. It never judges on the basis of the author or the interpreters. It believes in it. It's the public of childhood, the best."[41] In his role as a creator of spectacles, he attempts to create a theater that would affect him as the theater of his childhood did. "Such is my spellbound nature, so easily dazzled. I belong to the minute. It falsifies all perspective for me. It shuts me off from diversity. I yield to him who convinces me."[42] While there is a contradiction here between natural belief and the act of convincing, the issue remains the same. Against analysis stands faith as the ground for the appreciation of art.

The Artist/Child

Cocteau attributed childlike qualities to everyone he admired. Artists, authors, and musicians are all described as having a bit of the child in them as part of their greatness. One of the aspects of their "innocent" achievement is their ability to create their own worlds, to establish laws, principles, and an atmosphere that are integrated and entirely their own. Cocteau often writes of Picasso's "world" and, significantly, of his own. His ability to be convinced by a work of art, to believe in it, to have faith in it, coincides with his evaluation of good art. That is, a work is good when it enthralls us, makes us succumb to it, makes us enter its world. This way of speaking about art, poetry, and music is consistent with his notion of believability as the central tenet of an aesthetic.

In describing Picasso's set for *Parade,* Cocteau again resorts to the metaphor of childhood:

> If you remember the mysteries of childhood, the scenes it discovers surreptitiously in a puddle, views of Vesuvius at night, by the stereoscope, Christmas chimneys, rooms looked at through the keyhole, you will understand the soul of that set which filled the stage of the Opera House without any other artifice save gray curtains and a house of performing dogs.[43]

Today, Picasso's set for *Parade* seems full of "artifice," indeed. Cocteau, however, saw in it a rejuvenated approach to stage design that was awe inspiring. It evoked for him memories and fantasies that were highly charged.

Cocteau presents two distinct correlations of children and artists as if they were one idea. The acute sensitivity of children to the physical world is likened to that of the artist. In some cases the artist's abilities and subjects are presented as springing directly from his childhood. Cocteau claimed that Chirico was an autobiographical painter drawing on his childhood for his imagery.[44] Cocteau admired those who drew on their past and transformed it. He also was convinced by those artists who dealt with childhood as a theme theoretically rather than autobiographically. His protégé and mentor (in the kind of complex homosexual relationship Cocteau often had), Raymond Radiguet, earned a glowing epitaph on the twentieth anniversary of his death: "He turned a searchlight onto the darkness of childhood and revealed it to us with harsh clarity."[45] Those artists and poets who mimic the imagination and response of children in their lives and work are of the greatest interest to Cocteau. Cocteau describes Picasso's achievement as the refusal to grow up:

> Perhaps the first days of his astonishing enterprise were days of play, like childhood days. That is no one's business. They quickly become school days. But Picasso never professed. He never dissected the doves which flew out from his sleeves.[46]

That is, he never lost amazement at the world and the ability to amaze others with his world. He never tried to analyze it. Children are inevitably enmeshed in their own creations; as they grow they are less so. An artist retains his entanglement in his creative acts. "The world is suspicious of contrasting skills. Picasso, with his profound fantasy, proves how little he has tried to please. It gives his slightest gesture a fairy-like grace."[47] In Cocteau's view, there is a reciprocity between the artist's relationship to the world and its to him. It is perceived as a magic arena that never ceases to amaze the artist, and reciprocally, the artist creates objects that transform it once again. He occasionally defined children as poets:

> The words of children which get quoted are close to the dissociated words of poets, and there are some of them which I should be proud to have uttered.[48]

He then creates the unifying category for all poets, artists, and children:

> The poet? He is only the hand—the work of the schizophrenic in each of us, only he is not ashamed of it. Like the child, he only is entitled to genius.[49]

Defining the Artist/Child

The parallel of the child and the genius, no matter what his métier, is not original with Cocteau. Baudelaire made the point before him, and in reading Baudelaire, one understands better what Cocteau means. The specific attributes of the child's perceptions are described coherently in *The Painter of Modern Life,* in a way that Cocteau did only aphoristically.[50] Nevertheless, their conclusions are the same. In leading up to a rhapsody on the nature of the flaneur, Baudelaire describes a convalescent as the model for the artist.

> Now convalescence is like a return towards childhood. The convalescent, like the child, is possessed in the highest degree of the faculty of keenly interesting himself in things, be they apparently of the most trivial. Let us go back, if we can, by a retrospective effort of the imagination, towards our most youthful, our earliest, impressions, and we will recognize that they had a strange kinship with those brightly coloured impressions which we were later to receive in the aftermath of a physical illness, always provided that that illness had left our spiritual capacities pure and unharmed. The child sees everything in a state of newness; he is always *drunk*. Nothing more resembles what we call inspiration than the delight with which a child absorbs form and colour. I am prepared to go even further and assert that inspiration has something in common with a convulsion, and that every sublime thought is accompanied by a more or less violent nervous shock which has its repercussion in the very core of the brain. The man of genius has sound nerves, while those of a child are weak. With the one, Reason has taken up a considerable position; with the other, Sensibility is almost the whole being. But genius is nothing more nor less than *childhood recovered* at will—a childhood now equipped for self-expression with manhood's capacities and a power of analysis which it has involuntarily accumulated. It is by this deep and joyful curiosity that we may explain the fixed and animally ecstatic gaze of a child confronted with something new, whatever it be, whether a face or a landscape, gliding colours, shimmering stuffs, or the magic of physical beauty assisted by the cosmetic art. . . . I asked you a moment ago to think of Monsieur G. as an eternal convalescent. To complete your idea, consider him also as a man-child, as a man who is never for a moment without the genius of childhood—a genius for which no aspect of life has become *stale*.[51]

The freshness of vision and fascination with experience characterize the man-child of genius. Disorientation from the visual world becomes the sign of the refreshed relationship to that world.[52] Cocteau describes it as a matter of susceptibility and belief, Baudelaire as new attention and drunkenness. Both propose the visual as the key sense. In the elision of the quoted text from *The Painter of Modern Life,* one finds the primal visual experience the image of the mirror, Cocteau's own primal image. The one optical memory cited is that of watching the parent dress.

> A friend of mine once told me that when he was quite a small child, he used to be present when his father dressed in the mornings, and that it was with a

mixture of amazement and delight that he used to study the muscles of his arms, the gradual transitions of pink and yellow in his skin, and the bluish network of his veins. The picture of external life was already filling him with awe and taking hold of his brain. He was already being obsessed and possessed by form. Predestination was already showing the tip of its nose. His sentence was sealed. Need I add that today that child is a well-known painter?[53]

Compare Baudelaire's description to Cocteau's description of watching his mother dress. What is euphemistically spoken of as sensitivity and acute awareness is drawn, in both cases, from a primal scopophilia.

Antisocial behavior affords another means for analogizing the child and the artist. The child's misapplication of social forms and outright rebellion represents the dominance of imagination. In his description of the performance at the Nouveau Cirque in *Paris Album*, Cocteau speaks of children's love of clowns as stemming from contempt for authority.

Footit enchanted children; he achieved at the same time the tour de force of pleasing the grown-ups and bringing their childhood back to them. Children are at home with the nervous excitement of clowns when they learn a new joke and decide to try it out on a friend; they understand the chief rider's scolding voice, the refusal to work, the disobedience and the grammatical mistakes. . . . Footit brought into the ring the atmosphere of a diabolical nursery, where children could rediscover their sly malice; and where grown-ups were impressed.[54]

In a much later piece, Cocteau generalizes that point to include not only children but artists as well:

The spirit of creation which is the highest form of the spirit of contradiction, will abolish the modern "do what you like," that bad freedom of action that is taught to American children and that suppresses the essential resource of children, of heroes and of artists: *disobedience.*[55]

The cruel, warlike nature of groups of boys figures in the opening of *Thomas the Impostor.* Thomas is attracted to the army as a career partially because he is attracted to male cruelty. In all of the stories of Dargelos (especially in the opening of *The Holy Terrors*), Cocteau alludes to it. In Cocteau's summing up of the Dargelos character, he theorizes what is appealing about the stereotype:

I would prefer him to remain in the shadow from which I have substituted his constellation and for him to remain for me the example of everything which cannot be learnt, taught, judged, analysed and punished, everything that makes a person individual, the first symbol of untamed forces that dwell within us, which the social machine tries to kill and which motivate, beyond good or evil, those individuals whose example consoles us for the fact of living.[56]

In his response to Mauriac's attack on his play *Bacchus,* Cocteau wrote: "I accuse you, as you keep telling me that you are an 'old' child, of having kept nothing of childhood but its cunning cruelty."[57] With that response, Cocteau once again raises the malevolent side of childhood. But here he does not valorize "cunning cruelty" as he often does when speaking of children. Instead, he conveniently ignores his accustomed use of the phrase, and employs it as a polemic against his critic. The same ambivalence toward cruelty comes out over the course of his career. It is genuinely double-edged for Cocteau; he is both attracted and repulsed by it.

Seeing and the Invisible

The insistence on subjectivity and fantasy, and the rejection of order and reason as a method for the artist, has yet another facet. Cocteau considered realism, as a style, the enemy of art. The late work, *The Hand of a Stranger,* is a tract written almost entirely around this theme. In it, Cocteau deplores artistic creations that exhibit or explain actual life. He valorizes the affirmation of the "invisible." The invisible is Cocteau's alternative to the surreal. Never a part of the artistic movement of surrealism, Cocteau found his own terminology to set him apart from traditional realists. *"Le vrai mensonge,"* myth, and imagination are opposed to the superficial representation of the "visible." Cocteau puts forward a notion of an *other* reality to which artists and children are drawn. Their task and their achievement is to make believable this invisible reality.

Cocteau takes issue with several aspects of artistic realism. To reproduce the habitual order of things in an aesthetic form is, to his mind, not art. "After the school of botching comes the school of stage-realism. Now there is no question of living on the stage; it is a question of making the stage live."[58] Within that general method, Cocteau held that a living other reality would arise out of the given one through the careful subversion of the expectations of a reader or audience. To make "the stage live" is to endow it with qualities that can only exist under those very special circumstances. It has its own terms and, again, is taken on faith. Cocteau's insistence on contemporary clothing for his versions of ancient myths is a good example of the way in which he set up a given reality to be undermined. He makes an attempt to persuade an audience that the enacted events occur in the present time and space while really using costumes to make invented time and space more convincing. It is a strategy on which he relies extensively in the films.

The notion of the "invisible" has several meanings. It often stands for the author's imagination and emotional subjectivity. It is the place where the imagination resides. This concept provides a spatial model for the imagination and is used throughout Cocteau's plays and films. The "zone" of *Orpheus* is invisible unless one passes through the mirror. Usually, the events that occur within the arena of the "invisible" space take place in "no time." Within the fiction he composes, they take place during an instant. *Blood of a Poet,* for example, occurs within the instant of the demolition of a smokestack. Equally as often it is a euphemism for death, what Oxenhandler calls that "unnamed psychic disaster, a childhood terror which cannot be quite understood or expelled."[59] Its phases occur throughout childhood; it is reengaged by the use of opium, flirted with in art and poetry, and approached at death. The visible hides the "invisible" through a series of obstructions: bourgeois convention, law and authority, materialism. Aging is the vehicle for the construction of these obstructions.

One ends by reading Cocteau with a great deal of skepticism. His aphoristic style, his elusive language, even his subjects often mystify rather than clarify the themes he expounds. One has difficulty trusting the accuracy of his accounts as they range between reportage and fiction, and are modeled to fit various occasions. His signature—"I am a lie that always tells the truth"—urges the reader toward the dead end of uncritical acceptance of his oeuvre as a whole. Many questions remain unanswered; most importantly, why Cocteau, literary and theatrical prodigy that he was, turned to cinema? Yet if one steps back from the circular system of Cocteau's language to analyze its structure, and if one analyzes rather than accepts the metaphor of the child, then an unexpected reason arises for Cocteau's turn to cinema.

The notions of genius, innocence, authority, and invisibility—in fact, all of the characteristics that make children and artists similar—are discussed in the psychoanalytical literature on scopophilia. There are patterns that psychoanalysis evinces that make it easier to arrive at an understanding of Cocteau. Both Sigmund Freud and Karl Abraham have written on the psyches of artists: Freud on Leonardo,[60] and Abraham on the obscure Giovanni Segantini.[61] In Freud's well-known study, he points out and traces to their source several traits of Leonardo that converge with this discussion of Cocteau. The first and most obvious is the artist's love of looking and general sensual pleasure in the world. He attributes this scopophilia to primal curiosity toward the artist's own origin and a desire to see the mother's genitals. What is originally a natural privilege of the mother-child relationship becomes socially forbidden as the child grows. Nevertheless, the child's wish to retain complete access to the mother remains. This desire is repressed and transformed in two ways. First, it is generalized; whereas the child was at first interested only in looking at his mother's sexual parts, looking itself becomes fascinating, and the world is perceived with vigor and intensity. Abraham extends Freud's observation further by contending that artists' and intellectuals' seeking of the "unknown" as their life's work can be traced to the same primal curiosity.[62] Both the activity of looking (and investigating) and the elusiveness of what is looked for become important to the artist. Second, the love and curiosity that had been reserved for the mother is inverted toward the self. It is Freud's view that the child sees no other object as worthy as himself of the mother's love. From the point of view of the child, the mother-child relationship is exclusive and complete. When the mother rejects the child's sexual advances, he seeks the recourse of self-love. If she cannot accept his loving attentions, he will bestow them on what she loves best, that is, himself. Narcissism and homosexuality are two of the manifestations of this inversion. Both characterize Cocteau.

The child's relationship with the father as described in the studies of the lives of both artists is also illuminating. Freud describes Leonardo's unconventional life and his philosophy of creativity as antiauthoritarian. He traces this attitude back to the Oedipal conflict with his father for dominance in the eyes of the mother. Abraham makes a similar claim for Segantini's more extreme antiauthoritarianism. In another essay, "Transformations of Scoptophilia,"[63] Abraham describes certain extreme cases in which the Oedipal conflict is manifested by the desire neither to see nor to be seen. This phobia is traced to jealousy and fear of the father. Children often fantasize magic powers to make themselves "invisible." In that way they can both see what they desire and avoid being seen by what they fear.

In the essay on Segantini, Abraham also discusses, as a manifestation of Oedipal conflict, the way in which the artist described his own childhood and how that description is consistent with the mythology of heroes. Segantini valorized his childhood. Not only did he worship his mother, but he describes his own adventures as a child on an heroic scale. In referring to the work of Otto Rank, Abraham points to the history of accounts like Segantini's:

> Rank has dealt in particular with the myth of the birth of the hero. Every people in its myths attributes to the birth and childhood of its hero wonderful happenings which are in full conformity with the childhood phantasies of individuals. Segantini's childhood story reminds us in a striking way of these heroic legends.[64]

In glorifying the child as a gifted genius or hero, what the artist does establishes his right to be a hero as an adult.[65]

There is no way to superimpose the work of these two psychoanalysts onto the study of Cocteau. They do, however, touch on significant and relevant points. When Cocteau describes the particular sensitivities of the child to the world, by and large he is describing visual acuity, rather than emotional or bodily sensitivity. (There are two notable exceptions to this, and both deal with the sense of smell. His description of the circus and of his semen-filled boyhood classroom dwell on the memory of pungent smells.) He connects his love of the arts (the theater, in particular) to the sight of his mother dressing. He includes himself within the sight of her; that is, he sees himself and her in the same image, since the entire ensemble is described as seen in a mirror. In addition, he cites his first artistic perception as originating from a childhood game. The story of Sarasate, the "Tamer in the Cage" is a visual memory of framing that affirms his sense of the quality of children's perceptions, seeing without being seen, and redeeming powerlessness through the potency of vision.

Cocteau also extols the virtue of antiauthoritarianism in children and artists. In his accounts of his life, it is interesting to note that his father is omitted except with the perfunctory mention that he was a lawyer, and that he died when Cocteau was ten. There is evidence that he committed suicide,[66] but Cocteau himself rarely alluded to the means of his death. He does, however, describe his own near suicide a few years later, while traveling with his mother. He mistook opium for *poudre de Pavot* and nearly died of an overdose. One finds very little influence of the father on the son, except those occasions when Cocteau pleads his case, as a lawyer would. The opening of *Opium* is one such instance: "Here the Public Prosecutor rises. But I do not give evidence. I do not plead. I do not pass judgment. I merely produce documents, for and against, in the trial of opium."[67]

If one approaches Cocteau's relationship, or lack of one, with his father from a psychoanalytic point of view, it is possible to understand both the antiauthoritarianism of Cocteau and his interest in the "invisible." Further, it is possible to account for the repeated suicides in his films. Since his father died while Cocteau was still a child, his father's presence in his life was never demystified. He remained a powerful and controlling force in Cocteau's imagination. One of the ways in which a person with a heightened sense of the visual might deal with the problems of authority is to make himself "invisible," in his own mind, so as to be out of sight of the authority. Another is to rebel against the idea of any authority at all, and ally oneself with others who do so—that is, children and artists. And yet another is to try to gain that power and authority for oneself. To do that, one must go in search of the authority, to know it and emulate it. In Cocteau's case, death and the "invisible" were explored as the hidden wells of his father's power.

There has been other work in the field of psychoanalysis that touches on issues in Cocteau's writing and helps us to decipher images and structures in his films. In the area of research on the relationship of "primal scene" experience to scopophilia and sadomasochism in adults, Freud and other psychoanalysts have a number of things to say that are pertinent to Cocteau. First of all, they make a strong case that there is indeed such an interrelationship. Freud,[68] Fenichel,[69] Greenacre,[70] and others trace the origin of some of the manifestations of scopophilia and sadomasochism to the child's fantasized or actual witnessing of sex between his parents. According to Arlow,[71] Weissman "has described the connection between primal-scene trauma and an interest in producing or directing plays and spectacles."[72] The issue will become important here when the editing strategy (particularly of *Orpheus*) and the latent sexual content (particularly of *Beauty and the Beast*) comes under discussion. Love is seen in terms of power relationships. The privilege of vision is the sign of power.

One of the clearest ways to unravel the complex array of images and techniques with which Cocteau embellishes his films is by looking at scenes and whole sequences as obsessive reenactments of psychological realities present since early childhood. One can only speculate on whether Cocteau's witnessing his parents's lovemaking was the source for films. Nevertheless, evidence from the films in combination with the findings of psychoanalysis justifies such speculation. The case for the importance of Cocteau's father's suicide on his artistic career is more easily proved (if posthumous proof of psychical causes can ever be made). Both the reenactment of suicide in his films and the importance and superstructure of the "invisible" stand as forceful evidence.

As a mode of expression the cinema would be an apt tool with which Cocteau would explore his personal obsessions. He had a rare and privileged relationship with it. In the introduction to the screenplay of *Blood of a Poet*, he reveals his confraternity with the medium "that is the same age as I.". The cinema was a child when he was a child; it grew as he grew. Moreover, the cinema is firmly based in reality. It has verisimilitude. Those first films which permeated Cocteau's childhood were simple accounts of quotidian life. Yet they were not life, exactly. The viewing experience of cinema contains a controlled distance very similar to that which Cocteau describes in the "Tamer in the Cage" incident. Unseen, a viewer has a private, formalized encounter with the world, by watching it through a frame, at a distance. All the better if it is an adult so "caged" by the frame. As a creator of cinema, the filmmaker has doubled powers. Because of film's abilities to manipulate photographic reality by the use of deceptive sets, superimposition, rear-screen projection, and editing techniques, the fantasies of entering and revealing the "invisible" can be played out. Cocteau's need to seize power over the unknown by making it manifest, found the most appropriate means in the cinema. The "spectacle" to which he was admitted at the Théâtre Robert Houdin as a child was the school for his ultimate métier.

The Cinema of Cocteau's Childhood

Cocteau mentions childhood moviegoing twice in his memoirs. The name of the Théâtre Robert Houdin, the theater of Méliès, appears in *Paris Album* among a list of amusements available at the time. Like the Palais de Glace and the Nouveau Cirque, the cinema seemed immensely appealing to Cocteau as a child. The Lumière Cinématographe, on the other hand, is discussed at length. Its address coincided with the "Old England" shop where sailor suits and other accoutrements were bought for the young Cocteau. Its program is extensively described. Cocteau appears to have attended screenings with both his mother and his governess. As if to appeal to the children in the audience, the name of the hall in which the Lumières screened their films was changed from the original Grand Café to the provocative Salon Indien.

Cocteau makes reference to the Lumière theater first as a place and then as a film theater.

> Old England . . . made me welcome the exciting fever of measles, scarlet fever or appendicitis. (Old England, where they sold sailor suits with whistles, putty colored monkey-jackets and revolting gaiters which were lined with red flannel and scratched our legs, occupied an important place in our childish lives.[73]

He goes on to describe the many theatrical "spectacles"[74] of his childhood, including the films that were important to him. "For where is that innocent age when we saw *L'Arroseur Arrosé*, *Le Bock* and *Bébés au Bord de l'Eau* in the cellar of the Frères Lumières, near Old England?"[75]

Paris was alive with spectacles and cinematic events during the period Cocteau describes in *Paris Album*. Advertisements for "Around the World in Eighty Days" and the Nouveau Cirque, Cocteau's two most beloved shows as a child, appear alongside those for films. We do not know how much of Paris he was permitted to experience as a child, nor what he saw that he did not later write about. From his memories, he appears as a child singularly aware of the spectacles available to him. Although he writes that "I hated all circumstances which forced me on Sunday to come out of my comfortable nest of dreams,"[76] he follows that immediately with a statement of his delight at being permitted to go to the Châtelet or the Nouveau Cirque. His mother's dressing, the programs, the titles, the horse-drawn carriages, and the reputation of such actresses as Sarah Bernhardt and Loie Fuller are fused in his interest in the social world.[77]

In his sixth column in the *Portraits-Souvenirs (Paris Album)* series, Cocteau called for an animated film in fast motion to be made of the history of fashion. It is the Baudelarean tradition from which such an appeal arises. Here, however, it is interesting to note the direct source from which the proposal emanates:

> A . . . film should be made of the slow-moving periods and fashions that succeed one another. Then it would be really exciting to see at high speed dresses growing longer, shorter and longer again; sleeves growing fuller, tighter, then full again; hats going up and down, perching on top, lying down flat, becoming decorative then plain; bosoms growing fuller than

slighter, provocative and ashamed.[78]

Cocteau's proposed film could be made from the illustrations that accompanied the "Spectacles et Concerts" column. Above or to the side of the listings is the fashion column with an illustration each day of a blouse, dress, hat, or other article of clothing in the latest fashion. The two columns are juxtaposed in very much the same way that Cocteau intermingles his thoughts on spectacles and fashion.

The cinema of Cocteau's youth became a hidden part of his artistic formation. When the cinematograph seized Paris in 1896, Cocteau was seven. From his own account we know he saw films at both the Lumière and Méliès theaters. One can also assume he saw films at the Folies Bérgère and The Cigale though they are only briefly mentioned in *Paris Album*. The titles and subjects of the large part of his cinema come directly from the theater of his youth. In general, the cinema of Cocteau is a melding of the various cinemas of his childhood with the other spectacles he saw or of which he heard. An analysis of particular films of Cocteau shows how he drew his aesthetic from this mixture of childhood film experience.

The traditional distinctions between Méliès's fantasy and the Lumières' documents break down as they amalgamate in Cocteau's mind as *the* cinema. Though no credit is given or influence acknowledged (beyond the mention of certain favorite films), Cocteau owes the central issue of his film work to those first filmmakers (and to many others who have not been canonized by film history). But it is to them both, not to either singularly, that he owes his filmic creation. By offering him cinemas that were both fact and fancy they provided the ingredients for his cinema which was fact and fancy at once.

In his cinema, Cocteau applies the same notions of childhood that characterize his work in literature and theater. Autobiography, conviction in subjectivity, antiauthoritarianism, and innocent amorality carry over from his literary works. The same impulses that drive his novels, poems, and plays operate here. An emphasis on voyeurism, the "invisible," and death is underscored. His view of the artist as a child is sharpened.

Cocteau uses childhood in films in two ways. First of all, he seeks to locate the postion of children in the world. He proposes that children are oppressed by society and therefore antisocial; perceived as weak but manifesting real power; and advanced, rather than backward, in mental ability. Children explore the fundamental questions of language and existence. Secondly, Cocteau pronounces children the paradigm of his notion of the artist/poet. By presenting a seamless image of life and death, he seeks to "prove" the triumph of imagination over reality. In *Cocteau on the Film* and *Diary of a Film*, Cocteau defines himself as a child when either making or viewing the film. The central issue of his filmic endeavor is "believability"; the prologue to *Beauty and the Beast* asks the audience to accept the film, believe in it, as a child would. It is the most direct address to the issue of childhood in Cocteau's films. The nature of cinematography allows Cocteau to represent angels, personify death, and illustrate fantasy in a vivid and seamless way. He could create fantasies at one phenomenologically with the world on screen. The cinematic viewing experience (where mystification and identification are the rule) allows him to anticipate audience acceptance, no matter how incredible his imagery and concepts are.

Cocteau's cinematic style is characterized by the realistic portrayal of life and imaginary events. His rejection of the conventions for depicting dream, the afterworld, and fantasy owe something to the astute technicians with whom he collaborated. There are no misty transitions or hazy apparitions that are so often found in films dealing with the supernatural. His cameramen and technical advisors—Arnaud and Périnal on *Blood of a Poet*, Hayer on *Orpheus*, and especially, Clément on *Beauty and the Beast*—gave Cocteau the expertise he needed to create the subtleties of his films. The cameraman Périnal's excellent eye for atmosphere caught the effect of dust raised by the crew sweeping up the set of *Blood of a Poet*.[79] By filming through the dust, the scene of the Cité Monthiers was infused with veiled light. It is the mottled light that makes possible the transition between the artist's studio and the street scene. Similarly, in *Beauty and the Beast*, René Clément's technical advice about the creation of lifelike exteriors using natural light must have been invaluable. Clément was working simultaneously on his own film, *Battle of the Rails (Battaille du rail)* (1946), reconstructing striking documentary scenes of the French Resistance. Using the countryside, and intense sunlight and its consequent extended focal length, Clément contributed to the realism of the clothesline sequence, so necessary to the overall construction of *Beauty and the Beast*. It is in that sequence that the question of belief is sharpened. The sisters confront Beauty and are humiliated as a consequence of their incredulity. The realism of the set coupled with the issue of the scene form a nexus for the general concerns of the film.

Cocteau's urge to convince an audience of his world view and moral position is that of a storyteller. Walter Benjamin describes Cocteau when he writes that "the most extraordinary things, marvelous things are related with the greatest accuracy, but the psychological connection of the events is not forced on the reader. It is left up to him to interpret things the way he understands them."[80] In the most extreme case of his filmmaking, Cocteau resorts to the fairy tale, that form which "secretly lives on in the story."[81]

Just as the conscious metaphor for the child is reinvented in Cocteau's cinema, so are themes that linger from his own unresolved childhood experiences. More than any other medium in which he worked, the cinema was capable of depicting Cocteau's imagined reality. Death and the afterworld are structured like the adult world is to a child. That orders emanate from such a place, that hidden authorities dominate it, that its laws are unknown but all encompassing, make it truly an accurate rendition of Cocteau's personal obsessions.

The Films

Blood of a Poet: Dreams of a Child

Cocteau's first film was to have been an animated cartoon inspired by Chaplin's *His Profession* (1914), called *Cocteau fait du cinéma*. Funded by the count de Noailles, Cocteau was given free rein to make a film of the creation of a poem and the vocation of a poet. Cocteau claims the cartoon was abandoned after he discovered the technical deficiencies of French animators. One suspects, however, that the hundreds of thousands of drawings that are required to make a cartoon seemed prohibitive and forced the metamorphosis of Cocteau's plan. Instead, he organized friends, lovers, and high society into a small acting company to improvise the film.

Blood of a Poet follows the central character, the Poet, through a series of tableaux instructive of the possibilities of imagination and the dangers of choosing the life of poetry. The film is divided into three main segments: the artist/Poet who draws a mouth that comes alive and that, when rubbed on a statue, instructs him to enter a mirror; the Poet struggling down a corridor, peering into keyholes, and shooting himself; and the Poet playing cards and shooting himself again. The lack of narrative logic and the metaphorical quality of the imagery can be seen as parts of Cocteau's attmpt to make a film poem about the origins of the poet.

The film begins and ends with an image of a smokestack being demolished. It implies that *Blood of a Poet* occurs within the instant that it takes for a smokestack to break and tumble to the ground.[82] Thus the film's time is posed as equivalent to mental time (that time during which a great deal occurs but which often lasts only a moment). It is important to note this brief, parenthetically divided image, since the theme of subjective time and space runs through this film and others by Cocteau. After the smokestack begins to fall, but before the main segment begins, we see Cocteau himself, made up as a statue and as if offstage. He makes a theatrical gesture as if to commence the show. There are several shots of a doorknob. Cut between each shot of the knob is a text that pronounces the film as a "Coat of arms" and a "real documentary of unreal events." The dedications to "Pisanello, Paolo Uccello, Piero della Francesca, Andrea del Castagno" appear.

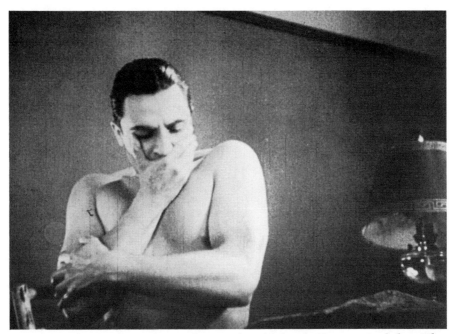

Blood of a Poet. The Poet embraces the mouth on his hand. *(Courtesy Anthology Film Archives.)*

The first of the three central sequences is titled, "First episode: the wounded hand, or the scars of the poet." The Poet, in a sparsely furnished studio, stands before his easel, drawing with charcoal on a sketch pad. The mouth of the head he had been drawing becomes shapely and begins to move. As a knock is heard, signaling a visitor, the Poet panics, smudges out the mouth, and answers the door. The guest (Jean Desbordes) falls back in horror (in an awkward reverse-motion fall) when the Poet offers his hand. The mouth is now embedded in it, a stigmatalike wound. The Poet, too, is horrified and tries in vain to erase the mouth and, finally, washes the hand. The mouth, unable to breathe (or "inspire") makes bubbles in the water and, when lifted out, calls for air. The Poet's attitude begins to change. After kicking out the window to provide air for the mouth, he becomes enamored and embraces his own hand. The embrace escalates into masturbatory lovemaking, after which the Poet sleeps.

An intertitle announces Cocteau's reappearance in the film. "The surprises of photography, or how I was caught in a trap by my own film." The Poet's face is replaced by a revolving mask and then a plaster cast of Cocteau himself. A question remains whether the Poet dreams his own creator, or if everything that follows is the Poet's dream. If he is just dreaming of his maker, almost no time passes from sleep to waking;

otherwise, the length of the film passes and the Poet becomes the ever-sleeping statute at the end.

The Poet wakes and presses his hand over the mouth of the armless Venus-style plaster statue in his studio. The statue's head is transformed. The windows of the room disappear and a mirror stands in the place of the door. The statue sneers at the Poet, who looks at the mirror and shouts, "Open it for me." The statue replies: "There is only one way left. You must go into the mirror and walk through." The Poet contends, "One can't go into mirrors." The statue retorts: "I congratulate you. You wrote that one could go into mirrors and you didn't believe it . . . Try, always try." The Poet presses against the unyielding mirror and, finally, climbs onto a chair and plunges into the surface, which splashes like water.

The second and longest main segment begins after the Poet's fall. The time spent inside the mirror is another layer of imagined time; its space, imagined space; its events are fantasized and reversible. The notion of passage through a mirror certainly was not original with Cocteau. His most notable predecessor was Lewis Carroll, whose Alice fell into the

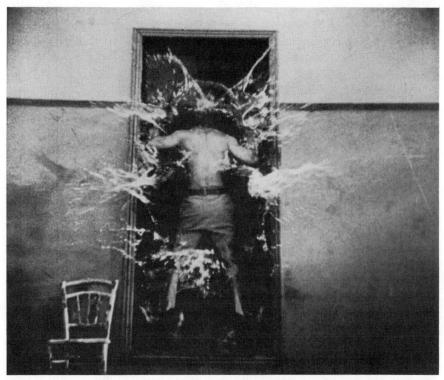

Blood of a Poet. The Poet plunges into the mirror.(*Courtesy Anthology Film Archives.*)

hallucinatory time and space of the mirror in *Through the Looking Glass*. Cocteau does not hide his debt, and his interpretation of Carroll's mirror offers a perspective from which to view Cocteau's own. In "Hommage à Lewis Carroll,"[83] Cocteau describes unknown tortures and tormentors of the girls in Carroll's photographs, "known only to the mirror that knew how to conquer Alice" *(connus du seul miroir que savait vaincre Alice")*. The willful and dangerous mirror is consistent with Cocteau's own.

The initial passage of the Poet who plunged into the mirror is through a dark void in which he swims and glides. A small man approaches the camera and disappears, as if in an early trick film.[84] This single effect of stopping the camera, is used in *Blood of the Poet* to mark the Hôtel des Folies Dramatiques as an extraworldly place.[85] There are two ways in which Cocteau signals the relationship of this place to his own childhood. One is by the use of disappearing, recalling the films he saw as a child. The other is in the name he gives to the hotel. The Folies Dramatiques was a movie–peep show arcade of his childhood in Paris.

Once the Poet enters the corridor, he peeps into keyholes. One knows from his memoirs that looking unseen played a large part in Cocteau's formation as an artist. The ability to encounter the world and enter into an empowered relationship with it, simply by watching it, is crucial to Cocteau's paradigm of the child and artist. The ultimate incarnation of this model is the Peeping Tom.[86] The cinema permitted Cocteau this characterization. As the vehicle for unseen seeing, film is remarkably suited to the metaphor of the voyeur. Cocteau emphasizes the voyeurism of movie watching by naming the hotel the Folies Dramatiques.

The first view that the Poet has is of the execution of a stereotypical Mexican bandit. The themes of death and resurrection, persecution, and antiauthoritarianism are all implied by this image and enrich the whole of the film. It is more interesting, however, if one knows its source. Like the image of Dargelos, it comes from a childhood fascination. In his description of the spectacle at the Nouveau Cirque, Cocteau contextualizes one of the attractions:

> One act we loved, aside from our clowns and acrobats, was the Mexican Sharpshooters—the term "cowboy" was still unknown. Men and women in fringed leather trousers put their lassos through calisthenics which ended, on Monday, at home with furniture broken, tearful scenes, and a session in the closet.[87]

Though Cocteau offers no explanation for his use of this particular image, it is of interest to see the way in which this scene of childhood pleasure and subsequent punishment manifests itself in a filmic image. The pleasure at being a bullet-strapped Zapata-like rebel is accompanied by the pain of execution. The pleasure at playing at being that character is accompanied by the pain of incarceration in a closet.

The second view through the keyhole is of a shadow of the preparation of opium, Cocteau's recently (but temporarily) conquered addiction. The scene ends with its spell broken. After the Poet makes a major attempt to see in a crack in the door by straddling it, he reverts to the keyhole. An Asian peers back and the Poet moves on.

The third scene is more explicitly concerned with a position vis-à-vis childhood than any of the others. The "Flying Lesson" is an image that explicitly deals with childhood and one that appears elsewhere in Cocteau's work. In *Opéra* (1927), Cocteau included the poem "Les voleurs d'enfants," a poem that plays on the word *voler*, which means both "to steal" and "to fly." It is a poem about the circus and the flight of childhood from parental authority, on the wings of the imagination. It joins the concepts of rebellion and fantasy through the metaphor of flight. Three years later he was to use the same interpretation of the metaphor in his film.[88]

In 1929, he wrote of a child who could fly in *Opium*:

> The boy at the Hôtel de la Poste in Montargis . . . knew how to fly, without the slightest play on words and without the slightest equipment.
>
> The proprietor's wife: "Anselme, fly a bit to show Monsieur Cocteau."
>
> I am noting word for word the transparent absurdities of morning drowsiness.[89]

Evidently, he is again using the French pun on *voler* to describe a conversation had in the half-sleep of morning. With Cocteau's penchant for literal readings of verbal plays on words, he translated the woman's order to the child from "fly" to "*steal* [emphasis added] a bit to show Monsieur Cocteau."

The "Flying Lesson" scene begins with the Poet struggling to the door, as he does to each door in the corridor. There is a sign that reads *Leçons de Vol* ("Flying Lessons"). Cocteau, in the screenplay to *Blood of a Poet*, accurately describes what ensues:

> A little girl in circus tights with a harness of bells is crouching by the fireplace, while an old governess in a black dress threatens her with a whip. . . . The old woman lifts her under her arms and sets her down on top of the fireplace. The bells tinkle. . . .
>
> Close-up of the poet. . . . The old woman is standing by the fireplace. The little girl, in the air above the fireplace, seems to be flying in the air, motionless, a kind of constellation of bells. . . .
>
> . . . The old woman climbs up the ladder and shakes her fist at her pupil.
>
> Close-up of the little girl, who is still on the ceiling, making faces and sticking out her tongue.[90]

Blood of a Poet. The Poet and the flying girl. *(Courtesy Anthology Film Archives.)*

Visually, the child's flight is strikingly like that of the Poet's movements. They both appear pressed against the wall by an unnatural force that distorts their movements. The similarity of their physical difficulties with their environs suggests that the girl is an aspect of the Poet, or at least a confrere. Cocteau chose to use the same technique to film them. By placing on the floor flats of the view of the corridor and of the interior wall of the room, and by filming the actors from above, their movements become strange. The girl represents an impossible defiance of gravity. The overhead shooting emphasizes both the characters' awkwardness and their subjection to an unseen power.

The girl seems harnessed and bound by the bell straps of her costume. She is being forced into an act that could be delightful, but coerced, she resists. It recalls Coceau's own experiences with skating. This activity intrigued him, but the lessons ruined all the enjoyment: "The prospect of lessons took all the poetry out of it for me . . . Dunce as I was by nature, the fear of a lesson spoilt the dream, as the magic of Christmas was destroyed by useful presents."[91] The masculine-looking governess, dressed in Victorian garb, is characterized as a sadist. The girl is at first recalcitrant, then rebellious.

The whip-carrying governess is inexplicably cruel. The child is uncooperative as she awkwardly rests pressed against the wall above the mantle, like a bas-relief or wall sculpture. When forced out of the frame by the threats of the instructor (and, in the next shot, onto the ceiling), she defies the gesticulations of the governess, moves even farther away, and grimaces. The close-up of her as she makes faces is the fullest close-up of the sequence. It fills the frame with defiance, so as to leave no doubt about the child's true feelings when out of range of the whip.

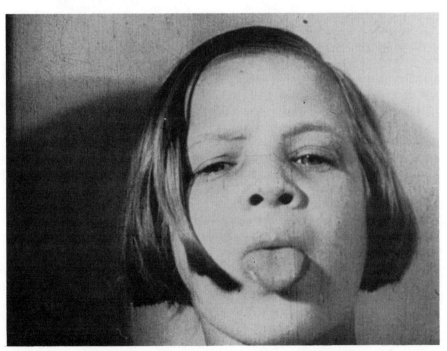

Blood of a Poet. **The defiant child.** *(Courtesy Anthology Film Archives.)*

It is interesting that Cocteau attempts to create an image of the girl as a constellation, marked by the bells on the soundtrack. The individual star and the constellation form one of his signatures. Many of Cocteau's drawings are made as if the figure were a constellation of dots or stars connected by a line. The scar on the back of the Poet is in the shape of a star. The opening title to *Orpheus* is drawn as if Orpheus were a constellation. He often writes of theatrical stars as if they were stars in the sky. This equation will also be made by Joseph Cornell (see chapter 2). In his description of Dargelos in *Paris Album*, Cocteau writes: "I have sub-stituted his constellation."[92] He qualifies the memory of him and disembodies him into the articulation of a constellation. The patterning of these two children is instituted for the same purpose: to make a symbol of rebellion out of a living being.

Cocteau ends the scene there with the child's grimace. The Poet goes on to see an animated and rather didactic hermaphrodite whose limbs appear through holes and whose genitals are hidden with a sign warning Danger of Death. In the two presentations of this character, once as a man and once as a woman, only the limbs and head are flesh. It is as if to say that the torso—the body and its blunt sexuality—were a surface cover for the real being. Cocteau often claimed that art was hermaphroditic, born of the copulation of the male and female elements in one being. What is more significant here is that this hermaphrodite is not of two sexes, but of no sex. It is a manifestation of a fetishism of the extremities in order to avoid seeing the genitals.

The "Flying Lesson" is the most elaborate of all the scenes in rooms, yet it remains a kind of aphorism in the film as a whole. It is a puzzling insert. Cocteau says he pulls images from "a kind of half-sleep,"[93] and even though he denies "deliberately" drawing on the unconscious, it is clear that there is a symbolic element in choosing such a charged image through a keyhole. As part of the sequence of scenes behind closed doors, it is of necessity a powerfully evocative image for Cocteau. The execution is a fanciful meditation on a childhood memory; the opium smoker recalls his recently squelched addiction; and the hermaphrodite depicts his own rather confused and fearful sexuality. All of them concern what Cocteau will later call "the difficulty of being." It is the child's option of rebellion in the face of this difficulty that is the purpose of the "Flying Lesson." Cocteau claimed earlier that "poets, in whom childhood is prolonged, suffer a great deal when they lose this power [of rebellion]. This is undoubtedly one of the reasons that drives the poet to use opium."[94] For Cocteau, this was a necessary point to make in making a film about the genesis of a poetic sensibility.

The scene has a powerful effect beyond Cocteau's personal obsession precisely because of its origin as an archetype. Flying, a symbolic image for sexual activity, and the Poet's voyeurism can, together, be interpreted as a reenactment of the primal scene. The Poet and the girl are

Blood of a Poet. "By breaking statues . . ." *(Courtesy Anthology Film Archives.)*

Blood of a Poet. ". . . one risks turning into one oneself." *(Courtesy Anthology Film Archives.)*

identified by their analogous physical and existential difficulties. This represents a union of the seer and the seen. The child's jeering response becomes the Poet's own while the exclusion of the Poet from the "flying" scene is symbolically remedied because of his identification with the girl. Psychologically, the Poet has a child's attitude toward sex: wishing to be included yet finding it repugnant and ultimately the cause for a negative attitude toward authority.[95]

As Frederick Brown convincingly points out,[96] the entire scene in the Hôtel des Folies Dramatiques is a variation on Cocteau's *Parade*. The "play within a play" and the characters of the opium smoker and the girl in a circus costume are direct holdovers from his earlier dance/theater piece. Yet in the film, the scene ends with the Poet carrying out the orders for his own suicide. He takes the gun and puts it to his head as if it were a logical next step in his passive adventures in the corridor, his punishment for repeating himself. While the blood streams from his head down his body, he is crowned with laurel and a voice proclaims, "Glory forever," as if he had become a hero. He rejects the costume, and presumably the glory, and makes his way out of the mirror. This final episode is interesting in a number of ways. First, it indicates an extreme of the tendency of the passivity that is first suggested by the Poet's voyeurism. He does not question the unseen voice that orders his suicide. He obeys. Secondly, Cocteau depicts the Poet as the crucified Christ, allegorizing his torment and suffering. And finally, the Poet rejects the heroic appellation in an act of rebellion against the unseen forces that guide him.

The Poet retreats through the corridor and falls out of the mirror. Angered at the snide remark of the statue that "mirrors should reflect a bit more before sending back images," the Poet smashes the statue into a pile of plaster rubble and dust. The leitmotif of plaster dust is a transitional one for Cocteau. While smashing the statue, the Poet becomes covered in white dust. As the scene changes, the narrator comments, "By breaking statutes one risks turning into one oneself." The final part of the film begins with the Poet covered in dust, having in fact become a statue. He is situated in a city courtyard, covered with snow. The snow, once plaster dust, will undergo several more transformations in the film. It will become marble in the hands of Dargelos and face powder for the statue/woman and the spectators.

The most moving scene of the film is one of the most compelling in all of Cocteau's films: the snowball fight. It is an enactment of a memory Cocteau retained from his school days of a snowy, dark street and a snowball fight that resulted in the death of a schoolmate who was hit by a snowball. He recounted this story in *Paris Album;* he recreated it in the opening of *The Holy Terrors;* he refers to it in poems and plays; and its hero/villain, Dargelos, is a character whom Cocteau mythologized throughout all his oeuvre. In *Blood of a Poet,* it forms the prelude of the final scene of the film and provides the basis for the second suicide of the Poet.

After the elegant beginning of the fight that destroys the statue of the Poet in the dusk of a Paris evening, Dargelos, a slightly older student, enters the fray. He walks on to watch the near strangulation of a boy by a group of others holding either end of a scarf.

> Dargelos, who tosses back his hair, throws off his hat and cloak and aims furiously at him. He throws the snowball.

> It hits the lens of the camera. Another snowball hits the friend in the chest. Shot of him from the waist up being hit, swaying and falling out of view.

> Shot of him lying on the ground next to his open satchel, and the books scattered in the snow. The top of the picture reveals several pairs of legs that come up behind the inert body, stop, and then run off. One pair of legs stays there, and unhurriedly walks away.

> The camera moves up the pair of legs—it is Dargelos. He walks to the entrance of the street, stops and picks up his satchel.

> Close-up of his face. He looks in the direction of the body, sticking out his tongue like a child concentrating in class, shakes back the lock of hair on his forehead and runs off, disappearing through the entrance of the street.[97]

Blood of a Poet. **Dargelos.** *(Courtesy Anthology Film Archives.)*

There is a poetic homage to Dargelos on the sound track. The image of the bloody student reappears, as if to emphasize the cruelty of Dargelos and the suffering of the boy. His head is shown in close-up, inverted, as blood streams from his mouth. His eyes flutter. There is an oblique shot of Dargelos studying his victim, and then the apparent death of the boy, as the blood continues to flow from his mouth.

Certain recurrent themes of Cocteau's work are repeated here. The dominant portrayal is that of boys as miniature soldiers, in school uniforms instead of fatigues, their games serious battles. The stance of the boys, their formation into groups, their cruelty, their wounds, and the way they are escorted off the scene—all are intended to reveal the larger scale on which they measure themselves. Their fight has some of the same qualities as the beautiful pillow fight in Jean Vigo's *Zéro de conduite*, made two years later. The nocturnal play of white flecks falling (snow and feathers) romanticizes the scene. The fight itself is a release from the rigors of the school day. It flies in the face of authority. The complex metaphor of Dargelos as the innocent perpetrator of a crime is made manifest here. The boys taking snow from the statue are taking the marble of the statue itself. (Conversely, in the artist/child analogy, sculptors are no more than the makers of permanent snowmen.) The snow is a kind of flaked marble; chunks of snow are pieces of stone. In the sequence of shots where Dargelos prepares to throw the fatal snowball, there is a brief shot of a rock in his hand, inserted between two shots of him holding a snowball. It is to emphasize his special nature. Whereas the other boys demolish the statue *as if* it were made of snow, their missiles are made harmless; in the hands of Dargelos, the material reverts to its original state and becomes hard as rock. By his special nature, he literalizes the gentle metaphor of snow and marble. The game dissolves for the other boys when one is seriously hurt. Dargelos alone remains in character as the victorious soldier who inspects his victim after all others have fled. He does not step out of his role. He lives what had been for the other boys only a temporary and imaginary foray.

Dargelos leaves the film. The child and the Poet remain. In the final sequence of the film, they again converge as like entities, as they did in the "Flying Lesson" sequence. The death of the bloodied boy prophesies that of the Poet. He stands for an aspect of the Poet. As the boy lies in the abandoned street after Dargelos leaves, it is transformed into a makeshift drawing room, as if a stage set, on which the Poet and the statue/woman now play cards. They are observed by an audience of men and women seated in loges that were formerly the windows of the street's buildings. Recalling Cocteau's fascination with the theater as a child and his desire to be among the celebrities in the audience at the Palais de Glace, this image rings with retrospective desire. The boy lies at the foot of the Poet, with traces of dried blood around his mouth and nose. The cardplayers are now suitably dressed in evening clothes; the

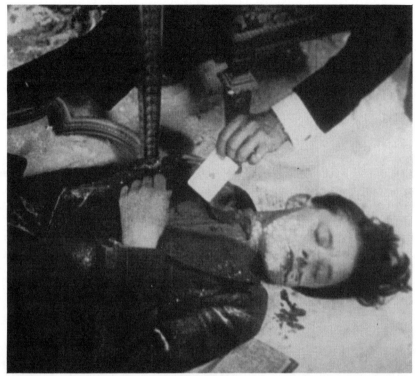

Blood of a Poet. **The Poet steals the ace of hearts.** *(Courtesy Anthology Film Archives.)*

woman wears long evening gloves (as his mother had for her evenings at the theater—again calling up provocative childhood memories). The friend who came to the door of the artist's studio looks on. The woman plays a card; the Poet considers his move. Cocteau interrupts the narrative flow with a comment on the nature of subjective time and on what is about to happen: "Documentary. Interminable, that's how the cheat imagines his gesture, faster than lightning." The Poet then reaches down and, in a medium shot of the dead boy, moves into the boy's jacket and pulls out the ace of hearts. A black "angel," with radio antenna-like wings (Feral Benga), slowly walks down the steps to the card table and lies down over the boy. In a marvelous effect of sound and image manipulation, the image switches to negative and the sound crescendos from a hum to loud buzzing sound. The effect electrifies the scene, as if the angel were dematerializing the boy. When the scene switches back to a positive image, the boy is gone. The angel rises, walks to the Poet, takes the ace of hearts, and limps back up the stairs. In a cool challenge to the Poet, the woman states, "If you don't have the ace of hearts, my dear, you're a lost man." The man's expression is transformed as if he realizes that what she says is true. In a medium shot over the shoulder of the woman, the Poet's chest bulges with exaggerated palpitations, a loud heartbeat heard on the sound track. He reaches into his pocket, takes out a revolver, and shoots himself in the head. He slumps onto the table and bleeds from the star-shaped wound on his head again, replaying the star-constellation motif. He first faces the friend leaning on the pedestal that had held the statue of the Poet, then in close-up, he faces forward, dripping blood, just as the boy had done.

The audience applauds. The woman is transformed again into a statue, now in a black cape. Painted facsimiles of eyes on her closed eyelids stare blankly before her. They appear to see without seeing. She glides off the set. She appears through a doorway and raises her gloved hand. A whistle is heard as if a taxi were being hailed. A bull slowly enters, covered with a torn map of Europe. His horns are a strung lyre, the sign of the ancient poet Orpheus. The statue glides off with him. The last scene is of the statue. Her profile is outlined in black, like a map. She lies draped in black cloth, next to the globe. The narrator proclaims, "The mortal tedium of immortality." The smokestack com-

Blood of a Poet. The woman transformed. *(Courtesy Anthology Film Archives.)*

pletes its crumbling fall, signaling the end of an instant.

No description of a cinematic sequence can meet the complexities of the clusters of images presented on the screen. Such verbs as *transform* or *appear* gloss over the shot relationships that are varied as a jump cut and dissolve. Cocteau's film style in *Blood of a Poet* is based on the clever use of editing to unify disparate spaces and times. Similarly the sound track, the harmonious mixture of music, narration, asynchronous and synchronous sound, and dialogue carries the film in very unlikely narrative directions. Cocteau was a newcomer to the use of cinematic language, but *Blood of a Poet* is evidence of a sophisticated understanding. In the shot of the artist's hand caressing his body, Cocteau's use of framing cleverly allows the viewer to speculate on the erotic goal of that hand as it descends out of the frame. The shot is a centered medium shot, fully continuous with those which precede it. After the artist reels in embrace with his hand, he sits down to continue the embrace. But the meaning of the shot changes as the hand progesses over the body. The shot becomes about what is *not* in the frame. A device usually employed to connect one character with another is here used by Cocteau to connect discreetly the artist's hand with his penis. The following shot of the artist asleep makes sense in consequence of the implied off-screen event.

In a similar fashion, the sound track reinforces the unity of the disparate elements of the film. The two distinct scenes of the film—the artist's studio and the double city/stage scene—are joined by the syncopated sound-image passage of the artist smashing the statue. The phrases spoken by the narrator are separated by pauses. Each phrase coincides with a new shot.

> The poet takes hold of a hammer and hits the statue. It breaks, and its head splits in two. He keeps on hitting. A cloud of plaster dust rises from the rubble.
>
> Still photo [photography substituted for cinema] of the poet holding the hammer, covered in plaster from head to foot. The author's voice: "By breaking statues . . ."
>
> Close-up of the poet's head, like a flour-covered character in an Italian comedy.
>
> The author's voice: ". . . one risks . . ."
>
> Shot of buildings in ruins, in the middle of which a white statue is sitting on a pedestal.
>
> The author's voice: ". . .turning into one . . ."
>
> Close-up of the statue. It is the poet's.
>
> The author's voice: ". . . oneself."

The camera moves back. The pedestal and the statue are in the Cité Mon-thiers.[98]

The phrases have a meaning that coincides with each of the shots they accompany and a second meaning that permits the transition between scenes. When we see the Poet's head covered with plaster dust, hear "one risks," and then see the white statue in the city courtyard, there is an ambiguous relationship to the "risk" involved. The Poet not only damages the statue but also himself, smothering himself in dust. The coincident risk to statue and Poet merges them, and the future destruction of the Poet/statue is foreshadowed. By the end of the sentence, the image is fulfilled. The demolition of the statue completes the transition.

To the extent that the film was meant to be a work of poetry, it is the subtlety and indirectness of Cocteau's approach to film structure that makes it so. The relationship of shots and whole scenes is, for the most part, based on detail, innuendo, rhythm, visual rhymes, and verbal puns. The prose conventions of fictional narrative are most often presented in order to be subverted by their application to taboo subjects—sex and suicide. While childhood is presented in the film as an aspect of the life of the Poet, subject to the structural permutation of poetry, it is through the elaboration of these two taboos that the more interesting manifestation of the subject may be found.

Cocteau offers very little interpretation of his film; he resists most of the interpretations of others as well. He does offer one note on *Blood of a Poet* in which he says:

I could tell you that the snowball fight is the Poet's childhood, and that when he plays a game of cards with his Fame, or his Fate, he cheats by taking from his childhood what he should be taking from himself.[99]

He is, of course, referring to the Poet taking the heart from the boy killed in the snowball fight. But how does one interpret such a claim? It is a warning against autobiography in art. In the distinction he makes between "his childhood" and "himself," the adult self seems to be separate from its past and, furthermore, seems to be of more value to the Poet than childhood is. It is a statement that one might read in light of the distinction between early and late Romanticism, between Rousseau and Nerval. Childhood is of interest to Cocteau only as an ideal. Autobiographical exploration of childhood per se seems dishonest to Cocteau at this point in his career. (He will succumb in a small degree to the autobiographical instinct in the making of *Testament of Orpheus* in 1960.)[100]

André Breton made the opposite claim in the first "Manifesto of Surrealism" (1924). In the opening paragraph, he describes the predicament of contemporary man, offering this qualification:

If he still retains a certain lucidity, all he can do is turn back toward his childhood which, however his guides and mentors may have botched it, still strikes him as somehow charming. There, the absence of any known restrictions allows him the perspective of several lives lived at once; this illusion becomes firmly rooted within him: now he is only interested in the fleeting, the extreme facility of everything. Children set off each day without a worry in the world. Everything is near at hand, the worst material conditions are fine. The woods are white or black, one will never sleep.[101]

When Breton speaks of "several lives lived at once," he is referring to discrete stages of one's life and the distinct otherness of childhood to an adult. He cites the cause of the grown man's insensitivity and superficiality as the "botched" work of his "guides and mentors." Clearly drawing on Rousseau's *Emile,* as he would eloquently do again in his "Lettre à une jeune fille américaine,"[102] he portrays children as living in the present and as models for adults. That passage forms a prelude to Breton's discussion of freedom. For Breton, the issue of childhood is merely part of the larger issue of the nature of man's perception of reality and the creation of imaginative responses to that reality. He does not identify the poet/artist with the child. He proposes an educated, analytical method unlike the naive intuitive method Cocteau espoused. Breton sought to air subjects—like sex—forbidden since childhood. By confronting an audience with issues like sex in such a way as to contribute to their analysis, literature and art can contribute to an understanding of the human mind. Cocteau sought to camouflage forbidden subjects, and to divert attention away from the raw, vulgar nature of the underpinnings of his art. Even while provocatively raising the issue of sexuality by placing the Danger of Death sign over the loins of the hermaphrodite, he refuses to explore sexuality in any but a joking fashion.

For Cocteau to offer the denial of sentimentality and autobiography in the written preface to *Blood of a Poet* is a defense against the accusations against him by Breton that his work was simply a veneer he laid over his life.[103] Even though he explicitly denied surrealism by making the convenient distinctions between dream and "half-sleep," when the film was exhibited Cocteau sought the approval of the surrealists and was disappointed by their attacks on him.[104] His claim that the Poet must suffer for "taking from his childhood what he should be taking from himself" is Cocteau's attempt to have his cake and eat it. And even then, the claim is not supported by the film, since by dying, the Poet, with whom Cocteau identified, becomes the child once more, bleeding from the head.

The film is an allegory. It is dedicated to such Renaissance religious allegorical painters as Piero della Francesca and Paolo Uccello. In refusing to call the imagery in his film symbols, by insisting that they are "coats of arms," Cocteau unfairly and inaccurately rebukes surrealism for a weak and tawdry use of an aesthetic phenomenon that earlier and greater artists had mastered. In his defense of his film, Cocteau found it necessary and convenient to distinguish his film from those of the surrealists—namely, *Un chien andalou* (1928)—by calling on a pre-Freudian tradition. Cocteau ignores the numerous times when he would find himself "taking from his childhood" experiences, stories, fantasies, and obsessions. Most significantly, he does not acknowledge the suicides in *Blood of a Poet* as the compulsive reenactment of a childhood experience that would oversee his life: the suicide of his father. The most significant fact to keep in mind here is that almost categorical repression of the event in all of Cocteau's memoirs. By its absence it draws attention to itself. Yet the issue of suicide as well as the function of authority—both of which can be traced to his childhood perception of his father—are pervasive themes for Cocteau. Because of his own severe repression of the event he does not wish his critics to search too deeply or analyze too vigorously the source of these themes. He establishes a critical theory against interpretation to prohibit the investigation.

Orpheus: Childhood without Children

Orpheus (1950) is another example of Cocteau's exploration of these issues. Though there are no children in the film (except the one as yet unborn to Eurydice), many themes appear that coincide with that of childhood. The nature of Orpheus's poethood, his relationship to the "zone" and its authorities, his love of death, and the mirror all point to the same concerns that have been discussed in terms of Cocteau's literary and dramatic works.

Orpheus is one of a set of plays and films in which Cocteau refashions Greek and Roman myths. *Antigone* (1928), *Orpheus* (the play) (1927), and *The Infernal Machine* (1934) (after the Oedipus myth) are all expressly modernized versions of the theatrical tradition since Sophocles. Part of the appeal of these ancient dramas lies in their classical themes and well-known plots. The manipulation of time in the concatenation of ancient and contemporary eras characterized Cocteau's treatment. The familiarity with the action even before it is performed, permits one to watch the process of the unfolding of the inevitable. Ubiquitous fate and the gods are the hidden causes for all that occurs; and Cocteau focused on them as the dramatic equivalent to the unknown, invisible forces of which he often wrote.

The film version of *Orpheus* places the myth in a contemporary setting. Rather than the charming musician, Orpheus is an aging poet set upon by youthful aspirants to his fame, a nagging wife, and a group of bohemian feminists. Rather than bewitching nature, he is himself bewitched by an Apollinairian poetic voice that recites brief lines and numbers over the car radio.[105] Through the scene in the Poets' Cafe, the

Orpheus. **Cegeste struck down.** *(Courtesy Anthology Film Archives.)*

domestic quarrels, the characters of the prefect and the reporter, and the riot of the young men and women, Cocteau creates an ordinary and plausible context for Orpheus's adventures in the netherworld of the "zone."[106]

The film begins with the title and credits written in Cocteau's hand, dotted with stars, like a constellation. This seems equally a part of Cocteau's iconography and a reference to the end of one version of the myth of Orpheus, in which Orpheus's head is thrown into the sky by Apollo and becomes a constellation. The overture to Gluck's *Orfeo ed Euridice* accompanies the titles. The first shot is of Orpheus (Jean Marais) at the Café des Poètes. The camera pans around the room, and Orpheus is seen getting up from his table and looking out the window that frames the Princess's (Maria Casarès) Rolls-Royce. The Princess and Cegeste (Edouard Dermit) get out; he is drunk. She moves through the cafe, evidently a friend and patron of youth. Orpheus is beckoned by an elder man, a former poet, who speaks the words that Cocteau heard as a young man from Diaghilev: "Astonish us." A fight breaks out and percussive jazz is heard on the sound track. Cegeste is struck by speeding motorcyclists.

Orpheus accompanies the Princess, with the fallen Cegeste, to her home. She resurrects the dead young man and, with his two assassins, passes out of her room through the mirror. Orpheus, frustrated by the unaccountable powers of the Princess and her unwillingness to answer his question, faints against the mirror.

Eurydice (Maria Dea), hurt and anxiety stricken by Orpheus's absence is consoled by her friend Aglaonice (Juliette Gréco) and the prefect of police (Henri Crémieux). Orpheus wakes from his collapse in a quarry, his face pressed against the poollike mirror in the sand. He finds the Princess's chauffeur Heurtebise (François Périer), who drives him home. Orpheus quarrels with Eurydice and her consolers, ascends to his bedroom and climbs out of the window. Heurtebise remains with Eurydice as Orpheus begins a series of listening sessions at the car radio. Eurydice goes to bed to rest. Heurtebise pleads with Orpheus to attend to her.

On the way to his interview with the prefect of police, who wants to question Orpheus about the death of Cegeste, Orpheus sees the Princess and chases her. After a series of frustrating sightings, he finally loses her, as he is surrounded by cloying autograph seekers. Orpheus's contemporaries from the Café des Poètes denounce him as a plagiarist to the prefect of police. Orpheus skips the interview and returns home to install himself again at the car radio.

Eurydice, pregnant and inconsolably hurt by Orpheus's irritability and lack of attention, leaves home, against the advice of Heurtebise. She is hit by two motorcyclists, like those who killed Cegeste. Heurtebise carries her to bed and tries to persuade Orpheus to go to her. The Princess and Cegeste arrive via the mirror and prepare to take Eurydice back with them. Part of the preparation is Cegeste's broadcast of the numbers and phrases to which Orpheus listens in the car. Heurtebise challenges the Princess's authority and vanishes in anger at her intransigence. Eurydice rises from her deathbed and she, Cegeste, and the Princess leave through the mirror, angrily broken by the Princess. The mirror is reconstituted, and Eurydice's body once again lies on the bed. Heurtebise brings the incredulous Orpheus to Eurydice's deathbed and persuades Orpheus to accompany him and retrieve Eurydice. Orpheus puts on rubber gloves that the Princess has left behind and passes through the mirror accompanied by Heurtebise. The time is six o'clock. They travel through the ruins of the urban "zone."

The Princess and Cegeste are questioned by a tribunal about the nature of their orders to take Eurydice. Orpheus and Heurtebise arrive through the mirror. The Princess is questioned about her love for Orpheus, which she admits. They leave together, embrace, and vow their mutual love. Heurtebise is questioned about his love for Eurydice. All parties are called back and the judges rule that Orpheus and Eurydice may go back with the stipulation that Orpheus not look at her. Heurtebise is permitted to accompany them. They return through the mirror as the six o'clock chime finishes its ring, and while a letter, delivered by the

Orpheus. Orpheus watches the arrival of the Princess's car. *(Courtesy Anthology Film Archives.)*

Orpheus. Orpheus and Eurydice exchange final glances in the rearview mirror. *(Courtesy Anthology Film Archives.)*

mailman while they entered the "zone," drops through the slot. The letter, in mirror writing, threatens to hold Orpheus to account for the death of Cegeste. After numerous ridiculous scares and avoidances of Eurydice, Orpheus storms out. At night, Eurydice, miserable about their life together, tries to trick Orpheus into looking at her. Just as he wakes, the light goes out. Finally, he catches sight of her in the rearview mirror of the car and she disappears.

A crowd gathers at Orpheus's gate, demanding that he account for the body of Cegeste and his poems, now published in Orpheus's name. A riot ensues and Orpheus is shot with his own gun. Heurtebise takes Orpheus in the car, as the two motorcyclists hold the police at bay. Heurtebise and Orpheus travel through the "zone" and further, into a large ruin. The Princess and Cegeste wait for them there. Orpheus and the Princess embrace and reaffirm their vows. The Princess proclaims that what they are about to do is necessary for their love. Heurtebise and Cegeste hold Orpheus as the Princess demands concentration and will power. Flashbacks of earlier scenes, now with Heurtebise and Orpheus traveling backward, reverse the time of the film. The Princess declares they are finished. Orpheus and Eurydice are seen in their bedroom. They are enraptured with each other, discuss their future child and embrace. The two motorcyclists arrive at the ruin to escort the Princess and Heurtebise to their unknown prosecutors. Cegeste remains.

The achievement of *Orpheus* is its incorporation of a speculation on the nature of death within an accessible narrative form. Cocteau uses an interplay between literalism and metaphor to guide that speculation. Death as a person and a place, as well as that aspect of life toward which we all are moving is illustrated in the film. *Orpheus*'s technique and structure facilitate the exploration of the idea of death, in the tradition of Nerval.

The death of Cegeste poses the issue as the literal negative of life. As Cegeste dies in the car, the landscape is transformed from a positive to negative image. The end of the film presents immortal life as the double negative of death. Orpheus dies twice and is pressed back to life by moving backward out of death, through the mirror. It is difficult to *describe* the nature of double negation as a metaphor for immortality, yet through the devices of flashbacks and reverse motion, Cocteau easily *depicts* it. Orpheus becomes immortal only after he is propelled out of the "zone" by death's agents.

The film's ability to glide between the literal and the metaphorical is its primary charm. The introductory encounter between Heurtebise and Eurydice is full of the amusing interpenetration of poetic and ordinary language and image. The scene is established by a high, omniscient, angular shot that takes in Heurtebise, Eurydice, and most of the room. Heurtebise jocularly accuses Eurydice of inviting him to stay in order to pump him for information about Orpheus's night out with the Princess: "You want me under your thumb because I'm part of the story." But the scene shifts quickly out of its sentimental conventionalism when Eurydice inadvertently boils the coffee. She praises Orpheus's attractions: He is "handsome" and "famous." The coffee boils over in orgasmic consequence of her rhapsodic description. The metaphor is subtle and comic.[107] The comic difficulty of the interview continues as Eurydice takes the boiling pot off the stove. She leaves the gas on. Heurtebise cautions her to turn it off and tells the story of his suicide. He qualifies his frank confession when he realizes how puzzling it is to Eurydice. Her ingenuousness and Heurtebise's blushing embarrassment at being one of the walking dead intensify the effect of the language at cross-purposes. It is both the initiation of Heurtebise's love for Eurydice (in the manner of a bedroom farce) and the first realization of the impossibility of consummating love between the living and the dead.

Cocteau often uses an elliptical editing style. The chase sequence is based on the disjunction of edited space and time so that Orpheus can never catch the Princess. The deaths of Cegeste and Eurydice are both depicted in an elliptical way. They venture into the street; the roar of motorcycles is heard; motorcycles zoom away; each character is struck. The scene of Eurydice's death is signaled by her loose bicycle careening down the road's shoulder. It is a sign of her fall. The nondepiction of the crucial event, the moment of murder itself, serves to increase the impact of the scene. In *Orpheus*, the slayings must be purposeless and random, and the murderers nameless and faceless, to promote the higher understanding of death as a purposeful and willful force behind even the most haphazard circumstances. Cocteau's elliptical editing serves that end. By refusing to include the incident itself, he emphasizes spiritual rather than physical death.

Cocteau tends to use the conventional cinematic structure of the shot-countershot in his films to confirm the psychological reality of the world he presents. The opening scene begins with a reaction to something not yet seen. Orpheus sees the Princess's car, then it is shown; the police and Orpheus see Cegeste killed and look horrified, then his assassins are shown driving off past the body that we see lying in the street. The reaction shot is placed before the action in the film. This gives the privilege of seeing to those within the film before extending it to the viewer. The entire film is structured in this way, creating a hierarchy of seeing: The Princess and Heurtebise see more than Orpheus (and there are judges who see even more than either of death's agents); Orpheus sees more than Eurydice (since he is a poet); and they all see before the viewer does. Cocteau represents a reality, but one based on a power relationship in terms of who sees things first. It is a reality peculiar to Cocteau. Rooting the mythological elements in quotidian life (and autobiography), he makes the lines between this and the other side of life virtually nonexistent.

Nowhere in the films of Cocteau is the power of photography to convince us of reality more in evidence than in *Orpheus.* By personifying death and creating an image of the afterlife, Cocteau asks the audience to believe in their actuality, in much the same way that Carl Dreyer asks one to believe in the resurrection of Inger in *Ordet.* By maintaining the same texture of image and sound, avoiding special effects often associated with dream and heavenly (or hellish) imagery (loss of focus, mist, flames), Cocteau insists on the continuous reality of life and death. Death acts the lady; her aides fall easily into our stereotypes of the military and policemen. The transport of the fallen Cegeste only momentarily transforms itself into his death by the switch from a positive image of a tree-lined boulevard, "the usual road," to a negative one. It becomes a shadow world, the inversion of the real. The continuity of the road, however, establishes the metaphoric convergence of the two worlds. Except for the passage via the mirror between the two, clarity of focus and normalcy of speed characterize both worlds. During the passage sequences, the focus shifts slightly because of the rear-screen-projection technique used to separate the gliding speed of Heurtebise from the ritardando of Orpheus and those others wandering in the decayed urban "zone." The passage is the only indication one is given of

Orpheus. Heurtebise and Orpheus in the "zone." *(Courtesy Anthology Film Archives.)*

the landscape of *Orpheus* as a fiction, because of its unorthodox cinematographic style. By insisting on conventional cinematography throughout, the continuity of being is affirmed.

The importance of photography for Cocteau comes directly from its ability to convince us of the verity of its subject. He writes of its ability to do the very thing that children do in play: It assembles scenes from life and asserts their truth simply by presenting them. His desire to be believed as a filmmaker is consistently linked to the notion that children inhabit the self-contained universe of their minds and believe in that universe. Certainly, credibility is something for which narrative cinema has always strived. Cocteau presses the limits by asking an audience to believe in impossible phenomena, much as science fiction does. He is speaking of cinema in general when he has Heurtebise tell Orpheus, "In order to go through glass it is not necessary to understand, it is necessary to believe." To support his demands as a filmmaker, he calls on childhood as an ally. In the name of childhood he upbraids those who remain unconvinced, abandoning them to a debased and unimaginative cinema.

While in *Beauty and the Beast,* Cocteau enfolds his film in the accessible wrapping of a fairy tale, in *Orpheus* he does not give the viewer such a clue to the forthcoming mysteries. As does Orpheus, the viewer must accept the events without sufficient explanation, with the faith that sense will be made at some later time. Yet the complex layering of simultaneous realities is never explained; the waking from the dream at the end of *Orpheus* holds no sure meaning.[108] One is not confidently grounded: Life, dream, and the afterworld are equally plausible. He does not dismiss dream and death as acts of imagination. In writing of *Blood of a Poet,* Cocteau insists on this principle for film: "that film contained visible proof that the unreal existed as an object, which I actually showed."[109] Even earlier he had asserted the *reality* of the unreal; the frontispiece of his book *L'ange Heurtebise* bore this inscription: "with a photograph of the angel by Man Ray."[110] He goes on to insist on this more emphatically for *Orpheus* (which he considers a more opaque film): "A film more closed, such as *Orphée,* has fewer entrances, so that many people butt against locked doors. And the speed inherent in any cinematic spectacle leaves them no time to try out different keys."[111] The scene in which Orpheus chases the Princess through the streets of Paris is "closed" in that way. It is edited to transform movement through space from a natural to a supernatural event.

The trip to hell (Cocteau's "zone") is incorporated in the Orphic myth that excited Cocteau's reinvention. As was discussed earlier, the exploration of invisibility and the representation of death were obsessions in his work. As he aged, he more and more stridently denied any meaning to this endeavor other than an arcane interest in the imagination and the delicate confluence of the imaginary and the real in the minds of artists and children. Though he unhesitantly used the classical and symbolical signs that had been interpreted by Freud to join the sexual content of ancient mythology with the mental life and behavior of contemporary man, Cocteau refused to acknowledge psychoanalysis in any but the most negative way. He insisted until his death that the images he used and the structures he created were innocent, intuitive, and true to some nameless inner reality that coincided with the myths themselves.

The passage into and out of the mirror is germane in this context. It springs from two sources: the childhood memory of his mother's dressing and Lewis Carroll's children's story, *Through the Looking Glass.* The links with Carroll's tale are manifold. Alice ventures into a world very similar to her own, but altered in remarkable ways. As she travels to the enlarged chess field, she and the Red Queen move, but the landscape remains the same, just as Orpheus and Heurtebise travel to and through the rear projection of the "zone" at very different speeds from one another and from the slowly receding "zone" itself. Heurtebise chastises Orpheus for always asking Why?; Heurtebise is as impatient as the Tiger-lily to the Rose: " 'I wonder how you do it—' ('You're always wondering,' said the Tiger-lily)."[112] Alice hears the disturbing news that she is but the Red King's dream. When Orpheus wants to find

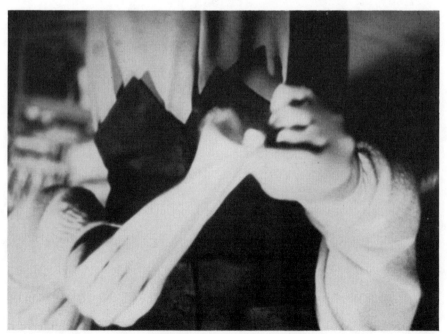

Orpheus. Orpheus puts on the gloves. *(Courtesy Anthology Film Archives.)*

Orpheus. Through the looking glass. *(Courtesy Anthology Film Archives.)*

the one who gives the orders, the Princess retorts that "he is nowhere. Some believe that he sleeps and that we are a dream, a bad dream." The Princess runs through the city streets like a frantic White Rabbit, checking her watch.[113] Any attempt to represent dream, imagination, and the afterlife in a quasi-realistic manner is bound to touch on areas that Carroll explored. The evidence that Cocteau knew Carroll's work and the similarity of their imagery and discourse is too great to ascribe to chance their parallel endeavor.[114]

Orpheus enters the "zone" through his own reflection in the mirror. He falls into himself, and by so doing has a brief meeting with death. The mirror is a symbol of narcissistic love. The key to the image is found earlier in the film, after the Princess has taken Orpheus for a ride with Cegeste. The death of the young poet recalls that of the boy in *Blood of a Poet;* they both bleed from the mouth. After trying to follow them into the mirror (in the abandoned building the Princess calls home), Orpheus faints against its surface only to find himself waking in a sand-filled quarry with his face on another, poollike, mirror. For the duration of that shot, Orpheus *is* Narcissus. Later, with the help of Heurtebise, he discovers how to go beyond his own image.

Since Mallarmé, there has been a thrust to depict, rather than describe concrete and abstract phenomena in works of literature and art. Breton's cry for works of *surréalité* is a continuation of that aesthetic.

Breton called for representation of a world that included the depths of the human consciousness and the mechanisms with which it operates. Although Cocteau worked within the same poetic tradition that sought to represent a world that included the interior reality of man, he refused to come to grips with a central area of subjectivity: sexuality. He used imagery and combinations that verged on the symbolic. Historically, he has sometimes been confused with the surrealists—significantly here, by Brakhage. But by elaborately denying any content other than the most elusively high-toned, and by disavowing the surrealist movement, he ignored some of the most interesting insights of his films.

Certainly, Cocteau's antagonism to surrealism was not unfounded. Breton despised Cocteau and said so in public. The surrealist movement, according to Breton, was decidedly heterosexual and emphatically antibourgeois. Cocteau, despite his several affairs with women and the few scandals he caused among the bourgeoisie, was primarily an upper-middle-class homosexual. The sexual issue was not publicly acknowledged by Cocteau, whose remarks on surrealism remained within the bounds of aesthetic factionalism:

> My break with the Surrealists . . . arose first, from my disobedience of official decrees, and second, from an instinct for value, stronger in me than the value itself which at that time I could put in to the service of a cause.[115]

More significantly, he disagreed with the surrealists about the nature of the other reality they explored in common and about the function of symbolic imagery. Cocteau vehemently argued against Freudianism, a method of analysis finally embraced by the surrealists. Cocteau's argument against Freud is based on his reading of "Leonardo da Vinci: A Psychosexual Study of an Infantile Reminiscence."[118] He was offended by Freud's ascription of sexual motives to Leonardo's life's work. It is characteristic that Cocteau would seize on Freud's most well known work on the analysis of an artist. It corresponded with his self-image as a Leonardo: jack-of-all-trades and a genius. As early as 1928, Cocteau attacked Freud for misunderstanding the nature of art and artists. In *Le mystère laïc,* writing on Georgio de Chirico, Cocteau offers the first of his attacks:

> There is no serious art without puns and riddles. That is to say, there is only serious art. Through the naiveté of Freud we can sense the greatness of Leonardo who flies in a dream with Uccello. Whenever Freud deplores his childish behavior Leonardo da Vinci flies.
>
> Every masterpiece is made up of concealed admissions, calculations, lofty puns and strange riddles. The world of officialdom would collapse if they discovered what was concealed by Leonardo or Watteau, to mention only two of the well-known secretive people. It is through the things which Freud regards as childish that an artist tells his own story without opening his

mouth, dominates art and endures.[117]

Cocteau's criticism stands on a casual reading of Freud's essay.[118] Cocteau berates Freud for his unwillingness to leave the mystery and "concealed admissions" of an artist's work alone. In this early critique, he does not take issue with Freud's conclusions, but with the nature of analysis when applied to art. Enigmas and the contradictory "concealed admissions" are at the very heart of what Cocteau, and therefore *his* Leonardo, are about. Cocteau does not mention homosexuality but implies it each time he refers to Leonardo's childishness. According to Freud there is

> a strong presumption that Leonardo, whose phantasy of the vulture was our starting point [and who was the painter of the enigmatic Mona Lisa], was himself a homosexual of this very type. (Brackets added)[119]

Cocteau performs an act of concealment even as he seeks to explore Freud's shortcomings.

More than twenty years later, Cocteau took up this same theme and elaborated it. The central theme of *The Hand of a Stranger* is invisibility. In that context, he discusses Freud's "vulgar" probings, again using the Leonardo essay.

> One should not confuse the tenebrosity of which I speak and that into which Freud asked his patients to descend. Freud burgled poverty-stricken dwellings. Out of them he got a few pieces of wretched furniture and a few erotic pictures. He never sanctified the transcendental in the abnormal. He did not offer a welcome to the great disorders. He offered the pestiferous a private confessional. . . .
>
> The Freudian key to dreams is most naive. Simple things are dubbed complex. Freud's obsessions with sex was bound to seduce an idle society to which sex is the king-pin of life. . . .
>
> It is easy to get at Freud. His hell (his purgatory) is scaled down to fit the mass of mankind. In distinction from this study of ours, all Freud wants is visibility.[120]

Cocteau was not interested in the therapeutic aspects of Freud's dream analysis. This much he shared with the surrealists. It is why he criticizes Freud's attitude toward "the great disorders." Clearly, one of those disorders was homosexuality, which Freud contended could and should be "corrected" through psychoanalysis. Cocteau was defensive to the extreme on this issue, refusing even to acknowledge it as the root of disagreement.

Homosexuality is not the only major issue that divides Cocteau from his contemporary surrealists. They sought to expose what Cocteau calls the "invisible." Under this umbrellalike word he included unconscious and conscious elements in life and works of art. To expose them destroys their power and aura. In the passage that follows the one just quoted, Cocteau chastises Freud for overinterpreting the shape of the vulture in Leonardo's "Saint Anne with Two Others," preferring to attribute it to a kind of art student's in joke, done with the intent of "tricking the dictatorial police of the Church." Cocteau's attitude reflects a great deal of anxiety about the interpretation of his own work. Preferring to evoke sexual issues rather than spell them out, preferring to tantalize rather than dramatize (as the surrealists were prone to do), and above all, preferring to see without being seen and, reciprocally, be seen without seeing the seer, Cocteau upholds "invisibility" as the banner of the true artist, and faith rather than analysis as the principle that should guide the understanding of works of art.

It is no wonder that he resisted the analysis of such works as *Orpheus*. To equate oneself with the protagonist and then depict that protagonist as a narcissist is not the act of one who is concerned with *meaning*. As in *Blood of a Poet*, narcissism (and in that film, the peculiar onanism that collapses masturbation with fellatio, the mouth in the hand) is an integral part of the life of the artist as Cocteau mythologized it. It is around this issue, too, that Cocteau stood apart from the surrealists. They sought to supersede ego involvement in art making by allowing the unconscious to become the moving force in their process. The exploration of one's self as an artist by making an image of that self was antithetical to the surrealist endeavor. Cocteau chose the opposite option. The mirror in which he watched himself at his mother's feet later became the paradigmatic image by an obsessive egoist.

Once Orpheus enters the mirror—the "zone"—the question of invisibility becomes inextricably linked with that of authority. Judges determine the consequences of all the passages into and out of the mirror by the Princess, Heurtebise, Cegeste, and Orpheus. Cocteau makes very little distinction between the tone of the judges and that of the Princess; those who speak do so with curt and impatient authority. Neal Oxenhandler, in *Scandal and Parade*, points to Cocteau's paranoia as the source of this picture of authority.[121] The universe, it seemed to Cocteau, is guided by a malevolent intelligence. It is very much the way a child might see the natural and social forces—unintelligible, arbitrary, but supremely powerful.[122] The Princess, the agent of universal forces, speaks to Orpheus in the tones of a sadistic mother, calling him stupid and ordering him about.

She establishes her power by forbidding him to act without her permission. When Orpheus enters her room, he changes the radio station to the obscure broadcast they heard in the car. The Princess changes it back to Eurydice's lament from Gluck's opera, as if to flash-forward to the next scene—Eurydice crying at home. The Princess angrily accuses Orpheus of interfering. Later, she exhibits her will by cracking the mirror as she looks into it with an angry glance. She destroys it—the

Orpheus. The mirror broken by an angry glance. *(Courtesy Anthology Film Archives.)*

object of the radio broadcast—saying, "Mirrors would do well to reflect more." It is a gesture that can be traced to the Snow White tale. In that story, the wicked stepmother destroys the mirror that reveals what she does not wish to see.

While Heurtebise leads Orpheus between the mirrors that connect his bedroom to the courtroom, Orpheus is amazed by what he sees and asks a number of questions. Heurtebise responds to him as an adult would to a child: "Why? . . . always Why? Don't ask me any more questions, just walk! Do I have to take you by the hand?" Cocteau was sensitive to his role as a child in the world, having lived with his mother until he was past forty. His work indicates an extreme distaste for women, especially of the motherly type. Eurydice is depicted as an insecure, whining nag. In *The Hand of a Stranger,* while eulogizing his own mother, he speaks of being treated like a child: "But what nobody will admit in us is a mixture of childhood and age, unless it be as a way of being spoiled. But I am not like that. Sometimes I am scolded and upbraided without people realizing that they are talking to me in the way families talk to children. I am, in a phrase, a damned nuisance."[123] Orpheus *is* a nuisance to Heurtebise at that moment. Heurtebise had developed an intolerance for those beings who want to understand what can only be experienced. His impatience mimics that of the Princess who had insisted that Orpheus not ask any more questions after the death of Cegeste.

The judges stun Orpheus into silent obeisance in the "zone." He responds to civil authority quite differently. In his contempt for the soft life he had been leading as a popular poet, he lashed out at his wife, her women friends, and the prefect of police. After his encounter with the Princess, he throws the prefect out of his home; when called for an interview at the prefecture, he skips the appointment in a frustrated attempt to catch up with the elusive Princess. He reserves his respect for those superiors who rule behind the scenes. Cocteau's repressed fixation on his dead father, omnipotence, and invisibility are collapsed upon a notion of God in this dual representation of authority. At each encounter with death (in the form of the Princess) his fascination reinforces her authority. When she says, "I love you," he replies, "You are all powerful." When he says, "I love you," she asks, "Will you obey me?"

One of the ways in which Cocteau talked about time was to use the metaphor of a child at play, for whom, once the imaginary process has begun, no time exists. When Cocteau writes that "a child's eyes register quickly—later on he develops the film,"[124] he speaks not only of quick-witted children who are first perceptive and later meditative. He is discussing the timelessness of subjective time and children's acceptance of that state as normal and desirable. The instant during which the events in the "zone" happen is the same kind of instant during which *Blood of a Poet* occurs. The unfolding of Orpheus's adventure through the looking glass is posited as both real and imaginary; the equivalent of a child's game. In *Blood of a Poet,* the confusions of time, space, and plot were produced to startle and disturb an audience, an aspiration of the French avant-garde in the 1920s and 1930s. In *Orpheus* these cinematic manipulations are domesticated to fit within the narrative and to gloss over the content of what is being shown. By eliminating references to masturbation and suicide, by casting the events on the other side of the mirror in the atmosphere of a decadent boudoir and Grecian-like ruins of Paris (as one sees in the last shot, which formalizes the chaos of the rubble into columns and arches) rather than a seedy hotel, and by making the difference between the two realms difficult to detect, Cocteau protects what are essentially the same obsessive concerns from the probing eyes of the viewer. In making an even more convincing allegory, he better conceals the admissions he felt compelled to make.

Beauty and the Beast: The Child's Genre

Beauty and the Beast was made in 1945, five years before *Orpheus.* It is the greatest act of concealment Cocteau achieved. He couched all of the issues discussed heretofore in the naive form of a fairy tale. The stylization (eighteenth-century realism) and the form (a fairy tale that permits the suspension of critical judgment in favor of witnessing the unfolding of a fantasy) both serve to formulate the game of hide-and-seek that Cocteau played so well. He makes a plea to the child in every adult. He uses the well-known fairy tale in the same way he had ancient myths: to allegorize his life. The "concealed admissions" are better made in the catchall of magic and enchantment. Insofar as it is also addressed to his peers, it explores questions of belief, omniscience, and sexuality in the same manner as his other films.

The story of *Beauty and the Beast* is well known. Cocteau made a new, but not radically different version of it. Beauty is the youngest in a motherless family, dominated by her two elder sisters. Her father leaves home to meet his ships and promises to return with gifts, including a rose for his best-beloved Beauty. His fortunes are seized by creditors and, despondent, he loses his way home, finally spending the night in the Beast's castle. Before he leaves in the morning, he picks a rose, not anticipating that it would enrage the Beast, who demands retribution. Father returns home, and Beauty goes in his stead to the Beast's estate. He loves her and wants to marry her. She softens toward him but continually refuses. He allows her to return home, where her sisters, brother, and suitor envy her riches and conspire to kill the Beast. Beauty, realizing her love for the Beast, returns to him, while her brother and suitor, Avenant, attempt to break into the temple housing the Beast's riches. The Beast dies as Avenant falls into the temple. Avenant is transformed into the Beast while the Beast becomes a princely Avenant, who revives and swoops Beauty up into the sky.

The style of the film is simultaneously realistic and fantastic. In the tradition of Reinhardt's *A Midsummer Night's Dream* (1935), there is a seamless interpenetration of reality and magic or fantasy. The Beast's estate is sparkling, misty, or shrouded in smoke; Beauty's home is starkly lit. But the transitions from one place to the next are fluid. The dialogue is literal and often humorous. There is a continuity of being from Beauty's to the Beast's estate that is similar to that of this world and the "zone" of *Orpheus*. Instead of a mirror (which has other functions in *Beauty and the Beast*), the passage between worlds is through the enchanted forest. Instead of Heurtebise, there is the Beast's enchanted horse, Magnifique.

The film opens with a powerful prologue:

Children have implicit faith in what we tell them. They believe that the plucking of a rose can bring disaster to a family, that the hands of a half-human beast begin to smoke after he has killed, and that the beast is put to shame when a young girl comes to live in his house. They believe a host of other simple things.

I ask you to have the same kind of simple faith, and for the spell to work, let

me just say four magic words, the true "Open Sesame" of childhood:
"Once upon a time . . ."[125]

This is as much an observation on the nature of childhood as it is an
introduction to the film. He postulates childhood on faith and belief. It
is the other side of children's ability to create a world in which they can
live with conviction. They can also participate in a world that is created
outside of themselves, if it is asked of them.

Cocteau used the magical "Open Sesame" on another occasion, in his
discussion of "tenebrosity" and Freud. After his proclamation that "all
Freud wants is visibility," he goes on to describe his own desires:

> The tenebrosity which engages me is different. It is a treasure cave. By
> courage—and the right password—it may be opened, not by either a doctor
> or a neurotic. But if the treasure makes us forget the *Open Sesame*, it is a
> dangerous cave.[126]

In the work of art, there is meaning, to be sure, and often secret and
hidden meaning, according to Cocteau. Concealed admissions, but admissions nevertheless. Content is the treasure; but Cocteau asserts that
one should never lose sight of the process by which this content is
revealed. "Open Sesame" is the whole range of aesthetic procedures,
stylistic devices, and ineffable resonances of works of art that distinguish one work from another and from explications and treatises on the
subject. The antagonist in this particular argument is Freud, but it is a
larger point he is making than just an antipsychoanalytic one. Cocteau
wanted to bolster the grounds for the artist to defy rationality. He
wanted to keep a place for the artist to create works that were mysterious even to himself as a kind of perpetual motion machine that generates
areas of inquiry as it investigates them. It is a dubious endeavor, but
Cocteau is not alone. The notion of raging creativity freed from the
limits of logic and analysis has been a mainstream current in thinking
about art since Romanticism.

In addressing the prologue to "you," Cocteau invites the audience to
mimic his idealized children. He makes a request for participation by
the spectator in the game that unites filmmakers with film viewers. It is
the game that was initiated as a paradigm in *The Holy Terrors* in which
those who participate are exempt from any authority other than their
own. As a participant, the viewer becomes complicit with the matters at
hand and, simply by watching, is implicated in their consequences. He
casts this demand for complicity in the charming light of childhood. In
saying of himself that he wanted to make "a film that would plunge me
into a lustral bath of childhood,"[127] he also wishes to share that shower
of illumination with his audience. He seduces the audience with the
offer to restore them to an earlier and more credulous relationship with
the world. Lydia Crowson bases her book, *The Esthetic of Jean Coc-*

teau, on the restorative power of his work. She contends that Cocteau's theater succeeds in establishing complicity between an audience and the author, and that it casts the audience back into childhood. Both by entering the milieu of the play and by losing oneself in the collectivity of the audience, one reverts to a childlike wonderment at that which is taking place on the stage. Crowson, like Stanley Cavell, gives a privileged status to the group phenomena of theater and movies.

> [Cocteau] wanted to create a private world and invite the public inside, much as children fashion games to play with each other . . . As the participant abandons his habitual adult mode of consciousness, he in a sense returns to a child's relationship with the world, in which the perceiver experiences *le merveilleux* for the first time. United into a single body with those around him, he loses awareness of himself as an individual and becomes a part of the work before him. For a short while solitude and fragmentation cease, and life assumes the form it had before man's consciousness of *le néant:* a primeval bliss where play was a natural process and did not simply function as a ploy against emptiness.[128]

In Crowson's system, "play" operates in the same way as Cocteau's "Open Sesame," to stand for the artistic process that is imaginative and beyond reason.

It is a fixed game, however. In choosing to work within a narrative mode that, no matter how much it strays from cinematic conventions, seeks to overwhelm and convince an audience, Cocteau does not allow freedom to respond in any other way than that which he prescribes. *Beauty and the Beast* is very far from *Blood of a Poet* and those films in the avant-garde tradition which have followed. The open-endedness of *Blood of a Poet* and its juxtapositions and evocative imagery allow the spectator to bring much of his own experience to bear in his perception of the film, including anaytical and critical judgment. One suspects that the critical response to *Blood of a Poet* (pointing out the fetishization of sex and suicide) set into motion yet another act of repression that resulted in the submersion of his personal obsessions in the descriptive form of the fairy tale.

As *Orpheus* would be later, *Beauty and the Beast* is set in a realistic manner. Cocteau attempts to invoke Vermeer in the style of his interiors. The intense light, the clarity of focus, the period sets, and conventional editing of the opening scenes establish a sense of objective reality that Cocteau will use to reinforce the believability of the Beast's domain.

The film begins with an exterior scene of Beauty's brother, Ludovic (Michel Auclair), and her suitor, Avenant (Jean Marais), in an archery contest. Avenant shoots an arrow that misses the target and enters a window. The scene changes to the interior of the house where Beauty (Josette Day) is serving her sisters Adelaide (Mila Parely) and Felicie

(Nane Germon) as they dress. Adelaide screams when the arrow flies into the room, nearly hitting her small dog. Felicie faints. The sisters quarrel with the men, and the scene continues as the women prepare to leave. Felicie and Adelaide call for sedan chairs and are clumsily carried off through the courtyard. While Ludovic ridicules his screeching sisters, Avenant is left alone with Beauty. He declares his love. She explains why she must remain at home as a servant, thereby establishing the foundation for the narrative that ensues. "If my father's ships hadn't been lost in a storm, perhaps I could have a good time like them [her sisters]. But we're ruined, Avenant, and I simply have to work . . . I want to stay unmarried and live with my father." She refuses Avenant's embrace. Ludovic enters as she does so and attacks Avenant. Beauty, again distressed by the disharmony around her, begs them to stop. They are interrupted when they hear voices. From above, they watch Beauty's father (Marcel André) enter with several men. He announces to them his good fortune. "We're going to be rich. One of my cargo ships has made port." Ludovic accuses Avenant of being a fortune hunter, of having previous knowledge of the news when he asked Beauty to marry him. Father is distressed that Beauty might leave him. She dotingly vows that she never will. The sisters enter and are delighted at the news of the prospective fortune. As he leaves to meet the ship, Father is asked by Felicie and Adelaide to bring them goods and jewels from the city. Beauty asks for a rose. When Father arrives at the port, he receives the news that his much-hoped-for fortune has been seized by his creditors.

The opening sequences of *Beauty and the Beast* establish the context for what will follow. All of the human elements conspire to reinforce the realism of the background. Injustice, sibling rivalry, money trouble, and unrequited love set up a very lifelike context for the forthcoming events. It is Cocteau's view that what it takes to "convince" an audience is realism and "facts," and that truth resides in the mind of the audience on the same plane as realism. Despite the fictional premise of the work as a whole, its acceptance by an audience is deemed dependent on its verisimilitude. By presenting a world established expertly within the cinematic conventions of realism, he hopes to seduce the viewer (transformed into a child by virtue of the prologue) to accept as real the fantasy of the Beast.

The double reality of the film is also carried out on the level of characterization. Beauty, who looks as adult as the other young people, is presented as a child. She is the cleaning girl while her sisters are women of the world. She is daddy's girl while they connive for husbands. Avenant and Ludovic chase women and cheat at cards; they call the sisters bitches and, sardonically, "Enchantresses! Goddesses!" All the while, Beauty remains pure and virginal despite Avenant's entreaties. Without any of the naughtiness or rebellion of Paul and Elisabeth, she is a child like those in *The Holy Terrors;* full of strength of

Beauty and the Beast. The Beast and Beauty seen from behind bars. *(Courtesy Anthology Film Archives.)*

Beauty and the Beast. Beauty serves the Beast water. *(Courtesy Anthology Film Archives.)*

character and immense internal resources; adultlike, but retaining some
of the spirit of childhood. In Beauty's case, she retains virtue and love
for her father.

After his disappointment, Father begins to return home and, losing
his way, encounters the Beast's castle. He walks toward it, up its curved
staircase, and is frightened by his own shadow as it grows and looms on
the entry. The eerie light of the woods and castle grounds and the
strangely animated shadow signal the difference between the normal
world and the Beast's enchanted kingdom. Differing cinematographic
styles divide the two. Father enters the vaporous hallway and calls out,
"Anyone there?" As he walks through the corridor, torchbearing human
arms unfold from the wall, lighting his passage. He calls out again and is
again left in silence. Human hands serve him from a richly laid table.
Living wall sculptures watch him. He sleeps and wakes to the sound of a
roar. As he searches for his horse to carry him home, he stumbles across
a slaughtered deer. Then, he sees a rose and picks it. The Beast (again,
Jean Marais) appears and accuses him of theft. The Beast offers to sus-
pend his sentence for three days, at which time either Father or one of
his daughters must come back to die. The cinematography reverts to its
earlier normalcy; when the distressed Father returns home and tells of
his misfortune, both the lighting and focus become more clear. Beauty
offers to go to the Beast in his place. Her sisters encourage her, but she
is opposed by her brother and Avenant. She steals out at night, however,
and rides Magnifique, the Beast's enchanted, sparkling horse, to her
dangerous rendezvous. She enters the estate and castle as her father did,
but continues through the dining room, gliding to a door that announces, "Beauty, I am the door of your room." The room has life, too:
The statues move their eyes, the bedspread rolls back, the arms of the
chair are human arms. The mirror announces its purpose: "Reflect for
me and I will reflect for you." It shows an image of her father lying ill.
She cries and runs out of the castle. Outdoors, she encounters the
Beast—the first of many meetings.

This scene is indicative of the intuitive relationship that Cocteau has
to cinematography as a tool to evoke sexual and voyeuristic themes.
Like the scenes through the keyhole in *Blood of a Poet* and the
hierarchical nature of the use of shot-countershot in *Orpheus*, the camera position here invests the shot with childlike, voyeuristic sexuality.
When Beauty screams and faints, the Beast is seen leaning over her,
staring and preparing to pick her up. The scene is filmed from a low
perspective, from behind the bars of a grate. Surreptitiously, like a baby
peering through the bars of a crib at his parents' lovemaking, or like the
boy Cocteau peering through the stair railing at the "Tamer in the Cage"
tableau, the camera peers at the Beast and Beauty. The shot passes
quickly, yet from it one is able to anticipate the relationship of the pair
and the importance of the cinematographic perspective in representing

Beauty and the Beast. **An exchange of glances.** *(Courtesy Anthology Film Archives.)*

the relationship that will follow in the rest of the film. After her initial shock, Beauty dines with the Beast, walks with him, and witnesses his passion for the hunt. Although she refuses his offer of marriage time

and again, she begins to treat him like a man and a friend. When he
needs help, she serves him water from her hands. When he appears at
her door bloody and disheveled from slaughter, she glares at him and
asks, "Aren't you ashamed?" She orders him to clean himself up and go
to sleep; in effect, to act like a man. He recoils, as if physically scorched
by her look. His eyes, his one tellingly human trait, are the most
sensitive to her withering stare.

In her relationship with the Beast, she operates with a childlike
literalism and matter-of-factness. At first horrified, she soon comes to
treat the Beast exactly as she perceives him—half man, half animal. She
is courteous and polite to the man in him; condescending, even scolding, to the animal. It is curious that in the end, when "la Bête" becomes
"ma Bête," this well-mannered condescension is called love. When the
Beast complains that she speaks to him like an animal, Beauty replies,
"But you are an animal," with a naive gravity very like a child.

The aplomb with which she responds to the mysteries of the Beast's
estate is wide-eyed but graceful. It is unlike the horror her father had of
the same phenomena. The candelabrum-holding arms, so like the arms
of the hermaphrodite that protrude from behind the sheet in *Blood of a
Poet*, give her light. She willingly takes the candelabrum from one when
she wishes to carry a light with her. The smoking bas-reliefs, whose eyes
scan the rooms, are her sympathetic witnesses. The unfurling carpets

Beauty and the Beast. **A caryatid watches.** *(Courtesy Anthology Film Archives.)*

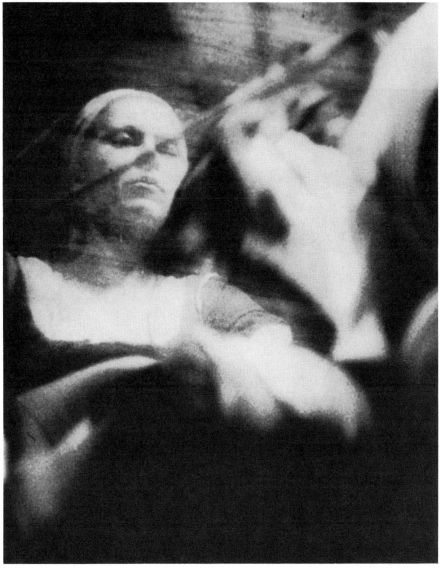

Beauty and the Beast. Beauty's reflection crossed by Avenant's love arrow. *(Courtesy Anthology Film Archives.)*

and bedspreads, and the serving hands, are all accepted, after an initial surprise, as ordinary aids to daily life. Once she is familiar with them she uses them with ease. The sense one has of unseen forces and invisible powers is magnified in the Beast's castle.'

The child Beauty is overseen by a hidden power. In the scene with her father, it seemed to be the malevolent power of the Beast. As Beauty inhabits the castle, one learns that it is a power at the service of the Beast, but not the Beast himself, that guides the animated furniture. It is an interesting metamorphosis of the workings of the enchanted house. The relationship of the image and sound when the Father is within is entirely different when Beauty lives there. As the Father sleeps in the armchair, there is a medium shot of his hand resting on a carved lion's head. A roar is heard that startles the Father awake and makes him flinch his hand, as if the carving had roared. He equates the sculptured chair with the Beast he has not yet met and assumes the causal interrelation of the lion and the roar. Yet when Beauty lives in the house, she dominates the animistic objects. They, as the Beast comes to do, serve her.

The film seems to be outgrowth of Beauty's world view. The interpenetration of realities guides the plot and is facilitated by Beauty's easy acceptance of the occurrences in both worlds. Though many of the scenes in the Beast's domain glow with spectral highlights, their interspersion with scenes of the promenades of this odd couple create an aspect of realism. There is an interesting balance of concrete and metaphorical shot relationships. While the magic of the Beast's estate is expounded by presenting the strange in the context of the familiar (for example, the disembodied arms that help Beauty as servants would), the realistic is given a metaphorical charge through its uncanny environs. The bridge with statues on which the Beast and Beauty walk takes on an aura of another, frozen, reality, transformed perhaps in the same gesture that created the Beast. It remains an eerily evocative image. They wander about as if in another time and space. The weather is different, overcast, unlike the sparkling sunlight at the pool's edge. The inserted shot of the deer, which explains the Beast's sudden trance, is filmed as if in a nature documentary. The scene serves to build another bridge across the gap between actuality and fantasy—one of the many the film erects.

Metaphor is consistently used in the film as the complement of the special effects that show the Beast's power. It is introduced casually in the beginning with Avenant's love arrow jettisoned into the room where Beauty works. One comes to know that the arrow was meant for her a short while later when Avenant reclaims it and proposes to Beauty, in a sequence of shots that begins with Beauty's face reflected on the floor next to the arrow. Avenant presses his "point" and sets up the transformation of the floor into a mirror: "Beauty, you weren't meant to be a servant; even the floor would like to be your mirror." The second and most hilarious metaphor is of the sisters as barnyard animals—chickens and goats. As Adelaide and Felicie enter the yard, the animals mimic their walk. They squawk and bleat in chorus with the women's "Let's go!" and "Yoo-hoo!" A duck roosting in the sedan chair is evicted by its replacement, the cackling sister.

Beauty and the Beast. The barnyard metaphor. *(Courtesy Anthology Film Archives.)*

Beauty and the Beast. The Beast's smoking hands. *(Courtesy Anthology Film Archives.)*

Metaphor is closely associated with the Beast, in the way certain of the special effects are presented. Morality is assigned to animated objects and body parts. The Beast's hands imply guilt by smoking after he has compulsively slaughtered his prey. He raises them like a surgeon would. The mirror serves numerous metaphorical functions, all centering on its ability to judge the character and desires of the one who looks into it. It is first of all the Cocteauesque mirror that reflects (thinks). Just as in *Blood of a Poet*, whose mirror is exhorted to "reflect more before throwing back images," this mirror has a consciousness, too. It speaks to Beauty using the same play on words: "I am your mirror. Reflect for me, I will reflect for you." It also establishes Beauty's centrality in the film. Each time she looks into it, she sees someone who longs for her and has fallen ill with longing: either her Father or the Beast. Further, it responds in kind to whomever looks into it. For Beauty, it makes her loved ones appear. For the Beast, it acts as a spy, exposing Beauty's hiding place, revealing her suitor Avenant. As the film continues, the mirror's powers expand.

The scene reverts to Beauty's home. Her family's fortune has descended further. Beauty begs the Beast to permit her to go home. He

Beauty and the Beast. **The mirror reflects for the Beast.** *(Courtesy Anthology Film Archives.)*

asks about her suitor, Avenant, and once again, distracted and inattentive to her response, rushes off. She hears a roar and cry in the distance. Finally, she is permitted to go home for a week. The Beast gives her the sources of his power: the mirror, the key to "Diana's pavilion" (which contains his fortune), and his teleportation glove. He collapses when she leaves. Beauty returns home and becomes the center of the family drama once again. Her Father appreciates her affection for the Beast, but the four young people conspire to keep Beauty home, kill the Beast, and steal his fortune. Adelaide steals the Beast's key, and the men ride off on Magnifique to the enchanted estate. Beauty, peering into the magic mirror sees the ailing Beast and resolves to go to him. She returns to the castle after a frantic search for the key. She cries out for "My Beast" now, and finds him lying by the pond, near death.

In this sequence, the mirror is again a metaphorical object. It responds to the Beast's catharsis, breaking apart (as the mirror in *Orpheus* does for the Princess) when his physical crisis is discovered. It casts back caricatures of the vain and ridiculous sisters when they try to see themselves. By investing it with morality, Cocteau seeks to impress his viewers with the immanent charm of one's ordinary surroundings. The diamond tears of Beauty when she cries, thinking of the Beast, and the transformation of her necklace into a charred rope when she tries to give it to her sister are variations of the same motif. The fact that they occur in the superrealistic setting of the Father's bedroom and the exquisite exterior landscape of clotheslines only puts into relief their power as fables within the larger moral tale of the film. They are examples of a kind of prelogical animism that assigns wills to things, very much the way a young child does.[129] Cocteau asserted that it is only possible to see the supernatural through ordinary things. In "On the Marvels of Cinematography" he describes the position he took in *Beauty and the Beast*:

> When one sees fairies they disappear. They only help us in a guise which makes them unrecognizable and are only present through the sudden unwonted grace of familiar objects into which they disguise themselves in order to keep us company.[130]

Beauty is forbidden by the Beast to look into his eyes. In the end, he is transformed by her loving look. The motif of seeing and being seen plays throughout the film. The wall reliefs watch with bemused expressions the comings and goings in the castle. Beauty's horrified stare when she sees him bloody and disheveled after the hunt burns his own eyes. He covers them as if to avoid bright light and asks, not that she lower her eyes, but that she close the door, as if the intensity of her judgment could not be dimmed simply by diverting her glance. Just as the objects that come to serve Beauty are invested with morality, so is her sight.

The final sequence of the film follows the simultaneous deaths of

Beauty and the Beast. The sister's reflection. *(Courtesy Anthology Film Archives.)*

Avenant and the Beast. Ludovic and Avenant climb onto the glass roof of the luminous pavilion. Avenant breaks a pane and hangs down, preparing to jump. The statue of Diana, suddenly animated like the

Beauty and the Beast. Beauty's horrified stare. *(Courtesy Anthology Film Archives.)*

statue in *Blood of a Poet,* turns and fires an arrow, slaying Avenant. He falls. Beauty, passionately gazing at the Beast, declares her love for him. The Beast is transformed into a princely Avenant, who rises up, and

Beauty and the Beast. Diana aims her arrow. *(Courtesy Anthology Film Archives.)*

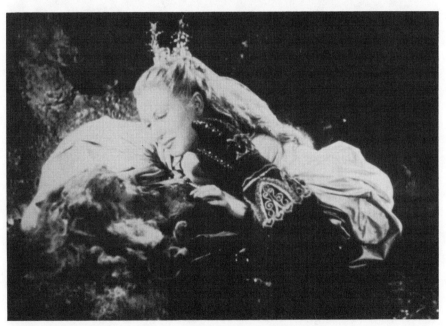

Beauty and the Beast. Beauty's loving look. *(Courtesy Anthology Film Archives.)*

Beauty and the Beast. "I like to be afraid . . . with you." *(Courtesy Anthology Film Archives.)*

explains his history as the Beast. Beauty is awestruck, but decides, "I like to be afraid . . . with you." The Prince sweeps Beauty up into the clouds to her promised fortune.

The theme of the power of sight is used to build to the climax of the film. It foreshadows the Beast's explanation of his mutation: "I could only be saved by a *look* of love . . . Love can make a Beast of a man. It can also make an ugly man handsome" (emphasis added). While this sounds like a maxim in the vein of "Beauty is in the eye of the beholder," in the context of Cocteau's pervasive obsessions, it can be read more profoundly. The power of vision is reaffirmed here.

If one looks carefully at *Beauty and the Beast* one sees a troubled interpretation of the classic fairy tale. Beauty's kindness is marred. Avenant is rather more of a sadist than a potential Prince, and the Beast is far more sympathetic than the unctuous Prince he becomes. The sisters and brother are caricatured in the traditional manner, but the Father is more weak and simpering than he ought to be. Beauty, who maintains a victimized and kindhearted surface character, is domineering. She clings to her Father, but when given power over the Beast, she uses it unhesitatingly. Her condescension to the Beast is an extension of the newfound sense of power she has over his estate. When she returns home, she seems to enjoy her enriched position vis-à-vis her impoverished family and Avenant. Part of her fortune, in the end, is to make her sisters her servants. Like the statue/woman in *Blood of a Poet* and the Princess in *Orpheus*, the female is a powerful sadistic force. In his journal of the making of *Beauty and the Beast*, Cocteau is explicit in praising Josette Day for her ability to represent this aspect of Beauty's character, which he certainly meant to include in her portrayal:

> And to explain this background away I make her say: "Who's done my washing?" Avenant replied, "We have," then she adds, "The sheets are badly hung and are trailing on the ground." . . .
>
> As Beauty she has naivety, simplicity and just that suggestion of superiority, as though she has seen things which her family have not even dreamt about. She dominates Ludovic, cherishes her father, but is not ashamed of them when she returns home. She has to say her line: "Who has done my washing?" dressed in pearls, tulle, silk and gold, yet even so, she does not lose her simple manner.[131]

He attributes her superiority, not to her riches or her conquest of the Beast, but to her having "seen things."

The relationship of power and vision is one that is explicated throughout Cocteau's career. From the "Tamer in the Cage" to the reviewing of his life's work in *Testament of Orpheus* (1960), Cocteau found vision to be the faculty that best illustrated the sadomasochistic struggle between power and impotence in which he was enmeshed. That this struggle coincided with that in which children are involved—their struggle with the omnipotence of fathers and laws, of a rationality whose logic they do not understand, and of the simultaneous urgency to grow into an adult and shrink back into the womb—serves to make *Beauty and the Beast* accessible to them on a profound level. That Cocteau never grew out of this struggle, but lived it and invested it in his work, makes its inscription in the film all the more compelling. Seeking to present innocence and fantasy, he cannot help but present the sadistic and malevolent reality that accompanies it.

* * * *

Beauty and the Beast brings into focus all the concerns that guided Cocteau's cinema. Baudelaire's prediction of a model for what is modern in art as a *"jeu d'enfants"* is the forecast of Cocteau's career. Since its invention, photography has been seized on by artists and writers as a metaphor for numerous modernist concerns, not the least of which is the revelation of unseen forces. Many of Cocteau's most notable contemporaries proposed photography and cinematography as the keys to understanding fleeting, even invisible, experience. Jean Epstein eloquently elaborated a theory of *"photogénie"* through which people and objects would be revealed in their essences.[132] Epstein contends that by filming the face of a defendant in slow motion, one can determine guilt or innocence. Similarly, inert objects can be shown to possess psychic forces if filmed with the aim of capturing their *photogénie.* Cocteau singles out the technique of slow motion to make a similar point. In *Paris Album,* he describes the thrill of the circus in terms of that effect.

> The safety-net was the no-man's land between heaven and earth; for the cinema had not yet proved that the most vulgar, crude acts embody an elusive angel, a rising smoke, a soft chestnut slipping from its thorns, if only because slow motion reduces the pace of life.[133]

For Cocteau, slow motion reveals something other than Epstein's truth; his "elusive angel" is often otherwise known as the child.

If one compares the two filmmakers' views, one comes to a possible source of their push to materialize the ineffable. Epstein speaks of cinema's ability to reveal the soul of people and things. Cocteau was equally impressed by the apparent animism of the visual world when rendered cinematographically:

> Mountains breathe, move, slide against one another, climb up and penetrate into each other, and the century-long slowness of this rhythm escapes us, revealing a static spectacle. The cinema has shown us that plants gesticulate and that only a difference in tempo between the animal and vegetable kingdoms led us to believe in the serenity of nature. We must change our minds; we climb down, now that those admirable fast-motion films have let us into the secret of a rose, the birth or the explosion of a crocus.[134]

Stop-motion nature photography was the one representation of overt sexual energy that engaged Cocteau. If one reads further, one comes to the passage of a time-lapse film of passing fashions. Cocteau chose to speculate on the application of this technique to the very phenomenon on which Baudelaire based his discussion of the modern.

Baudelaire, although rigorously opposed to photography as an art form (its immanent naturalism repelled him), establishes a definition of modernity from a study of passing fashion. In his discussion of the flaneur as the truly modern artist, he proposes for a student of history precisely that topic which Cocteau proposes as a film:

> If an impartial student were to look through the *whole* range of French costume, from the origin of our country until the present day, he would find nothing to shock nor even to surprise him. The transitions would be as elaborately articulated as they are in the animal kingdom. There would not be a single gap: and thus, not a single surprise. And if to the fashion plate representing each age he were to add the philosophic thought with which that age was most preoccupied or concerned—the thought being inevitably suggested by the fashion plate—he would see what a profound harmony controls all the components of history, and that even in those centuries which seem to us the most monstrous and the maddest, the immortal thirst for beauty has always found its satisfaction.[135]

While Baudelaire could see the phenakistoscope, the protocinematic toy, as a delightful amalgam of craft and imagination, the notion that one could combine its principles with the photographic image to create something beyond naturalism did not occur to him. Cocteau's hindsight into photography was to understand the possibility of subverting its conventions, established while Baudelaire was writing, to reveal the "philosophic thought" that Baudelaire seeks. Because of his position in history—his succession from Pre-Raphaelite and such other art photographers as Cameron and Rejandler, and from filmmakers like Méliès who defied filmic reality—Cocteau was well placed to revise Baudelaire and bring his acute aesthetic to bear on the most modern of arts.

Cocteau's good fortune to have been delivered *"une cargaison mal arrimée"*[136] coincident with the birth of cinema permitted him to collapse his life with the medium in a way not possible with any other. The double edge of the early cinema, that factual documentary traditionally associated with the Lumières and the magical fictions of Méliès, were amalgamated in Cocteau's double being and refashioned in his films. The significance of the child in Cocteau's experience of the cinema is not in the specificity of individual films, but is as a continuum from which he gleaned a principle that supported his entire aesthetic. The creation of fictions to support an expanded vision of reality is the "true lie" of Cocteau's cinema. He had a need to reassert the forms of his childhood as the work of his adulthood. As compensation for the insufficiencies he felt as a child, and as a translation of obsessions he was never rid of, he recast his childhood in much of his work. The unadulterated pleasure of the cinematic experience, watching the play of the world while hidden in the darkness of the theater, became an accessible model for his pervasive world view. The recognition that within the cinematic circumstance a childlike mold of fact and fiction was not only permissible but the very tradition opened the medium as a natural growth of his own being. As Lewis Carroll mistook an advertisement for "Roman Cement" to read "romancement,"[139] so Cocteau misapplied the separate realities of the early cinema toward the creation of his own.

He chose to use the possibilities of cinema to raise the issue of the "invisible." He never sought to come to terms with his own motivations nor did he try to analyze what he meant by the "invisible." He can be rightly accused of being defensive and anti-intellectual in his insistence on being believed, and on repeating rather than investigating his concerns. Restatement was his method of building a mythology over the course of his lifetime. The "true lie" became the Big Lie: fabrications told often enough came to stand in for the truth in his system. One may object to the means Cocteau used to make his career; nevertheless, without the process of obsessive repression and repetition, the most resonant images of his films could not have come into being. The snowball fight, the conscious mirror as portal, closed eyes painted open—all are original and engaging cinematic creations. Cocteau presents them as if they were self-explanatory or beyond explanation. They move us as viewers, to some degree, because they are not explained. The rich experience of many viewings of Cocteau's films is possible because they are not *about* what they seem to be. The high quality and pleasure of the experience of Cocteau's cinema is that it touched deep and highly individual chords without shocking or threatening the repressive mechanisms we share with Cocteau. Although we may not share his obsessions, we do share a common experience of socialized repression and sublimation. His films appeal to the profundity of the psyche without confronting it. In that way, they are very like stories, as Benjamin defines them, and Cocteau is an archetypal storyteller. Benjamin's eloquent definition of the storyteller as "the man who could let the wick of his life be consumed completely by the gentle flame of his story . . . the righteous man [who] encounters himself"[138] could be Cocteau's persona as a filmmaker.

2

JOSEPH CORNELL
The Symbolic Equation

The Place of the Films

Joseph Cornell is little known as a filmmaker. His audience is comprised primarily of those who value his work as a maker of boxes and a collagist, and those familiar with American avant-garde film. His films were generated out of his early hobby of collecting favorite movies, but emerged after Cornell's experience as an art-film goer in New York in the 1930s. A chain of enthusiasts, beginning with Julian Levy, have presented and preserved his films, which would otherwise have been packed among Cornell's vast legacy now resting at the Archives of American Art and the Joseph Cornell Study Center at the Smithsonian Institution. A debt of gratitude is owed to Julian Levy, who insisted that the films of the French dadaist and surrealist artists were a crucial aspect of their work in general. He encouraged Cornell to show his first film, *Rose Hobart* (1936). Parker Tyler was a proponent of Cornell's work, too. In his art and film criticism, he provided a bridge that united the endeavors of the European artist-filmmakers of the 1920s and 1930s with the insurgent, radical, individual filmmakers of the 1940s and after in America. He encouraged Cornell's filmmaking and led him to other filmmakers sympathetic to art film. Tyler's support ultimately led to the disposition of Cornell's films in the only place in America dedicated to the collection and preservation of the avant-garde film—Anthology Film Archives. The fate of Cornell's films has been fortunate; after more than ten years of screenings, they began to be viewed seriously. For the first time, in 1980, with the retrospective of Cornell's work at the Museum of Modern Art, the films were shown as an integral part of the exhibition.

There are a number of reasons that Cornell's films were slow to be recognized. His primary audience was that of the art world—dealers, curators, collectors, and fellow artists. Although now there is a degree of recognition of the individually made film as a viable art form (and even, sometimes, a salable commodity), this was not so when Cornell began to make films. He found an audience for his films very late, only after the rise of the American avant-garde. And for many years he was outside of even that incipient tradition. He was of the generation of Sidney Peterson and Maya Deren, but not within their circles. Nor was he of the circle of the younger filmmakers who received his work with enthusiasm—Stan Brakhage, Larry Jordan, and Ken Jacobs. His high reputation in the art world and his natural shyness kept him outside of the movement that was beginning to write its own history. And further, his work was unlike most of what was being done at the time. Both his lyrical-documentary style (in, for example, *Centuries of June*, 1955) and his film collages were peripheral to the psychodramatic mainstream of avant-garde film. With the growing fame of filmmakers like Brakhage[1] on the one hand, and the film collagist Bruce Conner on the other, a context was built in which Cornell's films could be evaluated and brought forward.

Eight of Cornell's films will be dealt with in this chapter. Although all of his films and scenarios share themes allied with childhood, these eight illuminate the issue most brightly, and account for other related concerns as well. The films are *Centuries of June* (1955), *The Aviary* (1954), *Nymphlight* (1957), *The Children's Party* (1940s–68), *Cotillion* (1940s–68), *The Midnight Party* (1940s–68), *A Legend for Fountains (fragments)* (1965), and *Vaudeville DeLuxe*.[2] They will not be discussed chronologically, but rather grouped in terms of the motifs they elaborate. Cornell draws on a broad set of traditions to bolster his aesthetic of childhood: German and French romanticism, surrealism, film history, Christian Science, nineteenth-century theater and ballet, twentieth-century popular amusements, and child psychology. All serve a child-oriented world view.

Sculpture and Collage

Since Cornell is thought of primarily as a sculptor, the question arises, what relation do his films bear to his other, better-known work? The answer can be found by looking at his approach to making things in general. Cornell did not generate his own material: he was an assemblagist and collagist in everything, including films. Engravings, magazine pictures, photographs, and books were the material he used to make collages. Clay pipes, cork balls, stuffed birds—an enormous array of objects and graphics formed the materials for his boxes. His own design and painting skill made them unique. Similarly, his films were created from other films, including ones he asked to be shot. He found film material or commissioned footage from other filmmakers. He was a joiner of things, and he grouped images and objects in such a way as to cast them in an entirely new light. He was influenced by the French surrealist tradition and followed its American turn in the figure of Duchamp. Unlike Duchamp, however, he carried the notion of the ready-made into film. He fashioned his own films by refashioning others.

But the relationship between his collages and boxes and his films stems from more than methodology. Images and themes carry over from one into the other. In her excellent essay on *Rose Hobart* and Cornell's scenario, *Monsieur Phot* (1933), Annette Michelson provided a list of a dozen ways in which *Rose Hobart* carried forward both formal and imagistic concerns from other work.[3] Michelson describes the very direct interrelationship between *Rose Hobart* and numerous boxes. Cornell created many different kinds of collages and boxes, meant for different occasions and audiences. He did this, too, with films. There is no question that Cornell held an obsessive interest in a few themes without ever exhausting their possibilities. Stellar imagery, birds, scientific equipment, and words (often written upside down or backward) appear in both kinds of work and are the pictorial elements that reveal the principles of Cornell's aesthetic. One of the most pervasive pictorial and thematic elements in his work was childhood.

There are a number of ways in which Cornell exhibited his interest in childhood in his noncinematic work. He used objects and images that were created for children. Marbles, miniature furniture, and dolls inhabit his boxes. Pictures of clowns and animals appear as if cut from children's books in both his boxes and collages. The titles and actual function of some of his works allude to children's games or places inhabited by children. The "Soap Bubble" sets, "Sand Boxes," and "Carrousel" series are named for childhood activities. There are numerous boxes in addition to the "Sand Boxes" that were meant to be moved and played with as if they were children's games. He gave many of these to the children of friends and relatives. Images of children appear in many works, and occasionally they are the central image. The "Medici Princess," "Prince," and "Boy" boxes are three of his finest. Those in which children are not the central but peripheral images are often biographical. Photographs of Lauren Bacall as a child are included in the "Penny Arcade Portrait of Lauren Bacall" (1945–46) for example. Similarly, the immense and timeless landscape of "The Last Prince of Urbino" (1967) is given specificity by the swaddled infant in the foreground. Often a box or collage is inflected with a lyrical quality by the inclusion of photographs, engravings, or other images of children, as in the "Portrait of the Artist's Daughter by Vigée Lebrun" (1960) or "Jungle Scene" (1966), in which children inhabit a space that is transformed by their emotion-filled stares.

Three Bases of Childhood

There is a thematic insistence on childhood that is, perhaps, inclusive of all of the above. Three major characteristics are contained within its venue: the Romantic and Victorian (in the figure of Lewis Carroll) representation of women and children as a motif; structures created in the spirit of play and prerational thought; and content that is veiled in the asexual innocence of the mythology of childhood, though it is as mature and sexually charged as that of the surrealists.

French and German Romantic poetry were the literatures with which Cornell felt most in harmony. Although an avid and catholic reader, he repeatedly pointed to Nerval and Goethe as epitomizing the highest achievements of literature. Their fictions share numerous qualities with one another, and Cornell saw them as harmonious with his own endeavor.[4] Each writes of the struggles of sensitive young men in a difficult world. Mood dominates events. The atmospheres of scenes are invested with the qualities of pathetic fallacy. The protagonist is in love with a young woman who is sometimes elusive, sometimes unapproachable. The desired woman is often an actress. She is boyish. Sometimes she is dressed as a man.

This unapproachable but beloved young woman is best seen in Nerval's collection, *Les filles de feu.* Glimpsed from afar, briefly encountered, but most often remembered and dreamed about, she is more a figure of the hero's imagination than a living woman. In the case of *Sylvie,* she is more important dead than alive.

The landscapes of the novels often reflect her desire and thus also that of the hero. Elements of nature are interpreted as signs of her. This agglomeration of the natural and mental superimposed on the figure of a young woman appeals to Cornell, for whom women exist as disembodied and spiritualized ideals. In *Sylvie,* Nerval distinguishes this figure from "the real woman" who "revolted our ingenuousness; it was necessary that she appear as a queen or goddess, and above all that she not be approached."[5] The most desired women in both *Angelique* and *Sylvie* appear as angelic children. Adrienne, the figure of desire in *Sylvie,* grows from a sexual ideal into another. She becomes a nun.

The erotic struggles of the hero in Nerval are most often set in motion by an obsessive adoration of an actress. *Sylvie* begins with the admirer sitting night after night at the theater. He is warned not to go backstage or pursue the actress. His father claims that her attractions are

Joseph Cornell. *Mignon* (c. 1960s). Collage, 11⁷⁄₁₆″ × 8½″ (image). © The Estate of Joseph Cornell. *(Courtesy Castelli Feigen Corcoran.)*

magnified by her unapproachability and her role and that she would be diminished in nontheatrical reality. In the course of the narrative, Nerval accepts, rejects, and ultimately draws the same conclusion himself. When he does lapse into pursuit of her, her function is to lead him back to his own childhood. He takes her to his home, compares her to the girl he admired as a child, and is alienated from her when she does not meet his ideal. Within the structure of Nerval's fictions, however, it is always the woman who is the conduit of the hero's return to his past.

Goethe's *Wilhelm Meister's Apprenticeship and Travels* is another of Cornell's sources that elucidates childhood in his work. It, too, begins with the young hero in love with an actress. In this novel, however, there is a variation on the theme that is important in relation to Cornell's work, particularly, *A Legend for Fountains (fragments).* The actress is dressed as a man, and Wilhelm's attraction is heightened by her costume. She is promiscuous and is exposed as unworthy of Wilhelm. The boyish-looking Mignon then commands his love. She had been a circus performer. Wilhelm's emotional relationship with her passes through many phases as the novel progresses. It is easy to see her attractions for Cornell. It is possible to draw a connection between early collages in the Ernst style with later collages from the 1960s, through Mignon—in particular, "Untitled" from *Story without a Name—For Max Ernst* (1930s) and "Mignon" (1960s).[6] Consider them in light of the following passage from *Wilhelm Meister,* noted by Cornell in his own edition. Goethe described a meeting with the Painter who paints scenes depicting the life of Mignon:

> And thus you might see the Boy-girl, set forth in various attitudes and manifold expression. Beneath the lofty portal of the splendid Country-house, she is standing, thoughtfully contemplating the Marble Statues in the Hall. Here she rocks herself, plashing to and fro among the waters, in the fastened boat; there she climbs the mast, and shows herself as a fearless sailor.[7]

Her ambiguous gender, her dramatic flair, and her mutability seem to be her major qualities. Cornell's early collage makes one image of two—a woman and a ship at sea. By and large, women and girls figure as elements to be cut and placed in context in all the collages. In "Mignon," she is intact, but her childhood is combined with an urchinlike appearance. She is very much a boy-girl.

Cornell also read and collected the works of Lewis Carroll. It is possible to see a further aspect of the kind of girl Cornell was interested in by looking at Carroll's depiction of Alice as a type. In *Some Versions of Pastoral,* William Empson points out the importance of the boy-girl figure in Carroll's work. In the first part of "Alice in Wonderland: The Child as Swain," his essay on Carroll's Alices, he describes the function of the child figure in the nineteenth century, replacing the swain of pastoral literature.

The essential idea behind the books is a shift onto the child, which Dodgson [Carroll] did not invent, of the obscure tradition of pastoral. The formula is now "*child*—become—judge," and if Dodgson identifies himself with the child so does the writer of the primary sort of pastoral with his magnified version of the swain. (He took an excellent photograph, much admired by Tennyson, of Alice Liddell as a ragged beggar-girl, which seems a sort of example of this connection.)[8]

He goes on to account for the child both in terms of Romanticism and Freudian psychoanalysis:

The child has not yet been put wrong by civilisation, and all grown-ups have been. It may be true that Dodgson envied the child because it was sexless, . . . It depends on a feeling, whatever may have caused that in its turn, that no way of building up character, no intellectual system, can bring out all that is inherent in the human spirit, and therefore that there is more in the child than any man has been able to keep.[9]

The notion of lost or unfulfilled potential was a crucial one for Cornell, as it was for those writers for whom he cared. Certainly Nerval found it to be the only subject worth writing about. But what is interesting in Empson's formulation is that he raises sexuality as a major factor in a Romantic world view. To gain sexuality is to lose one's "native poetry," he says of Wordsworth in the same passage. He cites Carroll as an example of this problem, and poses Alice as a boy-girl as Carroll's attempt to alleviate his dilemma. Cornell's recurrent creation of this type, especially in the films, indicates that the same claim can be made for him.

Insofar as any character in a work of fiction represents to some degree the author himself, Carroll is incorporated in the Alice figure. Empson points out how this can operate in the work of an elderly bachelor writing of a prepubescent girl. It involves a rejection of real sexuality and a collapsing of all gender into girlhood.

There seems to be a connection in Dodgson's mind between the death of childhood and the development of sex . . . but I think Dodgson felt it was important that Alice should be innocent of all knowledge of what the Knave of Hearts (a flashy-looking lady's-man in the picture) is likely to have been doing, and also important that she should not be told she is innocent. That is why the king, always a well-intentioned man, is embarrassed. At the same time Dodgson feels that Alice is right in thinking "it doesn't matter a bit" which word the jury writes down; she is too stable in her detachment to be embarrassed, these things will not interest her, and in a way she includes them all in herself . . . A desire to include all sexuality in the girl child, the least obviously sexed of human creatures, the one that keeps its sex in the safest place, was an important part of their fascination for him. He is partly imagining himself as the girl-child (with these comforting characteristics), partly as its father (these together make it a father), partly as its lover—so it might be a mother—but then of course it is clever and detached enough to do everything for itself.[10]

The reading that Empson makes of Carroll depends a great deal on a belief that Carroll was successful in repressing his desire for the young girls he wrote for and about. Not much is known of Carroll's sex life. One assumes he did not consummate his love for the Liddell sisters. However, the analysis of the Alice figure and especially, the conflation of all gender into girlhood, holds whether it was a function of pure repression or not.[11] A similar model can be applied to Cornell. Through the ambiguous figure of the girl, Carroll made a social critique, Cornell a Nervalian return to his childhood. The young woman who stars in *A Legend for Fountains (fragments)* is an example of the purveyor of that return. Although she is not a girl, she is only just a woman. She is young, boyish, and alone. Like Alice, she wanders through a landscape that is not familiar to her. Cornell will make of her a wanderer like Nerval's hero. Her type will reappear throughout Cornell's films to permit a vision steeped in nostalgia of the places he films.

The boyish girl is typical of much of Cornell's other work and reverberates through his collections[12] and "Dossiers." She stands as an icon that unites numerous themes: travel, Europe (particularly France), hotels, the theater, birds, and stars. The Baudelairean flaneur, the surrealist poet in an *"hôtel particulaire,"* the youthful adventurers of Novalis or Nerval traveling the European countryside seeking a meaningful focus to their lives—all come together in her image. Cornell's notable *View* article, "Enchanted Wanderer—Excerpt from a Journey Album for Hedy Lamarr," is illustrated with a collage of Hedy Lamarr as a Renaissance boy.[13] Cornell describes part of her charm as her ability to portray boys: "She has carried a masculine name in one picture, worn masculine garb in another, and with her hair worn shoulder length and gentle features like those portraits of Renaissance youths she has slipped effortlessly in the role of a painter herself . . . le chasseur d'images."[14] To imagine her as an enchanted wanderer, a man, and an artist is to make her a surrogate for Cornell himself.

There are a number of structural similarities between Cornell's work and children's behavior, particularly in play. One way of understanding how the works operate is to see them as founded on the same principles as the prerational systems of children. Aside from the childlike content and gamelike form of some of his work, Cornell used systems of collage that are nonrational and ludic. The breakdown of narrative flow and realistic space, and the use of repetition are characteristic of the collages, boxes, and films, and of children's speech and play.

One might usefully turn to the work of Jean Piaget to discover the principles of child behavior, in order to see just what Cornell's imagina-

tive assemblages share with children. It is, therefore, of special interest
to find at the Joseph Cornell Study Center, among the books from
Cornell's library, a volume of Piaget's *Language and Thought of the
Child.* Although one would not expect Cornell himself to have been
overly interested in Piaget's clinical and behavioral analysis of the world
of childhood, Cornell was an avid enough reader to have explored
Piaget's treatment of an area so intimately bound up in his own work.
The title itself is provocative. The book centers on the nature of the
question Why? in children between the ages of three and eight: what
brings a child to ask the question and how he deals with it once asked.
Reality consciousness, intention, and logic are all brought to bear on the
study of the development of the child's ego, as witnessed in conversation and experimental testing. Although Piaget's method and statistical
analysis may have seemed cold-blooded to Cornell, there are two passages in Piaget's volume that Cornell found significant enough to have
noted.

The first passage is brief. It is simply marked with the word "Nota-
tions" in the margin:

> The fact remains that many expressions, which for us have a purely concep-
> tual meaning, retain for many years in the child mind a significance that is
> not only affective but also well-nigh magical.[15]

The one word Piaget gives us an example of is *Mama,* which in a very
young child, is used to indicate anything that is desired.

If one added the phrase "and images" after "expressions" in the Piaget
quotation, one would arrive at a parallel to Cornell's work that is un-
avoidable. Certain words and images are obsessive in his sculpture and
films, and by their placement and repetition become iconographic
rather than merely representational. They mean much more than they
show. Sometimes they are metaphors, sometimes symbols, and frequently they stand for an undefinable and grand feeling or idea. Stars
sometimes represent the night sky, but more often they indicate a transition to a universal or cosmic mode. Birds are part of the ambience of a
landscape, but generally also point to ideas of freedom or grace or soul.
An amoeba, Rose Hobart reaching into her drawer for her pistol, little
Godiva on her horse, "The End" written backward or upside down—all
find a place in his films as signs of a far greater reality than that in which
they are fixed. To see the "signs" or "tokens"—as Cornell describes his
images in *A Legend for Fountains (fragments)*—as too full of meaning is
childlike, according to Piaget. This serves to reinforce Cornell's own
notion that his work would find a sympathetic audience in children.

The flaw in this vision of communality is that the "magical"
significance of a word like *Mama* is dependent on its intrinsic privacy;
that is, it is a word that fulfills its meaning only to the individual and

cannot be shared. When a child says "Mama," he does not mean anyone's Mama or anyone's desire; he means his own. There is an element of this private relationship to the images and words in Cornell's sculpture and films, in that the wealth of reference and oblique interrelationship between things may never be decipherable. For some works, Cornell himself may be the only key. Nevertheless, he was not an hermetic artist or filmmaker. However tentatively, he felt the need for an audience for his boxes, collages, and films and did not make them to be seen only by himself. The Romantic belief that the more one calls upon the depths of individuality, upon what is of significance to the self, the more universal the work created out of that private exposition will be, is perhaps what allows him to present his private iconography as if it were that of his audience.[16]

In his films *The Children's Party* and *Cotillion* there are one- or two-frame insertions of a cinematically irised nineteenth-century photograph of an ambiguously sexed child. These can be seen as charged traces of personally meaningful content that could not or were not meant to find a place in the obvious structure of the film. As flash frames, they do not operate on a formal level to bring into question the timing, framing, or tone of the images that surround them, as single frames in the films of Robert Breer, for example, do. The shot is too complex to be deciphered, and thus almost invisible. The film as a whole is disjointed enough without the need for such a device to point out its flicker. The shot is a private utterance, "well-nigh magical," hidden within the sixteen-frame-per-second flow of the film. Preferring to present rather than withhold such an image, Cornell asserts his privileged relationship to the films—as their maker—while at the same time offering the viewer entry, however narrowly, into that intimacy. At those moments, the films become demonstrative rather than communicative. Cornell's reach toward his audience withdraws into an acknowledgment that his is the vision that guides the making of the film, and the audience must itself reach toward that vision in order to participate in the film. Like deciphering what children mean by what they say, one must enter into their system to extract the content.

The second passage that was marked by Cornell in his copy of *The Language and Thought of the Child*[17] is singularly applicable to his work in film:

The Ideas of Order and Cause in the Expositions Given by the Explainers.—
Other factors are at work which help to render the explainer's exposition rather unintelligible to the reproducer. These are an absence of order in the account given, and the fact that causal relations are rarely expressed, but are generally indicated by a simple juxtaposition of the related terms. The explainer, therefore, seems not to concern himself with the "how" of the events which he presents; at any rate, he gives only insufficient reasons for those events. In a word, the child lays stress on the events themselves rather than

on the relations of time (order) or cause which unite them. These factors, moreover, are probably all connected in various degrees with the central fact of ego-centrism.

The absence of order in the account given by the explainer manifests itself as follows. The child knows quite well, so far as he himself is concerned, in what order the events of a story or the different actions of a mechanism succeed one another; but he attaches no importance to this order in his exposition. This phenomenon is due once more to the fact that the explainer speaks more to himself than to the explainer [*sic*], or rather to the fact that the explainer is not in the habit of speaking socially. When an adult narrates, he is accustomed to respect two kinds of order: the natural order given by the facts themselves, and the logical or pedagogic order. Now it is to avoid misunderstanding in others that we adults present our material in a given logical order, which may or may not correspond with the natural order of things. The child, therefore, who, when he explains his thoughts, believes himself to be immediately understood by his hearer, will take no trouble to arrange his propositions in one order rather than another. The natural order is assumed to be known by the hearer, the logical order is assumed to be useless.[18]

There are a number of interesting points here. First, Piaget claims that the child knows the real or logical order of events in a sequence, but does not consider that order important. Secondly, it is the egocentrism of the child that makes the logical order unimportant in recounting a story. His understanding is primary, his listener's secondary. And thirdly, there is a transcendent "natural order" that exists behind all accounts, known both to the teller and the hearer. These theses strike very close to Cornell as an artist and filmmaker. As an artist, Cornell gave new contexts to images that were once part of a rational or other-representational system. As a filmmaker, the order of events was altered as well as the context, and it is to the films that one can most accurately apply Piaget's understanding of mental sequence in children.

In his collage films, Cornell extracted brief passages from films in his collection and pieced them together out of sequence. His major achievement, *Rose Hobart*, uses this technique to create an atmospheric portrait of the actress of that name.[19] In a way, its simplicity is its genius. Hobart becomes an omnipresent figure, perpetually appearing and fading out in the exotic landscape of Borneo. The controlled disorder of the shots contributes to a mysterious and erotic representation of her character. Even if one has not seen *East of Borneo* (1931), the film from which it was made (with the addition of several other shots), it is evident that part of *Rose Hobart*'s power comes from our knowledge of its status as a disrupted narrative film. The sets, camera work, costumes, fades, and acting all contribute to the sense of its former life as a dramatic account of the adventure of this central female character. In choosing to make *Rose Hobart*, Cornell found the narrative of *East of Borneo* unsatisfying. He chose to emphasize the furtive and fleeting gestures of Rose (most often by placing them at the beginning or end of a shot). His is a study of gesture rather than possession, jealousy, or decadence. It is based on visual rhymes and rhythm. Like Piaget's child, by reorienting the viewer toward Hobart's gestures, he "lays stress on the events themselves rather than on the relations of time (order) or cause which unite them." This is a task that coincides with the surrealist push to disrupt the superficial order of events and to make mysterious and erotic the female character.

The other collage films are less thoroughly consigned to the surrealist camp. They do, however, find their parallel in Piaget's model. "Magical" expressions and iconography occur in *A Legend for Fountains (fragments)* as well. It is possible to see the "ego-centrism" of the filmmaker at work in the presentation and juxtaposition of images. The inconsequence of conventional narrative and the concentration on the "events themselves" follow the path of Romanticism insofar as they validate a subjective vision of the reality of what is represented. For a child, that reality does not come into question except to be short-circuited by his own intentionalism. That is, if the reality does not easily conform, he will reinterpret it until it does so. For an artist, especially one dealing with the given world of found objects and found footage, the task is to manufacture an aesthetic reality that wrestles with one that has already been internalized. The use of iconographic and subliminal imagery is an indication of that process.

The most outstanding characteristic of the collage films is their remarkable order. Some of them resemble one another closely. In the three films that make up *The Children's Party* trilogy, Cornell repeatedly uses footage from a Halloween party, acrobatic acts, and narrative film fantasies featuring children. The thematic difference among the three films will be discussed in order to set forth their identities as unique and articulate. Nevertheless, there is a way in which they circle around and cross-reference one another. Cornell's disjunctive editing style, which establishes a theme only by forays into its perimeters, is the decisive factor. In the Cornell criticism, much of his imagery is called "ephemeral" or seen as replete with superabundance of meaning. It can be understood in another, clearer way. He uses imagery to shift from one level of meaning to another. Once an image is established, any aspect or detail of it can be used as the basis for the improvisation (in the musical sense) of the rest. That the image is wrenched from its original narrative context for the sake of the film only makes it more fitting as material—that is, it comes packed with meaning to begin with. To place it in an aesthetic order, by virtue of its shape or reference or texture, is to add to its meaning and to redirect it and ourselves as viewers to its harmonious continuity with all other possible images. In Piaget's terms, it is to give priority to its "natural" order.

This is a complex notion. Piaget's terminology ("natural") is not at all clear-cut. What he seems to mean is the order of memory, in which events occur as a complex of simultaneities rather than sequences. If that is so, then Cornell's attraction to this passage derived from many personal preoccupations. He was a Christian Scientist. The passage might appeal to him as a parallel to Mary Baker Eddy's spiritual realm which hovers around our physical, limited beings. As a quasi-surrealist and Duchampian, the absorption of time into the moment—either the unconscious well of the past or the eternity of the present—would strike a particularly modern chord. And the attribution of understanding to children of an essential division between their inner and communicative selves, corresponds to a Romantic notion of man, while creating a unity between man and child that was antithetical to Romanticism, but never renounced by Cornell.

As an editing strategy, it allows him to take the position of both adult and child at once. As adult he has access to logic when it serves his end. In *The Children's Party*, Cornell makes a narrative connection between the first and last shots as if they were a shot and a countershot in sequence. A young man in the beginning pines for the young Godiva at the end. The interconnection of the two shots defies the rest of the ludic structure of the film. In order to unite them and therefore see what the film is about, one must be able to retain a complex structural picture over time. Similarly, Cornell makes fabulous causal relationships between shots that can be understood only by one who seeks causality. In *The Children's Party*, a shot of an Indian outlining a woman's figure with a set of knives is related to a shot of stars in the sky because both form dot patterns around a human figure. This is not an obvious or easily made connection. One must catalog the differences in the shots before one sees the similarities, and understand how the concept *constellation* unites them.

On the other hand, much of the humor and a number of the thematic elements of the films would be lost if they had to be seen as proceeding from a rational cause. Piaget's "simple juxtaposition of the related terms" serves as a model. For an acutely perceptive visual artist like Cornell, "related" takes on a special significance. An image could look like another, evoke another, have the same rhythm as another, the same shape, have existed at the same time, or have any number of other qualities that would permit him to place them together. In one way, Cornell's work stands as a criticism of Piaget in that what Piaget calls an "absence of order," Cornell posits as an irrational but aesthetic order. The absence is only the loss of narrative. What is gained is a richer construct of the "events themselves."

One of the conveniences of this Piagetian model for Cornell is that it allows him to deal with subjects that might be difficult, or too personal, in a way that defuses them by oblique reference or brief appearance. As a child substitutes fantasies for more awesome realities through either embellishment, distortion, or complete censorship, so Cornell in his collage films, touches upon themes he would never approach directly. Sexuality is enmeshed in a web of other imagery in order to camouflage its presence.

Cornell sought to reveal himself through the veil of childhood. His sexuality was massively repressed; nevertheless, it often shone through when he chose images of and for children. It was as if in the safety of fantasies and amusements surrounded by innocence, one would not notice the libido that drove them. And by and large Cornell was right. Although it has become commonplace to point to hidden motives for his work,[20] no one has made a systematic analysis of how sexuality operates in his boxes, collages, or films. Exhibitionism, voyeurism, and their repression are consistently at work when he presents children. They are equally at work when he makes things for children. In the films, both the quality of images and their juxtaposition to one another reveal his desire. At the same time, they also defend against it. It is not the intention here to make a detailed analysis of Cornell's sexuality. It is important, however, to point out those places in the films where a sexual analysis seems inevitable, and those unifying images which illuminate Cornell's sexual motivation, which extends beyond an individual film.

Cornell's editing strategy is based on the making of visual equations. People and objects are substituted for one another in playful succession. As he does in graphic collage by putting wings on a child or a woman's body in a ship, most often in his films, this kind of collage editing makes one thing stand for, be equivalent to, or be like another. The meaning of each is made richer in the context of the other. In the films, a child becomes a bird or butterfly; a child stands for a miniature adult; Cornell, as filmmaker, is like a boy-girl; and the viewer of the films is equivalent to Cornell. The fundamental content of those equations is hidden and sexual.

Titled in such a way as to be irresistible, the psychoanalyst Otto Fenichel has written an article that clarifies the study of Cornell's films: "The Symbolic Equation: Girl = Phallus."[21] In it, he describes a phenomenon linked with transvestism, in which men and women imagine themselves to be phalluses. In women, the fantasy stems from girlhood, when they imagine themselves inextricably attached to their fathers's bodies, small talismans of luck and power. In men, it often originates in rivalry with a sister who is seen as better-loved by the mother (her grown counterpart) and the father (her lover). In the fantasy, the boy becomes like his sister. It is a conflicted desire, however, since he does not wish to lose his penis in the transformation. He therefore imagines himself as a girl with a penis. In addition, since his penis is often referred to as "the little one," he also imagines his whole body as "the little one," a penis. Fenichel proposes the imaginary equation: "I = my whole body = a girl = the little one = the penis."[22]

Within his discussion of the varieties of manifestations of this equation, Fenichel brings forward cultural references that are particularly germane to a discussion of Cornell. One is the figure of Goethe's Mignon; the other is the status of fairy-tale elves, dwarfs, and miniature beings in general. Both types are of importance to Cornell. In both cases, Fenichel points to their phallic natures as the clue to their power as images.

After making reference to the work of Sarasin, "Goethe's Mignon,"[23] in which Mignon is described as a thinly veiled figure of Goethe's own sister Cornelia and as a bisexual, Fenichel draws further conclusions based on his own study of transvestism.

> That Mignon moreover represents not only a boy, but specifically his penis . . . becomes probable . . . if one takes into account, for example, the symbolism of her dancing.
> Other available analyses of little girls like these, needful of help, yet in the sense of a talisman, rendering it—infantile women—leave from the masculine standpoint no doubt that in such cases we are dealing invariably with a narcissistic object choice. . . . In my volume, *Perversionen, Psychosen, und Charaktersörungen*, I wrote in this connection: "In feminine men who during childhood or puberty liked to fantasy themselves as girls, the same mechanism is present as in heterosexuals. They fell in love with little girls in whom they see themselves embodied, and to whom they give what their mothers denied them. Very probably this mechanism is also the decisive one in pedophilia." To this we will now add: Basically this object choice in heterosexual persons also represents a homosexual type, in which the woman, chosen in accordance with narcissistic object choice, is usually fantasied together with a great man, a father figure (whom the person himself represents); in empathy with the woman the man thus unconsciously is loved homosexually. Always such fantasies are combined with the idea of mutual protection: the little woman is rescued by the great man in actuality, the latter by the former in magical fashion. . . . These women represent not only the man himself who loves them but, in particular, his penis. In the way in which the charm of such figures is generally described one invariably finds a suggestion of their phallic nature. They are *phallus girls*.[24]

Certain connections in Cornell's work become clearer after reading Fenichel. Although Mignon herself appears only once by name in Cornell's oeuvre, her type appears often. Rose Hobart, Suzanne Miller in *A Legend for Fountains (fragments)*, and girls dressed as boys in *The Children's Party* trilogy all bear a resemblance to Mignon as a boyish girl. Cornell's interest in women stars narrowed itself to some of those who dressed as men—Hedy Lamarr, Lauren Bacall, Marlene Dietrich, and Lee Miller (the female star of Cocteau's *Blood of a Poet*). And above all, Cornell was interested in dancing women: ballerinas. He was a cultured aficionado. But one only need look at the phallic spout of the teapot adorned by two sylphs in "Homage to the Romantic Ballet (Pour Philoxène Boyer)" (1967)[25] to see an illustration of "the symbolism of her dancing."

Moreover, his interest in girls in general was peculiar. He formed attachments to the daughters of friends and acquaintances, neighbors, and girls on the street. Some appear in his films: the girls in *Centuries of June*, Gwenn Thomas and the anonymous girl in *Nymphlight*, and Suzanne Miller in *A Legend for Fountains (fragments)*. The pathetic story that Lynda Roscoe Hartigan tells of his attachment to Joyce Hunter[26] indicates the extent to which Cornell's obsessive need for these friendships could overpower good sense. There is no evidence that any of these attachments was sexual. Cornell's known sexual history, in fact, leads one to believe that there were no sexual encounters in his life at all. His interest in these girls seems to have been that of preferred company. In Hartigan's analysis, there is a joining of Cornell's attentions to girls and young women with his aid to the underprivileged and the handicapped. That conflation is not far from Fenichel's analysis. The small and the weak are assisted in order that they may help their benefactor, to whom they are almost magically attached.

The conclusion that one draws after reading Fenichel is that Empson's category of the "least obviously sexed of human creatures"—the girl—is the type with which Cornell most probably identified and used as a model. The identification with a girl who is "detached enough to do everything for itself" is the same as the equation "I = my whole body = the little one = the penis = a girl." The cause of identification is the contradictory desire to be a girl but not to lose the penis. In Cornell's case this manifests itself in the types he presents to us again and again. Because of the repetition of this type, one gets the sense of one of the "least obviously sexed" of all artists engaged in a struggle to retain but hide his virility.

The opposing forces that underlie Cornell's object choice of boy-girl figures manifest themselves in some of his collage structures. The sculpture and collage call for sexual-metaphor readings, yet the ramifications of such interpretations are never acknowledged and are in fact inhibited by their placement within asexual contexts. For example, the bisexuality in the constellation of Cassiopeia as the crotch of a woman in "Vue par Tina (Mathematics in Nature)" (1962)[27] is obfuscated by her quasi-scientific context. While the implication is evident, by making the phallic vagina out of a group of stars and placing the figure amid data and diagrams, Cornell reveals and denies simultaneously his sexual anxiety.

Fenichel also points to the tradition of the dwarf as an aspect of the symbolic equation. Talismans, elves, dwarfs, and small children find a commonality in the motif of "the greatness of the little one."[28] In discussing a patient's Oedipal fantasies, he adduces the numerous points of contact with many often recurrent motives of legend and fairy tale; for example, little girl rescuers who protect great men in all their adventures occur not infrequently. Miracle-performing little companions (who do not necessarily have to be female) such as dwarfs, mandrakes, talisman figures of all kinds, have often been analyzed, and the "little double" has been recognized as a phallic figure.[29]

A number of images from Cornell's films operate as "little doubles." Sometimes a child is shot in such perspective as to make it equal in size with dwarfs and other small creatures. Viewed with Fenichel in mind, it thus acquires sexually governed content. It is not the universality of the child's image—its mutability and interchangeability with other people or things—but the smallness of the image of the child itself that is paramount. That a girl and a dwarf or boys and pigeons are equally small is not a simple realization for Cornell; it is a potent one. In *Cotillion,* there is an image of a tightrope walker that can be seen in this light, too. The woman dances across the tightrope, showing strength and dexterity and tantalizing the viewer with her raised skirt. Through the special effect of superimposition, a second image of her appears. It is a tiny tightrope walker, watched by her larger "adult" version, walking a rope tied between the hand and shoulder of the larger woman. The little one happily performs for her audience. She incarnates the equation "girl = phallus."

To see the sexual content behind the use of certain images of children is also to consider its relationship to the structures of the films. The distinction Piaget makes between "natural" and "logical" order, and the use Cornell makes of that distinction, is underscored. Cornell could accept the idea that the "natural" order of events was understood by both teller and hearer. In just the same way, the true content of images could be understood by maker and viewer, without ever being alluded to directly. There is a way in which the use of flash frames and obscure short takes operates in the same mode as sexual content that is consistently implied but never manifested. Priority is given to the filmmaker, who will appreciate the images in all their depth, but entry is given to the audience by way of metaphors, symbols, graphic "rhymes," and other hints that prod a common cultural consciousness. In *The Children's Party* trilogy a balance is struck between the revelation and concealment of sexual issues that is very similar to that between narration and "poetic" construction, allowing the films to be unified at a very vital level.

The Films

A Legend for Fountains (fragments) (1965)

Cornell's film portrait of Suzanne Miller casts her as a Nervalian wanderer through the landscape of the Lower East Side Manhattan neighborhood of Little Italy. A combination of posed shots of the heroine of the film and documentary-style sequences of the street life of children were used by Cornell to create a melancholic and lyrical portrait. The film is silent and in black and white. Lines from Federico García Lorca's poem, "Tu Infancia en Menton" intercut among the images, point to Cornell's iconographic representation of Romantic themes.

The film opens on a dark staircase, as can be found in tenements all over the Lower East Side of Manhattan. The following shot is somewhat lighter. A young woman descends, behind the banister railing. In a series of repetitive shots, she goes down stairs, as if from the top of a walk-up. She looks boyish; her short, dark hair falls into her eyes. She wears a trench coat. In this opening, Cornell presents us with an image central to his concerns and one upon which turns this investigation of the nature of his child orientations. This young woman is ambiguous. Just past girlhood, she is sexual; yet her sexuality is of ill-defined gender. She exists in a moody atmosphere that she poeticizes by her presence. She is a *type* of major importance to Cornell. She exemplifies the boy-girl.

A Legend for Fountains (fragments). The boyish heroine. *(Courtesy Anthology Film Archives.)*

A Legend for Fountains (fragments). The boys of Little Italy. *(Courtesy Anthology Film Archives.)*

The young woman moves out of the dark building, through a long courtyard. As she walks she is framed by a door-shaped rectangle of light. In the next shot, she comes toward the camera; the door is now behind her. Out on the street, we see the brick wall of the building. This is followed by a shot of two boys dressed for the cold (one has on a hat with earflaps), looking into a window, toward the camera. They move from the right side to the left side of the window frame, and a third joins them. This is the first shot of the film that disrupts the evident theatricality of the opening. The boys have an air of authenticity in their dress and curious stares at the camera. They are aestheticized only by their unwitting framing in the window. It is a confrontation of documentary reality with the dramatic one that preceded it, the first of many in the film. It is also the first sign that the heroine of the film might also be its mediator—that it is through her eyes that we see these boys. Our way of seeing is inflected by hers.

Cornell incorporated his narrative strategy into his working method. We see through the eyes of this young woman in the same way that Cornell saw through the camera/eye of Rudy Burckhardt. In the three films that follow young women through parks and streets of Manhattan—*Nymphlight, The Aviary,* and *A Legend for Fountains (fragments)*—Cornell worked with Rudy Burckhardt as a cameraman/

A Legend for Fountains (fragments). "I Love." (Courtesy Anthology Film Archives.)

collaborator. Burckhardt's accounts of working with Cornell[30] tell of the distance that Cornell retained from his cinematic subject, similar to the distance he establishes in the films themselves. Cornell would notice something—birds in the trees, for instance—and direct Burckhardt to follow their movement with the camera. Well aware of how any cameraman differs from any other in the personal quality of his recorded images, Cornell gave Burckhardt the freedom to shoot in his own manner. Brakhage, another of Cornell's cameramen, has speculated that Cornell was intimidated by the film equipment.[31] It seems more likely that Cornell needed to be distanced from the images he would later make into a film. The footage had to appear found in order to be manipulated, just as his boxes and collages were made of found objects, and his other films were made from preexisting found films.

The viewer is presented with a double perspective and a double reality. The young woman runs toward the camera and around the corner, out of breath. She looks to the left and to the right. She adjusts her scarf. She exhales puffs of cold air. She seems exhilarated and unsure of where she is. We see the boys again. The difference between the two kinds of realities we are faced with begins to become evident here. The boys are at home and curious about the intrusion on their landscape. That their notice of the stranger is directed away from her toward the camera only makes her more strange. The camera is diversionary. The young woman passes through the urban landscape while its inhabitants are held in the spell of the camera. In the next shot, we see her leaning against the wall, her eyes downcast. The children leave the window, and the camera moves toward it and then out to the children at play on the street. Little boys and girls play on door steps, ride bikes, run here and there. They are obviously at home. After several shots, the young woman is seen holding a cat up to a bakery window. The scene is shot from inside so that the lettering is backward.

In dreams and in other worlds (like Alice's through-the-looking-glass world), words appear backward. Cornell uses reversals to indicate the special, spiritual nature of the places he creates in his films. Freud's interpretation of linguistic inversions is crucial to any exposition on *The Children's Party* trilogy. Here, one must read the reversal as a sign of the young woman's status as an ideal. The shot signals a series of shots that emphasize mirror images, although it is not one itself.

The camera pans along a wall with graffiti, following it up to the cornice of a building and down to a reflection of a water tower in a puddle. There is another reflection with backward graffiti; then the young woman again, this time reflected in a window. The street is seen, also reflected in a window. She turns her head, as if to look. There is another shot, in close-up, of the same gesture. The camera pans up a building following the flight of a bird. It then follows the sweeping flight of many pigeons in the sky between buildings. These birds appear to be what excited her attention. They are, like children, the objects of her interest. They represent another kind of life, completely integrated into their environment. In juxtaposition to her, they magnify her isolation. As if to emphasize this point, Cornell interjects an intertitle. From Lorca's "Tu Infancia en Menton" he chooses: "Your solitude, shy in hotels . . ."

The intertitle carries with it the weight of Cornell's intervention in the film. Whereas up to now a delicate balance had been struck between the points of view—ours watching the young woman, hers watching the street—the voice of Lorca brings Cornell's consciousness directly to our attention. For Cornell, hotels were locations of imagination. It is probable that he never stayed in one. They are where travelers stay, and (except for his painful trips to and from Andover Academy as a youth), Cornell was only an imaginary traveler. Those figures whom he admired roamed the world; Lorca, in particular, was visiting New York when he wrote the poem from which the line comes. *The Poet in New York* is filled with poems of wonder and alienation from the city.

While for Lorca, New York was where one stayed in hotels, for Cornell, hotels meant Europe. His boxes and collages are littered with signs for hotels. Many are *of* hotels. Travel, through France especially, was a subject Cornell never tired of. The hotel is a poetic home, where

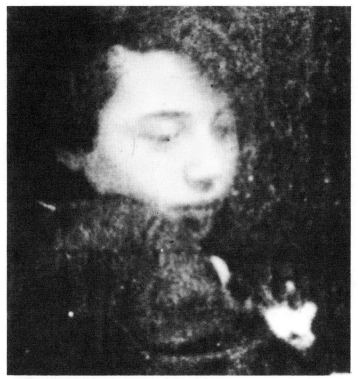

A Legend for Fountains (fragments). The young woman with the cat. *(Courtesy Anthology Film Archives.)*

Romantic and surrealist poets were brought together with society in the lobby, corridors, and lounge and distanced in the privacy of the room; it is a way station in the urban zone on the quest for meaning. To be "shy in hotels" is to choose the solitude of the room rather than the communality of the lobby (as the photographer in Cornell's scenario *Monsieur Phot* prefers). To make such a choice is to indicate one's purpose in travel as self-seeking—not tourism, sociability, or anthropological interest in other cultures.[32] The young woman in *A Legend for Fountains (fragments)* comes to represent this solitary stranger through the Lorca quotation. The intimate "your" (solitude) brings Cornell into direct focus. He addresses her as he might have read Lorca addressing himself. He describes both himself and her to us.

As if to emphasize the solitary nature of the young woman, the next shot shows her joined, not by another person, but by a cat. She kisses and fondles it, framed by a store window. She holds it in her coat to keep it warm. The next shot is of a bird in flight, first to the corner of a building, then back and forth between buildings. The young woman looks out of a window now, still holding the cat. The theme of urban

A Legend for Fountains (fragments). ". . . pure mask in another sign." *(Courtesy Anthology Film Archives.)*

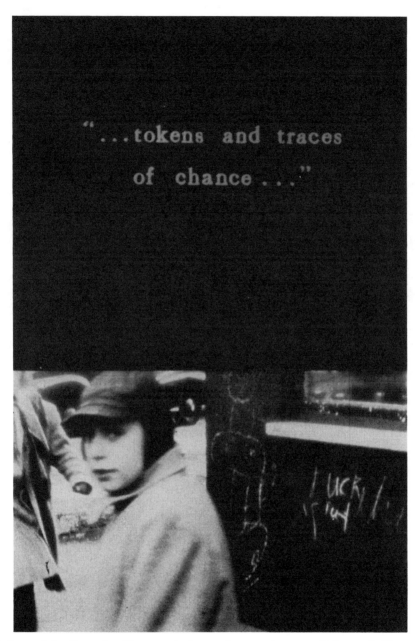

A Legend for Fountains (fragments). ". . . tokens and traces of chance." *(Courtesy Anthology Film Archives.)*

A Legend for Fountains (fragments). **The doll in the window.** *(Courtesy Anthology Film Archives.)*

pastoral begins to seem inevitable in this sequence. Instead of wandering the countryside of France or Italy, this young poetess roams Little Italy. Instead of encountering swains and sheep, she observes children and pigeons. As she looks out of the window of a café or bakery, holding her passing friend—a stray cat—the cityscape organizes itself harmoniously. The children and birds move as if choreographed.

The next intertitle—"Pure mask in another sign . . ."—keeps the nondocumentary thrust of the film alive. It extends its own meaning in a number of ways. It reinforces the sense that this young woman and this neighborhood are not really what they seem. She may be the mask; the cat may be the other "sign"; or the totality of the film to come may be the "mask in another sign." Its purity is both her purity and the absolute nature of the film's nonrealism. To be a "pure mask" is to be absolutely not what one seems. Moreover, the word *sign* underscores the notion that the whole film is a series of iconographic images, sometimes representing more than what we see. The literal signs in the film are but one type of sign. The images, too, must be read for their meaning.

The young woman and cat are again framed in the window, looking out from inside. The cat turns its head and looks around, in a gesture reminiscent of the young woman's turn of head earlier in the film. There is a second shot of them from another angle. The third fragment from Lorca's poem forms the next intertitle: ". . . tokens and traces of chance . . ." This seems to be the clearest suggestion of how to read the images. Like the previous intertitle, it may be predictive; that is, what is to come are the "tokens and traces of chance." It comes as the final intervention of the young woman. We are left on our own for the rest of the film. The intertitle, because it comes after the other two, must be interpreted as a kind of instruction for where to look for meaning. As the young woman (thus, Cornell) had been doing, so the viewer must now wander through the landscape of Little Italy seeking a greater

Joseph Cornell. *Untitled (Bébé Marie)* (early 1940s). Paper and painted wood box, with painted corrugated cardboard floor, containing doll in cloth dress and straw hat with cloth flowers, dried flowers, and twigs, flecked with paint, 23½ × 12⅜ × 5¼". (*Collection, The Museum of Modern Art, New York. Acquired through the Lillie P. Bliss Bequest.*)

reality through the "tokens and traces" and "signs." Not only does the phrase harken back to the place of the origin of the aesthetic of chance—France—but it reemphasizes the work of the film. The one who experiences these "tokens" must fill them with meaning. They are empty unless interpreted.[33]

The final section of the film occurs out on the street again, following the emblems of urban pastoral. Children walk and run past the camera. They are dressed in winter clothes. One little girl looks like a miniature European peasant woman in a scarf. A doll in a box in a window stands up, a modern version of Cornell's own "Bébé Marie" (1940s)[34] of more than ten years earlier. Buildings are reflected in the glass as the camera pans up the doll's torso. An old woman walks by. A boy carrying a laundry bag that is almost as big as he is walks down the street, hunched over. There is a double sense that this is only New York in the 1950s and, at the same time, anywhere at anytime. By concentrating on the timeless children and elderly, who (always out of fashion) are less of a particular place or era, Cornell universalizes his subject. Also, by making the children sometimes look like adults, he has them stand for all humanity. The film ends with the camera receding back into the alleyway from which it had emerged in the beginning, children running out of the rectangular, lit doorway that now forms its closure.

Centuries of June (1955)

Centuries of June was filmed by Stan Brakhage under Cornell's direction. Brakhage reports that he and Cornell walked together to and around the "Tower House."[35] Brakhage shot whatever Cornell pointed out.[36] The ostensible purpose of the film was to make a record of one of Cornell's favorite neighborhood sights before is was demolished. One senses the imminent destruction in the film; a pile of dirt sits next to the house, predicting the rubble soon to come. It is singularly out of place in the well-manicured, tree-lined street.

Cornell named the film with a line from Emily Dickinson's "There is a Zone whose even Years," although for a long time he had called it simply the "Tower House Film."[37] The poem is about the perpetuity of the present. The "centuries" of June and August are, for Dickinson, the temporal field for the recognition of "Consciousness." In Cornell's use of the line, he brings together both the Dickinsonian meditation on the time of consciousness—the now—and the simpler recognition of the timelessness of the June day he and Brakhage filmed. The filmmaking process is one that can prolong that June day. The title points to both the wish and the fulfillment of renewal.

Cornell did well to choose Brakhage for this film. By 1955, Brakhage was a young but experienced cameraman and filmmaker who had already developed a compositional sense that would suit Cornell's taste for subtle visual events. Often, the film image is framed obliquely or cut off. The camera movement is controlled; at times it strictly follows the lines of the house, at times it weaves and shakes as Brakhage walks toward what is before him. Some shots are framed to establish what is to come, as in the shot of the dirt pile over which climbs a young boy. Brakhage's agility with the camera allowed him to follow butterflies and birds in the same way he followed the children at play. And Brakhage did well to accept the commission. Cornell pointed out to him cinematic subjects that Brakhage had dismissed previously as insignificant. Cornell gave him the confidence to expand his cinematographic vocabulary by reinforcing filmic ideas that Brakhage had not yet felt the courage to affirm. For Brakhage the collaboration was certainly a formative one; for Cornell it was fortuitous.

The film begins with the major visual theme—the house and its tower, seen through the leaves of a maple tree. There is a medium shot of the tower and the upper portion of the house, followed by another medium shot of the house and an adjacent bush, and a pan up the tower. The next two shots are of the tree and a pan down the tower. The house is then seen through the trees. As an opening sequence, these first five shots are placed in almost didactic sequence. It is as if Cornell felt the need to establish the elements that will be used throughout the film: the house with its tower, the bush next to the house, the large tree, and the fact that in order for him to see the house he must look through the tree's leafy branches. The emphasis on the perspective from which the house is viewed is accentuated two shots later as the camera moves toward the porch steps. As much as this film is about the house, it is about looking at the house, sometimes from behind the tree, sometimes standing still, and sometimes prowling around it. The hand-held camera movement represents *looking*. It has a texture that can be described as subjective.

Centuries of June continues with a more controlled, almost documentary, study of the porch railing and the steps. Like the first few shots, it seems to describe what is there and of interest. The first inkling of the unhappy fate of the house comes with a shot of smoke in the tree's leaves. The juxtaposition of a pan from leaves to the tower with the smoke image, warns of its future destruction. One anticipates the "Centuries of August" of the Dickinson poem, the autumn of the leaves and the house. But as quickly as the viewer can sense danger, it is dissipated. Behind the leaves a boy appears playing in a pile of dirt. The smoke, like the boy and the house itself, becomes just another event behind leaves.

After Cornell permits this first image of a child near the house, the film is opened to many children. One sees children walking home from school passing by the house. After the continuous blue green color of the shots of the house in the trees, the girls' red dresses make the scene very festive. Some men working in the background are part of the

Centuries of June. **The boy and girl fling stones.** *(Courtesy Anthology Film Archives.)*

landscape, as the smoke had been. Because we have just seen the boy at play in the dirt, the men seem to be his grown counterparts. They also work intently near the dirt pile. An ambiguity between work and play is suggested: If the men do what the boy did, are they working or playing?

The interpenetrability of the child's and adult's activities comes into play in the next shot, when the children act out a small drama. In a medium shot of the street with a shaded sidewalk, a girl walks toward the camera followed by a boy, who ducks behind a tree, as if he were stalking her. Their glances meet and they both bend down to pick up stones and throw them in unison. It is a quietly funny shot. The scene begins as one very like those which had preceded it, of children walking home from school. We immediately reinterpret it as we see the boy, a shy suitor, following the girl. They seem too young for sexual interest in one another. The scene is humorous. He follows her in the manner of a hunter, stalking his prey. He plays at what he will later do as a man, though perhaps with more subtlety. The shot ends affirming that theirs in only a game, however, when their childish priorities reassert themselves. They end by playacting as adults and fling stones in one harmonious gesture that releases all the sexual tension that preceded it.

The next sequence of shots transforms the perspective of the film from an objective survey of the street and yard scenes to the perspective of a single, hidden observer. In a medium long shot, we see children

Centuries of June. **Children walking and playing.** *(Courtesy Anthology Film Archives.)*

walking on the far side of the street. It is a shot from a very low angle since, as the camera pans around, we see the tower through blades of grass. The shot that follows is from a very high angle, through an archway. The camera has gone from the lowest to the highest perspective. It is now in the tower, looking out over the neighborhood. A

sequence of shots follows that studies the architecture and yard from
above and explores the inside of the house. Light streams in through the
windows.

The film returns to the outside again. As the boy ducks behind the
dirt pile, a new visual element appears, in just the same place in the
frame. A butterfly flies up from the ground into the trees. The tower is
seen in the background. The simple parallelism between shots unites the
image of the child with that of the fleeting butterfly in rich metaphorical
juxtaposition. The unity is expanded as we see the roof of the house at
the moment birds fly away from it, continuing the line of flight of the
butterfly. The camera follows the line of flight to the corner of the house
but switches its path and follows the line of the house to the front porch
steps. The combination of parallel cutting and continuous camera
movement over disparate images emphasizes the nonobjective nature of
this "documentary" film. Through orthodox cinematic manipulation, a
unity is established that would otherwise go unobserved. This kind of
substitution is very characteristic of Cornell's films. In *The Aviary* and
The Children's Party trilogy, placement of succeeding images to make
parallels occurs frequently. Children come to stand for a spiritualized,
and sometimes sexualized, aspect of the world.

The film begins to be filled with children, walking and playing in the
dirt. A dog is held up to the camera, in the most direct encounter in the
film. The boys jump down the pile from the left to the right. The
children are then seen playing in the dirt, through the trees. The camera
pulls back to show the arch, framing the scene. The camera pans to the
right across a latticework pattern.

A subsequent series of rhyming shots forms the third repetition of the
theme of the abandoned house and seems strange after we have seen the
children who play around it. But the following shot brings us again to
the unitary structure of the film. A butterfly flutters in front of the
porch and flies upward. The house is seen through the trees, and the
camera moves shakily toward it. With the house in the background, the
butterfly hangs from a branch and then flies out of the frame toward the
left. A child's legs, shot as if the child were suspended like the butterfly,
stand in front of the house. The camera pans up to show a girl standing
in front of the trees.

In a medium shot, the girl walks down the stone steps from the left to
the right of the frame. The house is seen behind the trees. In an inclusive
gesture, the camera pans down the tower to the stone steps, passing
over the girl, to the sidewalk. The same shot is repeated, this time there
are children on the steps. The two boys stand up and walk away. The
final shot of the film follows three children: a boy on a bike, a girl in the
center, and another boy on the right—they all walk away down the
sidewalk, their backs to the camera. The butterfly, the birds, and the
children all abandon the house to its presumed destruction. The birds

and butterflies, as in Dickinson's poetry, are the soul of the place. Cornell includes children, as they all flee from the doomed place.

It is difficult to know how much of Cornell's film is an homage or a response to Dickinson's poem. The title was an afterthought, attached several years after the "Tower House" film was completed. The most that is known for certain is that the film represented an affinity Cornell felt with the poem. The poem presents a bleak picture of the human capacity for pure understanding, for "Consciousness." If it exists only at a moment, the instant called "Noon," it is barely perceptible. Cornell chose *Centuries of June* as his title rather than *Consciousness Is Noon*. He takes an optimistic position within a rather pessimistic tradition. While Dickinson's poem is the same valiant effort to fix the moment of consciousness by uttering it, *Centuries of June* seems to attempt to prolong and repeat the moment of day and place by fixing its image cinematically.

Although not an aspect of the Dickinson poem at issue here, the position of children in her work in general is mimicked in Cornell's film. Norman Talbot in his article, "The Child, the Actress, and Miss Emily Dickinson," described her use of the image of children and the theme of childhood as an "analogue of all human experience."[38] He goes on to say that Death, Love, Poetry, Nature, and Eternity, "the five crucial subjects of Miss Dickinson's poetry are constantly seen in terms that make the present finite life analogous to the life of the child," by which he means that adults are mere children in relationship to a vast, eternal future. Cornell's sympathy with this sentiment is evident in the series of shots that bring together the boys and men at the dirt pile as equivalents within the *Centuries of June*. In *The Aviary* and *Nymphlight*, Cornell makes a similar equation using children. One can only surmise his sense of the importance of that "Eternity" of which Dickinson often wrote. Although the history of the imagery of birds, butterflies, and children as emblems of the soul was not foreign to Cornell's intention, his is a much more subtle fervor than Dickinson's. His children remain firmly of the world.

The Aviary (1955)

The Aviary, made in the same year as *Centuries of June*, operates in a similar way. Rudy Burckhardt had an experience like that of Brakhage under Cornell's direction. They walked and filmed together, this time in Union Square in Manhattan. The film is shot in black and white on a late fall or early spring day. Although the film has a very different appearance from *Centuries of June* (because of its lack of natural and cinematic color), they share a wistful and moody air. The relationship of the children to the scene is very similar. They play within it and make it a meaningful place while they are there. And like *A Legend for Foun-*

The Aviary. **The statue of a woman with children.** *(Courtesy Anthology Film Archives.)*

tains (fragments) (which is also pure black and white), a young woman observes the children and the place, as she wanders fleetingly through the space.[39]

The film begins with a shot of leafless trees with buildings in the distant background. A pan to the left brings into the frame a statue of a woman holding a child in one arm and holding the hand of another at her side. She is draped in cloth, as if she were an ancient or biblical figure. The pan continues down to the pedestal of the statue, carved with lions' heads. A live woman sits at the base. Three sequences establish the major themes of the film: a montage of close-ups of the floral and animal carvings in the base of the statue (which includes bas-reliefs of butterflies and birds), the woman caressing the carvings in medium shots, and medium shots of the erratic movements of a pigeon walking in the bushes. Cornell will find numerous ways to combine these elements in order to create both the portrait of Union Square and the meditation on the mutability of children that is *The Aviary.*

After the beginning of *The Aviary,* the fleeting woman does not appear again. There is a sense that Cornell began by attempting to have her figure as the living counterpart to the statue, overseeing and protecting the children at play in the park as the statue/mother does her two.

The Aviary. Pigeons and boys are interchangeable. *(Courtesy Anthology Film Archives.)*

But the theme is dropped quickly, when the urban pastoral asserts itself. As in *Centuries of June,* the children, birds, and butterflies are interchangeable as the spirit of this rather ordinary place. The children are ever present like those in *A Legend for Fountains (fragments),* with or without the curious gaze of a wandering stranger.

The Aviary. Pigeons decorate the statue. *(Courtesy Anthology Film Archives.)*

The Aviary. Boys fly through the frame. *(Courtesy Anthology Film Archives.)*'

The Aviary. **A girl.** *(Courtesy Anthology Film Archives.)*

The Aviary. **A dwarf.** *(Courtesy Anthology Film Archives.)*

Pigeons, walking and flying, appear often. On its surface, *The Aviary* is about a sanctuary for birds. The same moving camera that followed the pigeon in the opening of the film follows the woman who had outlined the statue with her hands as she leaves the frame. A man feeds pigeons. Pigeons fly. Again the camera, as if catalyzed by their movement, gracefully follows them. The pigeons circle above and then land on the statue of George Washington on horseback.[40] As they land, the statue is transformed into a perch, so appropriate is the horse's back, the arm, and even the head to the birds's needs.

The point of relationship of the birds to the human sphere occurs when they are on the ground. Birds and people are made similar through the use of a moving camera and juxtaposition. After the sequence of the birds in flight, a group of young children is filmed in long shot so they are the same size on the screen as the pigeons. They jump over a fence, run, and tumble in a grassy area. They run away and jump back over the fence. In their grouping and their elegant, almost choreographed, movement, they are birdlike. This similarity is emphasized by the sympathetic tracing of their path by the camera. It moves gracefully, as it had following the birds's flight.

After the pigeons perch on the equestrian statue, a montage of shots describes the fullness of life in the park. People, dogs, and pigeons inhabit it. In a brief and very subtle set of two shots, a little girl runs and the camera pans to follow her; in the next shot, a dwarf walks toward the camera. Both occupy the same place in the frame. It is an amusing replacement of one miniature for another and brings our attention to an often repeated theme in Cornell's work. Children and dwarfs are equated as small versions of adults. Cornell's *Untitled (Object)* from 1933–35 illustrates the equation by its use of an engraving of a dwarf seated on an elegant sideboard, which is surrounded by dollhouse chairs.[41] Cornell was attracted to images of children dressed as adults (as the round-faced girls from Marken are in *Bookstalls* [1978]) and, alternately, to miniatures, like Thumbellina. It seems that Cornell was delighted by film's ability to conflate the two. By editing two shots together, filmed from such a perspective that their subjects were the same size, he contrived, in his poetic logic, to make them fundamentally the same.

The final sequence of the film comes back to the original statue. Some boys circle around it, hanging on to the rims of the fountains at the base. The trees surrounding the statue partially reveal the buildings behind them. Birds land on the leafless branches. Another shot, through bare trees with birds, shows the statue of Washington, from behind, its arm pointing to the left. A shot of small birds in the trees is followed by a close-up of the woman's head, as if looking up at them. Dry leaves blow on the sidewalk. The camera follows them, and pans up the back of the statue of the woman with children. From another lower angle, the child at her side is seen, towered over by trees with birds and clouds gliding by. The film ends with a montage of birds in the trees, flying from one to another. It is a series of eight shots that look like one. They are smoothly cut on camera movements that follow the birds in flight.

Cornell is obsessed with the unity of small flying creatures and children throughout all of his work. This can be accounted for in a number of ways. First, as a lyrical filmmaker, he chooses to represent reality with a vision of pastoral harmony. Empson's point that the child is substituted for the swain in late-nineteenth-century literature is applicable to Cornell. Children are depicted as having a continuous existence with animals and birds; they function as the conduit between the social and the natural worlds. Second, Cornell makes formal relationships on the basis of scale. Michelson's category of "the play with, variation on, scale" applies to the image of children. They are like birds because they are small. Third, the psychological implications of flight coincided with the sense of the sexuality of childhood present beneath the surface of Cornell's sculpture and films. One can find evidence of his sympathy with the equation of nature (here, birds) and the sexual forces. His reading of Walt Whitman, for example, was detailed and annotated. Many of the poems that draw together sex, nature, and childhood were especially noted by Cornell.[42] Further, there is an oneiric substitution of flight for sex. Omniscience and omnipotence are attributed to adults engaged in sex in the fantasy life of children, and the substitution of the metaphor of flight for intercourse is a common one.[43] Children's urge to fly has been analyzed by Freud to have its source in sexual curiosity.[44] And finally, the metaphor of the soul as a bird is employed in the flowery prose of Mary Baker Eddy, the major theologian of Cornell's religion—Christian Science. And in the history of Christian painting, the soul was often depicted as a bird. Equally often, until the seventeenth century, the soul was represented as a winged child, usually ascending to heaven from the corpse of an adult.[45] Insofar as Cornell was a serious Christian Scientist, he would find an agreeable coincidence of his religion with his art in this metaphor of the soul.[46]

Nymphlight (1957)

Nymphlight is a variation on *The Aviary*. It poses similar problems in terms of its narrative structure and point of view. In the way in which it combines documentary reality with dramatically enacted movements, it presents an image that is from two points of view at once. The central character watches the events in the park, yet some other observers—the cameraman, Cornell, we viewers—follow her as the center of interest. As does the woman in *The Aviary* and the younger one in *A Legend for Fountains (fragments)*, this young woman leads us to see the park from a

Nymphlight. The personification of the muse. *(Courtesy Anthology Film Archives.)*

Nymphlight. The bird's beak "touches" the Chrysler Building. *(Courtesy Anthology Film Archives.)*

fresh perspective. Cornell seems to have put her there in order to po-
eticize everything else in the film. One of the things to which she directs
our interest is another girl.

Like *The Aviary*, *Nymphlight* is the occasion for a set of transformations. Here the change involves a transmigration of spirit from the film's
first heroine to its second. A girl encounters and disappears from the
site of yet another urban sculpture—a fountain. Gwenn Thomas, a
pubescent girl dressed in a long, frilly dress and carrying a torn parasol[47]
runs along the park at the beginning of the film. Singularly out of
fashion, she has the air of one of the female figures of Romantic and
surrealist literature who appear in men's literary fantasies: the subject of
poetry and the personification of the muse. Not until well into the film
do we see her face, as she turns her head to watch the pigeons in flight.
In a beautiful work of cinematic framing, a pigeon lands on a branch in
the foreground; in the distance we can see the point of the Chrysler
Building. It is as if the bird's beak touches the top of that needlelike
structure. As they fly, the pigeons sometimes blend into the trees, like
leaves in silhouette. As they walk, they are anthropomorphic.

The girl turns her head to watch the birds. As she does, an ambiguity
arises as to who is perceiving the events in the park. It is like the
ambiguity in *A Legend for Fountains (fragments):* Either we, as viewers,
are following the distraction of the one who watched the girl, or we
have now entered the consciousness of the girl herself and watch the life
in the park with aestheticized fascination. The last two things she looks
at are the central fountain, which spouts water from its gargoyle heads,
and at another girl in a blue dress, younger and more up-to-date. Sitney
claims that at that moment, Thomas becomes the fountain, which like
the birds, children, and statue in *The Aviary* is invested with the spirit of
the park.[48]

While the evidence of the last shot of the film (of water dripping from
a fountain)[49] may point to that conclusion, it seems equally valid that the
first girl becomes the second, in that the attention of the filmmaker
shifts to this documentary version of his fictional muse. She is the more
timely picture of girlhood. She is younger and more genuinely belongs
to the park than the first, who although innocent enough, seems to be
acting. Yet the loss of the first girl is never quite satisfactory. The transition is made (either into the fountain or the other girl) only by a series of
glances, and the remaining parasol reminds us of her disappearance.
Further, the second girl lives up to no Romantic ideal. She is like the
pigeons: part of the park. She mimics their walk. In both *The Aviary*
and *Nymphlight* the birds are intercut with children only after the disappearance of the female observer, as if they doubly represented the continuing spirit of the parks, who remains even when unobserved.

No matter where one assigns the first girl's ultimate destination, there
is a sense of loss at her disappearance with the pigeons she watched in

Nymphlight. **The two girls.** *(Courtesy Anthology Film Archives.)*

flight. Although the park and even another girl remain, the pleasure of watching Gwenn Thomas is cut short. *Nymphlight* is by far Cornell's most explicit film about his love for young girls. The young women in

A Legend for Fountains (fragments) and *The Aviary* are older and much more suited to the quasi-autobiographical image of the boy-girl than is Gwenn Thomas. She was twelve at the time of filming.[50] In her costume, she appears to represent a fairy-tale image of a woman: old enough to be going to balls but always drawn as a girl—Cinderella, or more appropriate to Cornell, Thumbellina. Andersen's miniature woman is perhaps a good model for the girl in *Nymphlight*, whose disappearance is linked to the flight of birds. In the illustrations to Cornell's scenario, "The Theater of Hans Christian Andersen" in the Hans Christian Andersen issue of *Dance Index*,[51] there is a picture of Thumbellina carried over a city on the back of a bird. In the puzzling sequence in which Thomas watches the birds, there is much less identification with her than with the young woman in *A Legend for Fountains (fragments)*. More than watching with her, we watch her. She is objectified; because of the lack of identification, it is possible to watch her passively and with more distance than in the later film. The viewer's position and Cornell's position are voyeuristic. We look upon this presexual, harmless, and therefore desirable girl, but we do not identify with her. It is necessary that she be prepubescent and oblivious, like Alice, in order for her to be watched without threat.

The Children's Party Trilogy and *Vaudeville DeLuxe*

The Children's Party, The Midnight Party, and *Cotillion* (1968) form a trilogy that is at the heart of Cornell's nonnarrative cinematic achievement. There is no elusive girl who mediates between the viewer and the image. There are only the participants themselves, those children at the party, who—asleep and awake—are the image and the viewer at once. Cornell's idea was to make films that were both for an audience of children and about children. It was his sophistication that led him to create structures that would mimic the mental organization of a child.

These films, which are analogous to his graphic collages, are comprised of a number of films owned by Cornell. He found the basis for his films in material created by some other hands. As Jay Leyda illustrates in *Films Beget Films*, the tradition of the reuse of film footage is almost as old as cinema itself;[52] for Cornell the coincidence of cinematic discovery with his own work as a plastic artist provided an outlet for a great deal of artistic energy. Popular imagery, pedagogy, and fantasy congealed in his collage films. As the cubists had employed newspapers and advertisements in their paintings, as Ernst had used nineteenth-century engravings, and as Cornell's contemporaries Marsden Hartley and Edward Hopper used popular imagery, so Cornell reorganized seemingly disparate and "unaesthetic" film material to his own purpose.[53]

Cornell believed his films would not be understood or appreciated. It is tempting to ascribe his insecurity to the films' insistence on amusing scenes and seemingly slapdash organization. Particularly the central segments of *The Children's Party* and *Cotillion* have an accretion of shots that are very difficult to comprehend in one or two viewings. They seem anarchic. Perhaps Cornell feared that the films would be misinterpreted, that his mode of editing[54] would not be considered seriously by viewers who saw the films as merely amusements for children. Moreover, the images themselves have a direct relationship to children, and on one or two viewings might seem to be *only* what they are. Their resonance would be overlooked because of their illusory simplicity.

Further, the films are repetitive and have been viewed as variations on the presiding theme of a children's party. The use of the same material of acrobatic performers, children at a Halloween party, scientific- and educational-film footage, and the technique of stop motion tend to support that view. In fact, the editing strategies and the principles on which all the films are based are very similar. The three films contain a series of self-contained activities—stage acts, apple dunking, and children sleeping or dancing—intercut with a great variety of other imagery, as if the completion of any single activity was assumed and therefore unnecessary to show. But the three films are different from one another and about different things. *The Children's Party* centers on the theme of stars: stars in the sky, child stars, circus stars, and starlight. *The Mid-*

The Children's Party. **The End.** *(Courtesy Anthology Film Archives.)*

night Party describes the mystery of night: the power of light in the darkness, fear, and sleep. *Cotillion* is about performance and sight: seeing and being seen, being able to see without being seen, and blindness.[55] They are separate films that form a coherent trilogy, not because of their use of common imagery, but rather because of the premises of their editing.

The Children's Party begins with "The End" written upside down and backward. There are two aspects to such a beginning that are of interest.[56] To have the end at the beginning is to make a film that can be projected forward and backward. Cornell had undertaken such an inversion of narrativity before, in the making of *Gnir Rednow* (1955).[57]

In *The Children's Party,* the end is literally the beginning. One assumes that if the film were turned around and projected from the end, "The End" could also be its finish, its inversion canceled. For a man who worked with glass and mirrors in his box sculptures, a word written backward suggests a large range of possibilities. The viewer is meant to see through the film, as if through a window with writing on it, as in *A Legend for Fountains (fragments).* Also, the screen is a kind of reflecting device. The film is a mirror for the audience. Certainly, Cornell used those kinds of techniques consciously in his boxes.

There is more to it than that, however. Although there is no indication that Cornell read Freud, their similar interest in words written backward leads to the possibility that *The Children's Party* is introduced, however unconsciously, as a dream. In Freud's "Antithetical Sense of Primal Words,"[58] he points to the dream phenomenon of non-negation—That is, in dreams, there are no opposites, only simultaneities. He uses words in ancient Egyptian that reverse their sound and spelling as well as their meaning as a linguistic model to argue that it is an early human invention that we retain in dreams. By extension, this included inverted writing. As an example of what he points to as "a factor of deeper origin," Freud says, "We remember how fond children are of playing at reversing the sound of words, and how frequently the dream-work makes use for various ends of a reversal of the material to hand for representation."[59] By inverting "The End," Cornell uses a mechanism common to dreamlife and childhood. If this interpretation of Freud is correct, the subsequent film can be seen as rooted in a system of unconscious order. Even though Cornell did not consciously work from a Freudian model, he would perhaps not have rejected that supposition. Both dream logic and children's logic were of interest to him. Instead of exposing the hidden content of dreams, as Freud sought to do, Cornell saw the dream structure as a way of presenting meaning in a veiled form, the most base content in a modest way. It is an attitude inherited from his Romantic progenitors, particularly Nerval. Rather than take unconscious structures apart, he built conscious ones based on unconscious models, in order to present his own secrets.

The Children's Party. **The boy stares offscreen.** *(Courtesy Anthology Film Archives.)*

After its oxymoronic title, the film becomes an educational film, temporarily. A drawing of a window, its shade drawn, is animated; the shade rises onto a night scene, the sky dotted with stars. This is followed by a shot of a boy, on the extreme left of the frame, looking off to the left, in profile. It is lit as if he were looking out of an open window with light streaming in. The shot sets the tone of the film. A boy, almost a young man, placidly looks out the film frame at something we do not see. It is an opening similar to that of *Bookstalls*, where a boy reads; but in that film, the opening serves as a parenthesis that is closed at the end of the film by the young reader closing the book and moving on. Here, the film will close with a shot of a young girl wistfully looking off in the other direction and passing out of the frame. It is a mystery why the boy appears at the beginning of *The Children's Party*. Only at the end do we discover that his function is to set the stage for a story of star-crossed lovers.

The shot of the boy is followed by an intertitle that speculates on the origins of constellations. It was "the Ancients wondering what the stars were" who created constellations in order to find places in the sky for their heroes. As it comes after the shot of the boy, it poses him as one of the ancients, or at least his type as an ancient one. It also introduces the theme of stars and constellations in their literal sense. Through a series of dissolves between animated drawings and intertitles, we see the constellations of Orion and the Great Bear (the Big Dipper), with its smaller constellations of the Little Dipper and the North Star. The sequence is presented in a very conventional manner. It seems not to have been altered at all by Cornell.

Cornell comes to the subject of constellations from a very different perspective than that of Jean Cocteau, whose signature was often a drawing in the form of a constellation. It is interesting to compare their repeated use of stellar imagery as a metaphor in their work. Cocteau drew portraits of his personal "stars" (Dargelos, for example) by connecting star points with lines. He often signed his name with a star. In the "Flying Lesson" sequence of *Blood of a Poet,* he strung the little girl with straps of bells, placed her high and flat against the ceiling, emphasizing her nature as a human turned constellation. He made her an archetype of rebellion. In the boxes, Cornell often used stellar imagery as an atmospheric and graphic device. Through it, he both organized the visual elements formally and gave a context to the other objects in the box. And Cornell shares Cocteau's literalization of the relationship of stars in the sky to stage and movie stars. From Cornell's other work it is clear that he made visual puns from verbal constructs: star-struck, stars in his eye, and star-crossed.

With the next shots, Cornell presents two of the possible aspects of stars. There is a four-frame image of a girl and boy standing posed,

The Children's Party. Girls dressed as boys. *(Courtesy Anthology Film Archives.)*

looking to the left. Then a slightly longer one of four children at a table. Two of the girls are dressed like boys.[60] Because of the brevity of both of these shots, they are nearly still. This is followed by a lengthy stop-motion image of a girl with a wincing smile holding a doll, a bottle, and party paraphernalia. She looks at the camera. Because of the effect of stop motion, the image is as two-dimensional as the graphic ones. It emphasizes the surface nature of the image and its flatness. Like a constellation, it is a graphic representation of something that was once thought to be human. The mythological proportion of a hero or god is honored in his constellation. In this shot, the graphic representation predicts the girl's mythologization. Cornell was very interested in child stars. He kept dossiers on them. He followed the careers of "Baby Peggy" and "Baby Marie" Kiernan, child stars of the 1930s and 1940s through press clippings and movie announcements.[61] His dossiers on women stars often included photographs of them in costume as children. The trilogy of which *The Children's Party* is a part is comprised of material from "Our Gang" serials along with some of a party of children who could be child actors themselves. By being filmed, they become prospective stars. This is one of many shots in the film in which children stare out of the frame. Their fixed stares through stop motion transforms their changing features from humorous and spontaneous to quizzical and sometimes serious glares. Their acting ability is thus enhanced by Cornell.

A man carrying a chair in his mouth interrupts the child's gaze. His type in the film is representative of live performance, one of the many "acts" we see in the film. He is what the children stare so intently to "see."

If Cornell based his notion of what would appeal to children on his own experience, then the combination of film and performance was a natural choice. Stage shows and other theatrical entertainments were things he actively enjoyed as a child. He went to matinees nearly every Saturday.[62] The two large theaters of his childhood in Nyack, New York, were combinations of vaudeville and movie theaters. The Lyceum and the Broadway featured matinee and evening performances by major vaudeville personalities, acrobats, and dramatic stars, interspersed with short films. As he grew older, the shows were transformed to all-movie sessions; by the time he was fourteen, the theaters booked movies rather than vaudeville acts. Predictably, Cornell retained a love for film and performance in combination, and in this film he seems to have wanted to include variety acts within (rather than along with) the movie.

The shot has another function in addition to this introductory one. It is the first showing objects in people's mouths. In a montage of seven shots, the man swings a chair in his mouth, the boy carries an apple in his, and the man then turns a woman on his head, on an apparatus supported in his mouth. There is another stop motion shot of the small

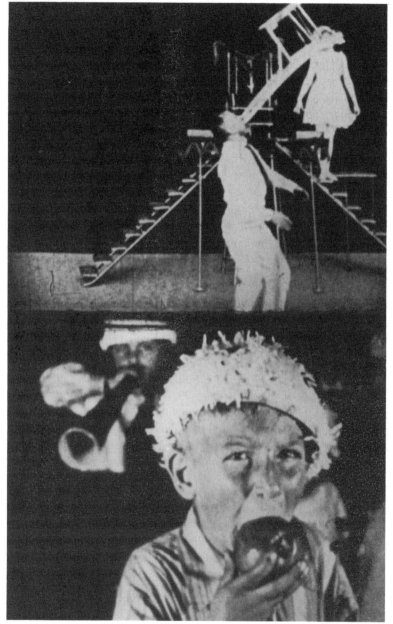

The Children's Party. **Objects in mouths.** *(Courtesy Anthology Film Archives.)*

girl staring with her tongue slightly out. As the sequence continues the performers are intercut with the children either staring or clapping as if for the acrobats and knife thrower. They are never purely spectators since Cornell also makes them equivalent to the performers (for example, the cut from the man to the boy with objects in their mouths). And we are never completely passive as viewers, since the children stare out at us, often with facial gestures of poignant appeal.

The material of the Indian knife thrower here is particularly interesting. It is presented as another act incorporating skill, danger, and amusement. It is intercut with shots of children responding. The thrower outlines a woman's body with knives. He makes a dangerous constellation around her form. She extricates herself, and all that is left are the blades. After he wraps her in paper and throws more knives, a brief title appears, only thirteen frames long, which emphasizes the accuracy, danger, and trust involved in the act: "Two inches out of the way and Chief Zat Zam would not need to apply for a divorce." The Indians represent the nature of the creation of constellations, and an implicit pact between the creator and the subject.

As in the Andersen fairy tale, the human performers in *The Children's Party* are interchangeable with animal performers. The influence of Andersen should never be underestimated in Cornell's work. Not only did he make a collaged "Homage to Hans Christian Andersen," several collages using Hans Christian Andersen characters, and innumerable references to him in letters and notes, he also owned no fewer

The Children's Party. **A constellation of knives.** *(Courtesy Anthology Film Archives.)*

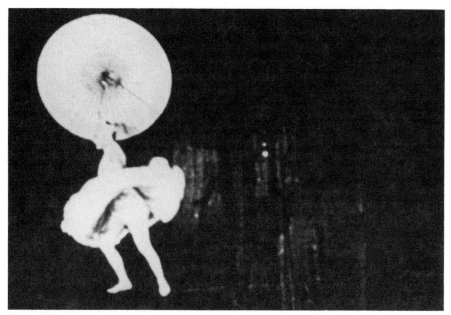

The Children's Party. The tightrope walker. *(Courtesy Anthology Film Archives.)*

than eight volumes of Andersen fairy tales and novels. The antimoral-
istic tone and the personification of animals coincided with two of
Cornell's aesthetic issues. Seals replace the acrobats and knife-throwing
act, in a way reminiscent of each of them. The seal has things thrown at
it—a ball, a chair—and suffers from them as little as the "Indian squaw."
In fact, the seal balances a chair on his nose just as the acrobat had done
with his mouth.

Cornell then shifts back to the human realm. The seal, balancing a
spinning ball on its nose and clapping its fins, rolls forward on a caisson.
Within the tonal range of the film, it is a densely black shape on a light
background. The next shot is of a woman, hanging from a rope by her
mouth, spinning, as the ball had. Both images are centered. The spinning movement unites them. As she stops, she contorts her body and
makes gestures with her arms and legs that strive for grace but look as
ridiculous as the flapping seal fins. The figure of this woman appears
again in *The Midnight Party* and in *Vaudeville DeLuxe,* always as a
grotesque, objectified image. The awkwardness of her movements, her
complete whiteness against the black background, and the inhuman
posture of hanging from a rope by her mouth all contribute to her
dehumanization and flattening. Not only is she interchangeable with a
seal, but she is just a moving shape that can be visually rhymed with
other shapes. Sometimes she is star shaped, like a starfish caught by one
arm.

The next woman in the film has a different function. The tightrope walker ludicrously prances across a rope with her umbrella. She wears a white dress on a black background, like the hanging woman. But she has a shadow. She comes in from the right, walks across and back. The title "High Jumping" flashes on the screen, written backward. In close up, we see the rope and her legs and feet bounding twice in slow motion. Her skirt flies up, but as soon as it reveals her panties, it descends and covers her again. It is a shot similar in function to that of the ballet dancer in *Entr'acte* (1924), a film Cornell had certainly seen. It tantalizes the viewer with an unusual perspective. Both films present the view up a woman's skirt as an image of unfulfilled fantasy: *Entr'acte* offers a lengthy look from below a glass floor up a dancer's skirt, but spoils the pleasure when it reveals the "ballerina" to be a bearded man; *The Children's Party* never completely indulges our voyeurism because of its discreet timing.

It is a childish thing to do to lift up a woman's skirt. To include such an image in a film is at once to entertain an assumed audience of children with an act relevant to their experience of humor and to admit, however tentatively, the perpetuation of childish desire in an adult.

There is a one-frame insert of a superimposition of the tightrope walker with rope strung between her hand and her shoulder, carrying her own image. This will be a much longer scene in *The Midnight Party*. It seems to function as a brief optical trick to lead back to the hanging woman. The tiny double of the tightrope walker is the same size as the hanging woman at the beginning of the next shot. As if to indicate that all of these acts go on in perpetuity, the hanging woman reappears, again spinning. She is quickly replaced by a full trapeze act, three men and three women. This seems to be the most modern footage in the film. Its tonal range is much greater than the other material, indicating fewer generations of prints before Cornell obtained it for his own use. It looks like documentary footage of an actual circus performance, shot from below from close range. The tent is quite small, and the film could have been shot from a seat in the audience. In any case, it is not as staged as the other footage is. Significantly, it appears to have been filmed so that the lights form a background to the performers, like stars in a night sky. The trapeze artists perform various exchanges with one another from several camera angles. A woman swings forward and drops down on the bar to hang from her knees. It is shot from below so it seems for an instant that she is falling toward the camera and us. Her arms swing forward, as if she is reaching out toward her audience. It permits us to look down her costume, this time from the top. Although it is only for a second, she offers her bosom, twice, barely concealed in her scanty costume. She then hangs from her arms and swings toward the camera feet first.

Cornell's presentation of these three women—the hanging and spinning one, the tightrope walker, and the trapeze artist—is abbreviated in the editing. Because of their context in the film, as part of the show ostensibly performed for the children's party, it would be easy to overlook any trace of sexual innuendo in their presentation, in favor of seeing their costumes and performances as ordinary acrobatic paraphernalia and gesticulation. The very look of the film begs us to pass over an analysis of those images to the more strange and out-of-context footage. Yet Cornell did not make works—boxes or films—that were not considered in every detail. Not only the imagery but its juxtaposition was the core of his achievement. Carter Ratcliff offers the idea that a wine glass or a cork ball is "the emblem of a presence too elusive or too vast to be enclosed in a box."[63] This is perhaps true. But in that light, it is also true that an image of a robust woman nearly exposing herself can be the emblem of a presence too sexual, however immature, to remain on the screen for long.

In a box, an image persists indefinitely; in a film, it passes. It can be cut off at any point. Cornell's abbreviated editing style has often been attributed to avant-gardism and surrealism. It must also be considered as repression. Although there is some evidence to argue that by the middle 1960s, his collages became much more overtly sexual in dealing with women's bodies than before, by and large Cornell continued to the end of his career in discreetly presenting women as Romantic objects and

The Children's Party. **The trapeze artist.** *(Courtesy Anthology Film Archives.)*

muses, even when they are naked (as in *The Sorrows of Young Werther,* 1966). Cornell's repetition of two of these three women in other contexts is indicative of his attraction to them. In a film, time can contribute to repression by quickly replacing one image with another, especially if it is one that looks like the one that preceded it. The troublesome view becomes merely an image like the next. For Cornell, however, it must reappear again and again.

At this point in the film, a puzzling scene functions as a caesura. A pulley wheel attached to a door begins to turn and the door opens. The image freezes. It is similar to the shot near the beginning of the film of the window shade rolling up. A dark rectangular opening is created, inviting speculation as to what is out there. The shot is related to those which preceded it by the rope of the pulley and the rotation of the wheel. It is possible to see them as part of the trapeze apparatus. The rope extends off the bottom of the frame. Within a conventional editing structure, they could be viewed as the top and bottom of one elaborate mechanical device. The next shot reiterates the star theme: An amoeba made of thousands of points of brilliant light slowly descends diagonally across the screen. Its position after the shot of the open sliding door and its value as bright white on a black background lead the viewer to conjecture that it is what is beyond the door. As a Cornell image, it is typical. A microscopic organism is transformed into a macroscopic galaxy (a mass of slowly moving stars) by its placement next to a framed opening.

The emphasis of the film changes here, from the entertainers to the children. The perspective changes also. Most of the camera angles are now from above rather than below. Suddenly, the children are being watched instead of watching. Instead of being briefly interspersed between the adult entertainers, they are the center of attention themselves. They perform for the camera, and as he had done for the acrobats, Cornell gives dramatic intensity to their actions by cutting to and away from shots at decisive moments. A group of children dunk for apples; one of them, the shiny, round-faced boy (like an apple himself) gets one and turns his face up toward the camera. A baby, dozing in a chair compulsively gnaws on a half-eaten apple, and in cranky discontent, throws it away and cries in his half-sleep. Another baby sits caged in a crib alongside a jack-o'-lantern larger than he is. He stares out dumbly from behind the bars. Again, we see the baby in the high chair eating the apple. The self-contained world of this child is emphasized by repetition throughout the rest of the film. It is as if the baby sleeps, wakes, and eats in perpetuity as the clamor of the party goes on around him.

A chorus line of young women bow and kick up their skirts in a Busby Berkeley-like shot. Their flimsy costumes fill the frame in sequence from back to front. The camera is at eye level, and lower in the next shot to be level with their legs. Then a bare-legged line performs a

The Children's Party. **Two hidden shots.** *(Courtesy Anthology Film Archives.)*

tap-dancing routine. The camera returns to its higher position. Children, well dressed and cheerful, sit at tables of four in the background. This is the first shot of the film that contains within it both performers and audience. It grounds the notion of a children's party in actuality. It places the camera, and the viewer, distinctly outside or above the party. No longer do we see the women's skirts. To make the party footage all the more appealing to Cornell, half of the girls are dressed as boys in jackets and pants. It is by their "banana" curls that we recognize them as girls. They dance with the femininely dressed girls as naturally as if they were boys. The way they rush through the frame glosses over their sex except to the attentive viewer.

The children's party is in full swing now. Shots succeed one another in a montage of festivity. A baby eats an apple spastically; children in weird party hats dunk for apples; and the well-dressed children dance and throw streamers. There is a puzzling insert within this sequence, only really visible if one studies the film frame by frame. Between a fast-paced shot of the chorus line and one of the baby dozing in his chair, there are two shots that wrest the film out of its objective distance and bring it back to a more personal meditation on childhood. The first is an image of two hands holding a turn-of-the-century photograph of a young person (it is difficult to tell if it is a boy or girl), who has short hair and wears a dark suit, with very loose pants or a skirt. The child carries a riding crop and sits on a dark draped background. The photograph is within a floral frame with an elegant pattern. This shot is followed by one frame of a photograph of three babies in a bed together, looking out at the camera. Hidden by their brevity, these two shots recall Cornell's own boyhood. Although they do not seem to be images of him, they have the look of family photographs. They bring to mind his childhood. He is alone in the first, with his two sisters (his siblings closest in age) in the second. They are meant to be overlooked, by all but perhaps Cornell himself. Unlike the other brief images in the film, they are not repeated or elaborated (although they do appear again in *Cotillion*). Like a secret compartment in one of his boxes, they are not meant to be unpacked. Nevertheless, once discovered, they reinforce the autobiographical in the film.

After these barely discernible inserts, there is a close-up of the baby's face staring into the camera. The light seem excessively bright. His eyes shine. He sneezes, blinks, and turns away. It is the first time in the film he has made any response to the glare of the party, and he seems to be responding at that moment to the brilliance of the movie lights, in the manner of a child who looks into the sun. He looks amazed. The space of clear leader that occurs after is brilliant light on the screen. If one speculates that he watches the performers at the party while sitting in his high chair, then he, too, could be "star-struck." The dancers, the boy who successfully holds an apple in his mouth and beams with pleasure, and the children who barrage a woman with confetti all perform for him. There is another shot of the boy dunking for apples that interrupts the direct connection between this astonished baby and the final performances, the real stellar performances of the film. By reiterating the

The Children's Party. **The dance before the judge.** *(Courtesy Anthology Film Archives.)*

space of the party, it allows the final sequence to be integrated as part of the event.

The last sequences of the film are of little girl stars. They are from narrative films and feature girls cast into films while very young, like those girls whose careers Cornell followed in his dossiers. The first is of a pair of blond twins doing a dance number, accompanied by a boy and a girl trumpeter. It recalls the shots of the chorus line earlier in the film as they have their hands around each other's waists and they turn while kicking. Two of the four shots are filmed from above, and we see in the final shot that there is a judge on his high bench for whom they are performing. Up until then it can be assumed that it is for the baby that they dance. Sitney describes the judge as a "child judge" in his metaphor of "The Emperor's New Clothes."[64] It is a questionable assertion. It looks equally possible that he is a grown man, a severe figure that recalls the seal trainer and knife thrower. It is a long, wide-angle shot and not clear. One can see a policeman and matron in the background. The girls perform for the judge as did the seals and the "Indian squaw." Followed by the lonely and sad ride of Godiva, one has a sense of the dark side of performance and stardom. Godiva, like Mignon in *Wilhelm Meister,* must exhibit herself for a difficult master.

The Children's Party. **Little Godiva.** *(Courtesy Anthology Film Archives.)*

The end of the film is somber but not tragic. The four shots of Godiva cast her as the personification of a star. She glitters in the night as she passes slowly across the starry landscape. Sitney's equation of the image with a phrase from Cornell's rhapsody over Hedy Lamarr—"the gaze

The Children's Party. Little Godiva. *(Courtesy Anthology Film Archives.)*

she knew as a child"—is correct. From the earlier discreet exhibitionism of women in the film, there seems no reason to doubt that Cornell would use the same extension of meaning here. But the shot functions in another way, also. It unifies the circular structure of the film, bringing the end back to the beginning. Godiva rides slowly into the frame on her pony. In close-up she turns and looks back over her shoulder. An extreme close-up of her face emphasizes her wistful sadness. She turns forward again and rides off. Within the logic of the film, the gaze that she meets as she turns her head is that of the young man at the beginning of the film who had been looking out into a starlit night. His wistful expression matches hers as if they were star-crossed lovers. Cornell's oblique way of leading us from that opening image through the film turns out to be his unique way of creating a romantic fiction of a Nervalian young man in love with an inaccessible actress.

Vaudeville DeLuxe (unfinished), presents in a more direct and clear way some of the underlying sexual content of the other films. It is perhaps for this reason that it was never released. The film is based on the material in *The Children's Party* series. It was discovered in 1978, among a series of film collages Cornell had given to Anthology Film Archives in 1969. There is no indication that he considered it complete. Nevertheless, because of its complex editing, one can assume that if it was not completed, it was very nearly so.

Vaudeville DeLuxe. The wagon wheel and the spinning woman. *(Courtesy Anthology Film Archives.)*

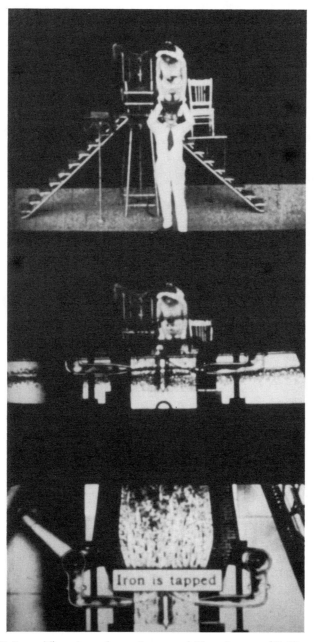

Vaudeville DeLuxe. The triangular staircase and "Iron is tapped." *(Courtesy Anthology Film Archives.)*

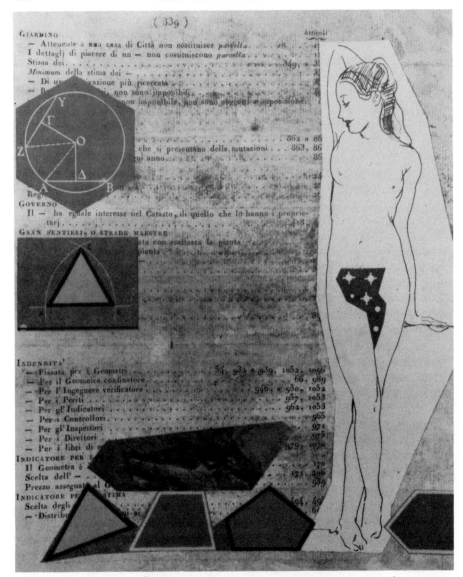

Joseph Cornell, *Vue par Tina (Mathematics in Nature)*. Collage. 9⁷/₁₆ × 7½". Copyright © The Estate of Joseph Cornell. *Courtesy Castelli Feigen Corcoran.)*

As has been seen, in much of Cornell's editing many metaphors are created by substitution. In this film, these substitutions were presumably made for the sake of amusement—children's, his brother Robert's, and other adults's. The first series of shots presents the acrobatic woman as a protean creature. The man who carries things in his mouth first carries her, as she sits primly on a straight-backed chair, up one side of a set of stairs and down the other. He then lifts a wagon wheel and turns it. This shot is followed by one of the women hanging by a rope, spinning. She swings forward, poses with outstretched arms, and the shot fades to black. The man continues to lift the wheel and place it in his mouth. The substitution of the woman for the wheel takes place because, as they are both carried in the mouth of the man, they both spin. The use of the very staid camera work that centers all subjects in this found footage is obvious. Whatever is in the center of the frame is in the man's mouth. One can be substituted for the other. In this case, it is the woman who is transformed into a wheel. A little later, she will reappear on a motorcycle.

The design of the acrobatic set was also noted by Cornell and played against the other kinds of footage he chose to include in *Vaudeville DeLuxe*. After the woman sits on the motorcycle, which is spewing exhaust, there is a brief montage in which she makes a cinematic leap from the top of the triangular staircase onto the man's shoulders. She reclines on an apparatus on his head. Cornell cuts to an instructional film. The diagrammatic image reads "Iron is tapped" next to an animated drawing of a funnel shape with tubular protuberances. An arrow points down through a hole. Below that, a white cone shape extends down. The point here seems to be the relationship of the triangular staircase to the inverted triangles of the funnel and cone shapes in the diagram. Moreover, there is a sense of human physiology in the tubular shapes in the diagram; and further, a sexual innuendo in the arrow thrusting through the hole and the tubes running into the funnel. In this seemingly nonsensical montage of disparate elements, Cornell plays with a set of factors that begin to bring into focus the hidden content of the film. As in his late collage "Vue par Tina (Mathematics in Nature)," in which the constellation of Cassiopeia is substituted for a woman's pubic region, geometry (particularly the triangle) is put to the use of sexuality. This segment of *Vaudeville DeLuxe* ends with a series of shots of a woman tightrope walker, including one shot from below as her skirt lifts up in slow motion.

The first title of the film occurs: "The End," written backward, in a gesture similar to its insertion upside down in the other films. It indicates both the end of the first act of the vaudeville, and the beginning of the next; that is, the reverse of the end. In an image that borders on the macabre, a woman hangs suspended from a rope, holding on by her teeth. Although this is the same image as in *The Children's Party*, here it is no longer funny. As she prepares to swing, the film cuts to another title: "The Great Vulcano—The Marvel of the World. The Most Sensational and Original Act of Its Kind in the World." There is a drawing next to the title of a spouting volcano, triangular again like the staircase and the diagrams. This shot is followed by one of a camera iris opening onto the man and the woman on the motorcycle. They look toward the

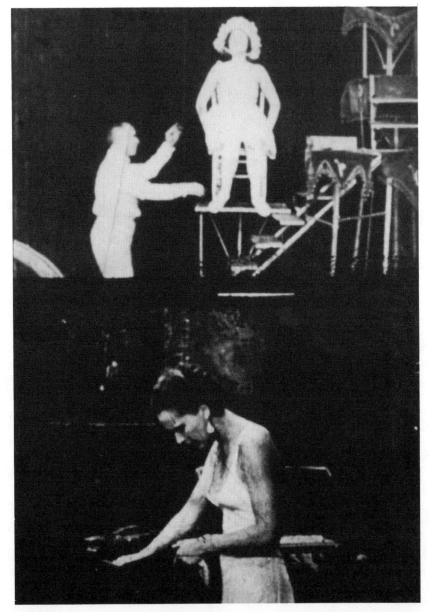

Vaudeville DeLuxe. **The outstretched hands.** *(Courtesy Anthology Film Archives.)*

camera and the iris closes. The sexual innuendo of the film is most obvious here. The object of the volcano, simultaneously phallic and vaginal, is the vulnerable, suspended woman. The result is the common ride, straddling the motorcycle. In this brief sequence one comes to see the appeal of cinematic vaudeville for Cornell. Through a seemingly random series of filmic acts, he can infuse an order that points to his repressed obsessions and desires without having to acknowledge their explicit content. The woman is another version of the boy-girl.

The film returns again to the acrobatic manipulation of the woman spun by the man. She changes into a chair. But the underlying theme is not long in resurfacing. The man comes in from the right to the frame with an outstretched hand. The next shot is from *Rose Hobart,* Cornell's other source for volcanic imagery.[65] Rose reaches into a drawer and picks up an object. Her hand appears where the man's had been. For those familiar with Cornell's films, the power of that shot is in knowing that what she finally extracts from the drawer is a gun. In *Vaudeville DeLuxe,* Cornell follows this shot with a two-frame intertitle, tinted yellow that reads, "The microscope shows how each grain of pure iron is surrounded by a film of rust-proof slag which gives to genuine puddled wrought iron pipe its ability to resist corrosion." The next shot is of a pointer moving across a yellow patterned field, presumably of grains of pure iron. The grains then take up the burden of continuity, as the scene switches to the desert, with men loading the backs of camels. The structure of this sequence is more complex than the preceding ones. There are several different modes of connecting shots. The plastic cutting of the man to Rose Hobart is a simple visual strategy to make them continuous and complicit. Cornell seems to have reached the limit of sexual explicitness in having Rose reach for the phallic pistol, for the next shot trails off to explore the composition of the metal of which the pistol is presumably made. Significantly, the description is of the production of iron. The following shot traces even further the decomposition of the material that makes up the iron/phallus; grains that, poetically, could fill a desert.

Vaudeville DeLuxe ends darkly. Its title appears: "Vaudeville DeLuxe—Four Acts." This is followed by a montage of the Disney cartoon, "Mickey's Circus"[66] with a live-seal act. In the end, the film returns to the image of the woman hanging by a rope, as if she were a dangling fish about to be fed to the seals. Although unreleased, the film forms an interesting link between *The Children's Party* and *The Midnight Party.* Its humor and poetic editing are put to the service of serious themes. While it uses entertaining and even childish imagery (the Disney cartoon, for example), it does so in a very disturbing way. The image of the hanging, spinning woman is the object for Cornell's sexual and morbid ruminations. *The Children's Party* dealt with some sexual content. In *The Midnight Party,* sex is linked with terror and death, and is submerged again in the theme of childhood.

The Midnight Party is as unearthly in its use of stellar imagery as *The Children's Party* is bound to the human sphere. In the bizarre and often terrifying juxtapositions of scientific, dramatic, and fantasy footage,

Cornell creates an awesome construct of the hidden forces of nature at night. In one way, the film can be seen as another part of the Halloween party events initiated in *The Children's Party*. If indeed it is Halloween, then what better entertainment than a horror story, with flashes of lightning and unaccountable gusts of wind? Although its "story" is obscure, there is an unmistakable atmosphere of uncanny causality that places the film in the horror, or at least the Gothic, genre. Using many of the same punning and plastic editing techniques, Cornell creates an image of a darker, more stormy side to the child's imagination.

The film begins with the title "The Amoeba," followed by the galactic amoeba from *The Children's Party*. It descends slowly, diagonally across the frame from left to right and is cut as its forepart reaches the lower right corner of the frame, its body in the center. A brief title appears: "The Stentor." This is followed by the woman who hangs from a rope, swinging in her weirdly contorted way, her white body replacing the brilliant amoeba. Since the amoeba had been preceded by its name, one assumes that this woman is the stentor: either the herald of the *Iliad* who loudly proclaims the opening of the film or just a primitive undulating protozoan. She hangs in the air and flaps her arms. Her movement is mimicked in the next shot by seagulls flapping their wings, as seen from below. In an economy typical of Cornell, in these first five

The Midnight Party. The "little double." *(Courtesy Anthology Film Archives.)*

images he collapses the micro-macro-cosmic universe of the amoeba with the mythological past, the human condition, and the natural world. By the use of visual rhymes and the brief interjection of a title, the natural images become supernatural, the scientific cosmic, and the entertaining mythological.

An atmosphere of impending storm and danger follows the opening. Smoke sprays upward, continuing the white-on-black design of the amoeba, the acrobat, and the gulls. A four-frame title appears, upside down and backward: "and of the eye." Besides implicating the film as a dream (as "The End" had in *The Children's Party*), this shot makes a new connection possible between the human and the scientific. A lens appears as if to show what the title describes. Its iris closes and opens. The obvious allusion is to the iris of the eye, which opens and closes in response to less or more light. Cornell makes a parallel of the human eye with the lens instrument. Further, by the movement of the lever that controls the opening of the iris, the air becomes another element integrated into the construct. The shot that follows is of a weather vane, which begins to swing from exactly the position at which the lever had ended its movement. The wind in which the gulls, and presumably the acrobat, had been buffeted is now registered by the eye and recorded. As the smoke had blown violently, so in the next shot, the smoke from the oil lamp billows upward, carrying heat enough to char dangerously the drawn window shade. The wind that had flown the birds and the woman is now on the edge of causing fire. An ominous tone has now replaced the cosmic/scientific one of the film's beginning.

The acrobatic theme seems like that in *Vaudeville DeLuxe* after such a beginning. A three-frame title written backward—"Bird Millman has been 'walking the wire' from childhood on"—introduces the energetic tightrope walker seen in *The Children's Party*. Here she looks windswept, gusting back and forth and up and down in the same sequence seen in the other film. Transformed into a miniature of herself, the image of the acrobat with a tightrope strung from her shoulder to her hand emphasizes the supernatural. She is either a miniature of herself watched by a human-size version (with the extension that all miniature adults are children, as has been seen in *A Legend for Fountains* [*fragments*] and *The Aviary*), or she is a human watched by a giant. In either case, instead of a comic scene, it is a disconcerting image of transformation caused by the wind or by the force that guides the wind. The laughter of the woman directed toward her smaller self has an air of the diabolical. In light of the work of Fenichel on "the little double," it is possible to interpret Cornell's use of this image as unconsciously sexual.

"The End" appears, in a backward title, with the Pathé Frères insignia of a rooster crowing in a bright sun. It divides the film into two parts, forming an inclusive end to the first part. The rooster is the token of

The Midnight Party. The furtive woman. *(Courtesy Anthology Film Archives.)*

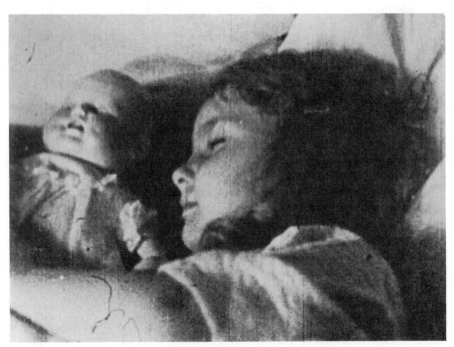

The Midnight Party. The sleeping child. *(Courtesy Anthology Film Archives.)*

dawn, and the shot could be seen as the promise of the end of night. However, the film continues in its night mode, and displays a fervent interest in the night sky and the heavens.

A three-frame title introduces a telescope: "The merest hand-push is enough to turn the 7,000 lb. telescope in any direction." An ironic, one-frame intertitle begins a metaphorical rendition of the use of the apparatus: "Photography is the best means of studying the heavens. Very long exposures are required." The brevity of the title contradicts its own advice. Yet it raises a heretofore hidden issue. Not only is the night sky being explored, but its spiritual nature as heaven must play a part. Cornell worked very much in the tradition of Emily Dickinson, who decried in several poems the reduction of the notion of heaven by science. The poem that begins " 'Arcturus' is his other name—"[67] is expressly concerned with the diminution of nature and space by science. The verse—"What once was heaven, is zenith now. / Where I proposed to go / When time's brief masquerade was done, / Is mapped, and charted too!"—is her eloquent complaint that astronomy is destroying the notions of heaven and God by its investigations. Charles Kingsley made the same complaint in his wonderful child's tale, *The Water Babies*, a book Cornell had in his library.[68] While Cornell does not champion the negative attitude of Dickinson or Kingsley, his manipulation of science to the end of art (here, the visual poetry of film) reveals a less than reverential attitude toward the achievements of that discipline and a sense of the balance that must be asserted between the natural and spiritual (in this case, Christian) sciences.

The scientific is theatricalized by the next two shots. The pulley wheel that had appeared to operate the trapeze in *The Children's Party* now spins as if it were connected to the swinging telescope. In fact, it appears to come from the same original film, opening a door in the roof of an observatory. It is optically printed to halt the wheel dramatically before and after the door slides open. This is followed by a very brief shot of a blond woman in a kimono, bent over as if reaching for something, getting up, and turning away. It appears to be at night and lit by moonlight coming from outside of the left side of the frame. As she turns away, the image fades to black. The type of footage is reminiscent of *Rose Hobart*, although the woman is evidently a different actress. But its mystery—Who is she? What is she reaching for? Why does she turn away?—is similar to those manufactured in Cornell's filmic masterpiece, and the fade recalls the numerous fades he cut to and from in that earlier film. With the subsequent shot, the woman may be interpreted to be the mother of the sleeping child with the doll we now see, turning to look at her in the darkness of the room. However, it is not a benign image. Because of the furtive movement of the woman, there is a sense of danger surrounding the sleeping girl. Compounding that feeling is the notion that this film may be the child's dream, and that the dream verges on nightmare. Certainly for a filmmaker who can put "The End" at the beginning or middle of a film, it is not impossible that he would put the unifying mediator of the film in the center of it. As was pointed out earlier, it is possible that the film could be a dream. Although one may see the shot as demonstrative of the implacability of a child asleep through the most ominous of circumstances, it also must be considered that the free-ranging imagination of a child's dream could piece together such diverse material. The vague knowledge of science combined with a literal notion of heaven in the sky is characteristic of children's perception of outer space. The personification of natural phenomena is also characteristic of them. Like constellations (human and other forms of star patterns), so the stormy events that make up the end of *The Midnight Party* reflect an anthropomorphic rendition of natural processes.

"A speed maniac in a world of speedsters,—a comet caught in the act" is the title that begins to bring the film to its climax. As if the comet were a race-car driver, it is described speeding through the heavens. A still of the comet is shown. It looks like another version of an amoeba, thereby reiterating the micro-macro-cosmic theme of the film. In a brief montage sequence, there is a shot of the moon in a starry sky, blocked by a triangular wedge, perhaps the roof of a house. A whirling metal device in a glass globe spins furiously. A stylograph begins to move. There is a very dark shot, with two lights that fade out. The sequence is an accelerated accumulation of recording instruments responding to turbulent conditions. A rising storm is predicted, but we know it only by the response of the sensitive devices.

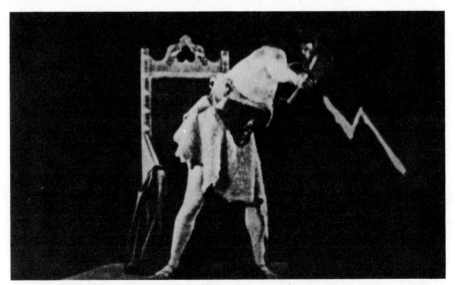

The Midnight Party. **Thor.** *(Courtesy Anthology Film Archives.)*

The Godiva sequence that follows is made up of the same four shots as in *The Children's Party.* After the brisk pace of the preceding montage, it serves as a ritardando in the film. Unlike *The Children's Party,* here Godiva seems a truly heavenly being, riding luminously through the starry sky, like a comet in slow motion, her hair its tail. She seems to be the bearer of bad news; her quiet sadness predicts what is to come. Within the structure of this last part of the film, her appearance is like the eye of the hurricane, a brief period of unnatural calm in the midst of a furious storm. She retains the aura of the other girls who wander through Cornell's films and are fixed in his boxes. She carries with her "the gaze she knew as a child,"[69] that of an older man on a young girl. She opens the film up for the real personification of nature—Thor, casting lightning bolts from his throne upon a cloud.

In the most intense sequence of the film, fantasy footage of "Thor" is combined with dramatic material of rescue in an electric storm and other, less recognizable, footage. Thor stands and swings his cudgel. From it emanate bolts, scratched directly into the film's emulsion, so they appear both hand drawn and brilliantly luminescent. The branch of a tree rustles over a wire connected to the roof of a house. It is night. Men scramble about in the dark in the brush of a fallen tree. Some try to climb a ladder. Then, in evidently reversed order, the tree falls and breaks the wire. From a rational perspective, it seems a gratuitous reversal. Coming so close upon its result, there seems little reason to switch the order of the shots. The sense of danger, however, would be lessened if Cornell had left the sequence intact. As it is, an irrational fear is instilled in the viewer, who sees men scrambling every which way, as if in response to Thor's angry jettisons. This irrational fear is much greater than if the men were merely rescue workers running to save the inhabitants of the endangered house. It is much more like the hysterical fear that many people suffer during electric storms.

We see a washerwoman in a wretched room with a window, as though she were in the house around which the men dash. It is the window that unites the two shots. In the center of the exterior view, there is also a window. Here, it is darkened as if it were night. As in Porter's *Life of an American Fireman* (1902), one can infer that there are parallel events going on. The cutting unites the inside and the outside events as if they were occurring simultaneously. Although barely discernible, in the last frame of the shot of the washerwoman, a figure appears on the left side of the frame, costumed as an elf. As part of the supernatural events of the film, it is not surprising. Instead of the logical course of events that would have the rescuers come in through the window, this elfin figure materializes to aid the abject woman.

In light of the next image, the elf is perhaps a sign of another, greater, force. In eleven frames, a cloudy night sky is superimposed with a text: "He shall transform the households/of drudgery into homes of ease/

The Midnight Party. The woman, the elf . . . "shrouded in mystery." *(Courtesy Anthology Film Archives.)*

and happiness/He shall work unceasingly night/and day,/And yet his origin shall remain/shrouded in mystery." The text fades out and leaves the clouds streaming violently by. "He" could be the elf, or Thor, or God. It is a text that seems to provide the meaning and antidote to the image of the woman, dangerously threatened by the storm. It is her "drudgery" that will be transformed, by this mysterious being who evidently resides in the sky. The most obvious persona of this "he" is Thor, who for the final four shots of the film casts lightning bolts from his windy throne. To those below, especially children, the origin of lightning is "shrouded in mystery"—but the language of the text is biblical and seems to be about God, not Thor. Cornell makes pantheistic equations here, personifying an angry god, as if he were *the* angry God. The electric storm seems to be the result of a supernatural temper. The film ends in darkness and mystery, as a horror story told to a midnight party of children should.

This central section of *The Children's Party* trilogy elucidates better than any of the others the sexual undercurrent of these naive-looking films. The presence of the paradigmatic image of "the little double" in the tightrope-walker superimposition is one indication that *The Midnight Party* can be read as another example of Cornell's reworking of the boy-girl theme. The fact that the film is situated at night makes speculation on the sexual nature of the imagery plausible. The furtive gesture of

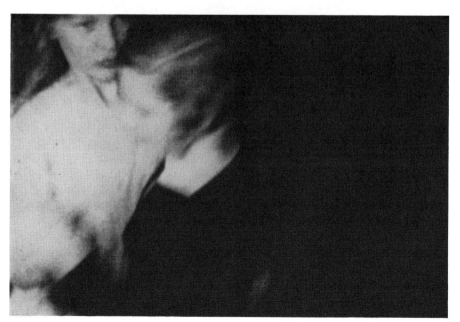

Cotillion. Girls dancing with other girls dressed as boys. *(Courtesy Anthology Film Archives.)*

Cotillion. **The sequined woman and babies.** *(Courtesy Anthology Film Archives.)*

the woman, the sleeping child, the importance of looking (as evidence in the image of the telescope/iris) all point to a voyeuristic fantasy of nightlife. The combination of those kinds of images with cosmic/

Cotillion. The critics and their subject. *(Courtesy Anthology Film Archives.)*

religious images and titles and sexually symbolic images of lightning bolts and knives being thrown at women indicate even more strongly Cornell's imaginative direction. As was discussed in chapter 1, fantasies about flying, gods, and heaven can be seen, from a psychoanalytic point of view, as displacements that substitute vision for sexuality. While the film poeticizes many of the events within it, part of the horror of *The Midnight Party* is the violence of sexuality.

Cotillion explores a number of the same themes as *The Children's Party*, but without the narrative elements, and without some of the terrors of *The Midnight Party*. It is the most difficult film of the three and the most explicitly Cornellian. In its insistence on the montage of disparate elements to create an atmosphere and a structure built on a nonrational order, it most rigorously espouses Cornell's brand of surrealism. While in the other two films there are identifiable subjects, here the subject is only transitory; seeing and being seen make up the primary level of organization. Because of its inability to arrive at a central image, the film seems the most superficial of the three. Yet the shot relationships unify the film and lead to a conclusion hidden in *The Children's Party* and *The Midnight Party*. Whereas in the others, it is difficult to ascertain in what respect Cornell meant these films *for* children, in *Cotillion* it is possible to see that a direct appeal is made to the pattern of thought of a child, as he imagined it.

From the very beginning, the division between entertainer and audience breaks down. The performers exist in the same space as the "party" from *The Children's Party;* or rather, the children and the stage show are all part of the performance. The heads of the chorus line pass quickly through the frame. The children—girls dancing with other girls dressed as boys—circle around, shot as if from the perspective of an adult looking down. A small black boy, dressed in a turban and harem pants, dances on a vaudeville stage.[70] Streamers are all around him, and a line of bare-legged white women chorus dancers are behind. The curtain falls, and he turns as if to go through it but runs off stage left. Two acrobats on a horse are led around a circus ring by a female trainer. A brief title—"Olive Charmion—the star that was twinkling for the last time—Paulette Duval"—appears, followed by a shot of a woman who looks like a peacock, glittering with sequins as she slowly waves an enormous feathered fan. She is large and looks slightly masculine, like a transvestite. The title seems to have been a description by Paulette Duval (an actress herself) of Olive Charmion, the sequined woman we see. Her ludicrous costume conveys both her star status and her "twinkling." She smiles obsequiously at the camera. In a one-frame insertion is an image of a gaudily dressed woman at the top of a staircase lined with chorus girls. It is probably Olive Charmion. This shot is followed by one of four babies looking at the camera. The sequined woman and the babies seem to exchange glances; her condescending smile and their amazement coincide. At this point, it appears that the babies are the audience for what has just occurred. With the next shot—a still image of two children looking off in either direction—children are again placed as images to be studied. The stop motion dehumanizes and stabilizes them into observed objects.

After distancing us as viewers from the children and other actors, Cornell makes our distance both judgmental and childlike. He presents a court of peers. Three girls, with hands on their hips and big voile bows in their hair, look severely off frame right. The camera pans across their faces from left to right. They may be studying the previous image—the stop-motion shot of the two children—although it makes equal sense to say that they, like the two children, are looking at something else entirely. They are, however, definitely *looking,* and disparaging of what they see. There is a one-frame insert of a chorus line of boys and girls in a courtroom. It is clear that these shots come from the courtroom sequence used in *The Children's Party.* There is a medium shot of the three girls, all seated, looking angrily off to the right, then one of a boy and a girl looking nervously off to the left. This couple seems to be what the girls were studying, and as if to emphasize their objectification, the frame freezes and they are suspended in stop motion. Cornell displaces his viewers (the three girls) in a shot different from that of what they see (the couple). Thus he makes an equation between their critical distance and our critical distance from what goes on in the film. We can see no more than those girls. They take over for us, and inflect the shot of the child couple with their negativity.

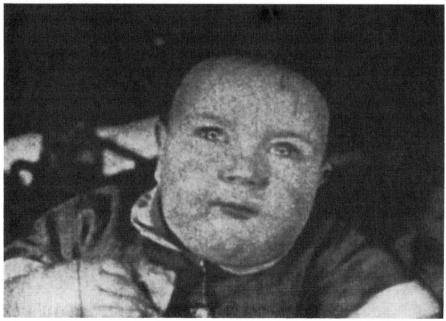

Cotillion. **A stop motion stare.** *(Courtesy Anthology Film Archives.)*

The shot of the girls is followed by a whole section of the film edited on the basis of roundness. It begins with the mysterious shot of a nineteenth-century photograph, centered in an irised frame. It is the same shot that was used in *The Children's Party*. Here it is four frames long instead of one. It is followed by only one frame of the photograph of the three babies in bed, looking at the camera. They place the subsequent shots in an obscure, undecipherable context. The iris coincides with the other round shapes, and the babies' heads with the other round heads, but their reference is opaque and their brief duration unaccountable. As in *The Children's Party*, they add a personal wrinkle to the fabric of the film. The other footage in this sequence is the most standard of the trilogy. Babies asleep in chairs or staring out at the camera, children dunking for apples, a jack-o'-lantern—all are interchangeable on the basis of the round forms they contain. The heads, apples, and pumpkin form a kind of mutable single figure that condenses all of them. Cornell's more frequent use of stop motion emphasizes the graphic quality of the images also. The still image of the boy with an apple in his mouth is a study in circles. It is followed by a shot of a baby in a chair, asleep, who appears in the frame just where the apple had been forming an expanding series of round shapes within round shapes. It is, then, a hilarious jolt to see in the next shot the baby replaced by

Cotillion. The spinning woman. *(Courtesy Anthology Film Archives.)*

Cotillion. **The rolling seal.** *(Courtesy Anthology Film Archives.)*

another, but next to a huge pumpkin that reorganizes the scale once again. By using roundness as a formal principle for the sequence, Cornell can manipulate the footage for its humorous effect. While it looks like a random juxtaposition of views of the party, its secret is in its unity of shape, and its comedy is the transformation of a baby into an apple or a child into a pumpkin. The order of events is determined by their usefulness in the visual scheme. They form a harmonious continuum. The events themselves exist simultaneously and constantly. This type of poetic shot relationship is illustrative of Piaget's notion of the narrative patterns of children, discussed earlier.

The film moves back into the realm of entertainers. We rarely see the children. The acrobats and actresses take on the changeability of the children. The woman who is carried seems to fly. Her image is cut from standing on top of the triangular stair (three frames) to on top of the man's head. It appears as if she leaped. Then she is transformed into a seal. She has been spinning on his head; the seal, in rhythm with her, turns and rolls on a caisson. Other acrobats appear, some upside down. A flurry of activity replaces the mechanical calm of the preceding images. Streamers and confetti fill the frame. It is an abrupt break in the rhythm and texture of the film, as if the party burst into life at just that moment. The final shots of the sequence are of the children throwing paper at a grown woman who, laughingly, defends herself. She is the link to the next shot of a woman with a feathered fan who leans over backward toward the camera. The waving white fan and her womanliness unite her with the previous image. Again, this is an editing strategy that works on a free-floating association. Despite the order of the appearance and logic of the sequence, shots are connected by one or another aspect of an image that is reminiscent of the previous image. The natural order is that which is visually or thematically harmonious.

The importance of this issue for Cornell should not be underestimated. This is a subtle transference of identification from those who are being watched to those who are watching, and equally subtle rejuvenation of the viewer who becomes identified with girls in white dresses. Nevertheless, it is a vital theme he reaches for in this kind of editing. Cornell had a penchant for voyeurist activity. We know from Stan Brakhage that Cornell's criticism of Brakhage's *Wonder Ring* was that it remained too much inside the elevated train and did not peer enough into the windows passed en route. As it was for Cocteau, to be able to see without being seen in return was a tantalizing activity in Cornell's imagination. In Cornell's cinema, the normal shot-countershot relationship established between two close-ups of faces with intersecting glances is broken. The convention is to posit the two people in the same space. Here, they are clearly not in the same space, and there is not an equality of interchange. By their expression, it is the girls who watch the couple. By establishing them as the temporary mediators of the film, we as viewers are identified with them, or at least, Cornell as filmmaker is collapsed with them. Once again, a central place is made in the asesthetic for an androgynous identificatory figure who supplies us with a point of view.

The last sequence of the film is of the Indian knife thrower. It forms the disturbing, suspended end of *Cotillion*, a final circle. It is often interrupted by brief intertitles, four or five frames, describing the technique and the emotional sadomasochism of the relationship of the two Indian performers. After the fan dancer, there is a four-frame title: "His wife taps on the board with a small hammer and his acute sense of hearing guides him to make an accurate throw." This is followed by two shots, one wide angle, one medium, of the blindfolded Indian throwing knives at a brown paper box, presumably with his wife inside. This image is important in light of some of the other characters we have seen previously. The other couple that has appeared—the boy and girl who look so nervously at and away from the camera—were regarded with scorn by the tribunal of young girls. The irrational negativity of that exchange of glances is redoubled in this image of potential violence. A knife appeared earlier, in the shot of the toddler holding one up to the face of a carved pumpkin. And the act of throwing is predicted in the children's throwing confetti at one another and at the grown woman.

While there is no programmatic message in these cross-references, there is a kind of holistic vision created between play and violence—violence toward things in general, but particularly toward couples and women.

Another title briefly appears, grotesquely underscoring the potential violence: "Two inches out of the way and Chief Zat Zam would not need to apply for a divorce." More knives are thrown at the paper, and the woman emerges and furtively bows. Two very brief titles follow one another in a speed that makes them nearly unreadable: "Still the best of friends!" and "His wife—also an Indian—takes great pains to keep on the good side of her husband." She stands at a board as he throws more knives at her, and she extricates herself from her outline. Another title: "The blade of each knife imbeds itself two inches in the board." He wraps her in paper and walks to the table with an array of knives on it. He blindfolds himself and picks up knives. The same title that began the sequence reappears to end the film. The entire Indian scene is an elaborate loop, then, forming another kind of circle in the film.

Cotillion is a strangely formal film. By redefining *roundness* to include also circles in time, Cornell creates an abstract aesthetic unity. The film is about its own structure. Considered alongside of the passage from *The Language and Thought of the Child*, it becomes analogous to Piaget's description of the mechanism of a child's narrative. For Cor-

Cotillion. Play and violence—the Indian knife thrower and his wife. *(Courtesy Anthology Film Archives.)*

nell, "natural" order is that which comes about through the unity of
visual aspects, major or minor, or the unity of one shot with the next.
He gives natural order precedence over the logical order of the films in
their original state; or rather, he reveals a natural order by casting away
the screen of conventional narrative. The playful free association that
permits him to make a continuity of a spinning ball and a spinning
acrobat is childlike. In reading Piaget, he found a theoretical groundwork for his intuitive model.

*   *   *   *

In *The Children's Party* trilogy, Cornell was able to integrate many of
the themes that drove his artistic practice. All of the major elements are
present: scientific, natural (especially bird), and fantastic imagery appear with dancers, acrobats, and children to create an interpenetrating
cluster of films. The theme of childhood is more elaborately presented
than in his dramatic and documentary cinema. The personalization of
the images of girls seen in *A Legend for Fountains (fragments)*, *Centuries of June*, *The Aviary*, and *Nymphlight* occurs here also. But it is
placed in a context of many other themes coincident with Cornell's
sculpture. The three films most thoroughly represent the complexity of
Cornell's creative imagination, and the driving force of childhood in his
aesthetic.

The films are less elusive than they seem. The imagery, editing, and
repetition are no longer unaccountable. One must permit metaphor,
symbolism, and other poetic devices to carry meaning, and one must
read between the lines to get at their real subject. When studied for
connecting theme and analyzed for manifest and implied content, they
are as meaningful as the stories children tell.

While their style appears to be unique in the history of cinema, it is
possible to see both their influences and their influence. The surrealists
and Cocteau were precursors to Cornell's film style. Their nonverbal
and nonrational juxtapositions of highly charged imagery set the prece-
dent for the later film collages. The critical response, which interpreted
the imagery as symbolic and sexually evocative, was well known to
Cornell. Moreover, the possibility of a cinema of rigorous rhythmic and
formal structure was opened by the films of the 1920s in Europe. Cornell incorporated the notions of both freer content and poetic structure
into his films. He applied them to material from the popular culture and
generated unprecedented filmic possibilities. He was an attentive and
courageous editor. The freedom with which he reconstructed the preexisting film culture inspired a whole generation of American avant-garde
filmmakers. One of them, Stan Brakhage, became committed to the
editing practices of Cornell and extrapolated even further their roots in
childhood.

3

STAN BRAKHAGE
The Family Romance

The importance of childhood in the work of Stan Brakhage cannot be overestimated. At almost every juncture in his prolific career, he calls upon childhood to represent an aspect of film theory, perception, artistic creation, universal history, or autobiography. Childhood represents the Romantic Self and the Other. The child is a being and a metaphor; he is present and remembered; he is formed by society and in turn forms society; he is the most literal and the most allegorical of creatures. Brakhage promotes childhood as a rich field of exploration for the artist. He incorporates his other themes—dailiness, mythopoeia, light, and vision—in the theme of childhood. There is no area of his writing about film that does not make use of some manifestation of childhood, and there is no period or genre of his filmmaking (except the very earliest) that does not use some image of children.

Brakhage does not subscribe to a specific theory of childhood. Rather, he invents a peculiarly Brakhagian system of connotations around the notion of the child, made up of ideas derived from Gertrude Stein and Charles Olson, as well as Ray L. Birdwhistell and Sigmund Freud. Not content to deal with childhood as that period between birth and adolescence, Brakhage extends its temporal limits from life in the womb (perhaps even before conception) to death. For Brakhage, the child lives on through adulthood.

Children appear in Brakhage's films in profusion. Four films characterize the general trend of Brakhage's treatment of childhood from his early to his latest period: *Song IV* (1964), *Song IX* (1964), *The Weir-Falcon Saga* (1970), and *Murder Psalm* (1980). In addition, *23rd Psalm Branch* (1965) forms an important backdrop to all four films. By concentrating on only a few films, one risks losing the subtleties of Brakhage's representation of the theme of childhood. Brakhage has given us probably the most complete history of family life recorded in cinema. Certainly, any longtime viewer of Brakhage films feels an intimacy of unusual proportion with the lives of the filmmaker's children. Their physical appearances, manners, and habits of play and sleep are remembered, as they have been presented over and over again in Brakhage's films.

By studying the evolution rather than the nuance of their image, however, it is possible to trace more easily Brakhage's own development as a filmmaker. One can see the continuities and the change in his general stance reflected in his changing treatment of childhood. The idealism of his early films and writings coincided with the birth of his children. His career, as their lives, stretched out before him and was the object of projective fantasies. Perception (including fear as a function of it) and play were represented in the early works that use children. Sexuality is depicted in terms of child's play. The independence of children is presented positively. His writings reflect the valorization of the "untutored" child. They initiate the notion that his films and his children were "given to" him.

The middle films—here represented by *The Weir-Falcon Saga*, but also including *Scenes from under Childhood* (1967–70) on one end of the chronology and parts of the *Sincerity* and *Duplicity* series (1973–80) on the other—shift away from the grandest idealism of the early films. As the children are less easily subsumed in his project, so the films become less comfortable in their representations. The consciousness of the complexity of his endeavor rose in Brakhage. What had initially been chosen to free himself of the limitations of film history—to film daily life—began to have its own constraints. In recognizing his need to hold the image of his child before him in order to understand his own being, he also recognized the frustrations in store for him when that image would no longer be available.

And most recently, Brakhage has come into the position of his own parents—removed from his children's daily lives. In contemplating his achievement—their adulthood—there seem few rewards. His introspection, his struggle to, as he describes, "deeply perceive" them, his efforts to remove them from the dominant culture, have only resulted in *his* continuing alienation. At this stage of his career, it is evident that the films up to now have used the children in the making of a continuing self-portrait. Brakhage's attempt to connect to *their* lives, in a way he never could retrospectively, with his own parents had sustained him through their childhoods. The bitterness of the loss of them is revealed in *Murder Psalm*.

Literary Precursors

Where does Brakhage's interest in childhood originate? We know little of his background other than what he presents. Until such time as a biographer delves into the circumstances of his birth, adoption, and upbringing, there is little hope of measuring Brakhage's own accounts (and there are very few)[1] against other evidence. In his evolution as a filmmaker, childhood appears as a major trope one year before his marriage, in *Anticipation of the Night* (1958).[2]

It may be argued that Brakhage's maturity as a filmmaker coincided with the birth of his first child and the establishment of a family. In his films, childhood is almost always depicted as part of family life. In rooting him, in forcing the issues of home, birth, and growth to his attention, children became the catalyst for Brakhage's slowly arrived at, antidramatic sensibility. His interest in the poetics of new American poetry, stemming from Pound's exhortation to "make it new"[3] and Stein's elevation of "things" and "daily life"[4] had been incipient in *In Between* (1955), but this interest extended itself fully into his films only when Brakhage began to see his home and family as subject.

At least two of Brakhage's mentors had a deep interest in childhood. The poet Robert Duncan introduced Brakhage to a serious consideration of children's literature—L. Frank Baum's *Oz* books and the Andrew Lang collections of fairy tales—as well as to the writings of Gertrude Stein. When Brakhage left San Francisco for New York, Joseph Cornell provided much the same influence, going so far as to have Brakhage film children for *Centuries of June.* Neither Duncan nor Cornell were actively involved with children on a day-to-day basis, and Brakhage made a significant departure from their version of childhood when he began to create his own family. Duncan and Cornell both maintained a romanticized distance from childhood that soon broke down for Brakhage.

The difference between Duncan and Cornell, on the one hand, and Brakhage, on the other, is crucial. Brakhage developed an analytical stance with regard to children. It is evidenced in films of children's sex acts; for example, *Vein* (1965) and *Lovemaking* (1968). The films can be seen as a search for the meaning of children's behavior, including sexual behavior. Brakhage's point of view in reading the fairy tales recommended by Duncan and Cornell would be substantially different from theirs, and much more in line with the analysis of fairy tales in Bruno Bettelheim's *Uses of Enchantment.* Bettelheim shows how sexuality is an issue in fairy tales and discusses its importance in the lives of children. The idealization of children is shown to be based on a false sense of their sexual innocence. Duncan and Cornell subscribed to the fiction of innocence. Brakhage, when presented with the marvelous stories, incorporated them into his own sensibility of childhood, which included a Freudian analysis of the sexuality of children.

It is also possible to trace the origins of Brakhage's interest in child-hood to the more distant past, which would form the substratum of influence, even on those who influenced him (Pound, Stein, and a myr-iad of young poets and filmmakers). Brakhage's individualism, Roman-ticism, and modernism jell if one considers them in light of the one figure who represents the core of a distinctly American philosophy and aesthetics, a writer who was perhaps the most widely read American philosopher for more than a hundred years—Ralph Waldo Emerson. If one reads Emerson in order to better understand Brakhage, one can find the same analysis of the subject of art, a similar valorization of sight as a primary sense, and an elevated regard for daily life and childhood as exemplary fields for study. Moreover, Brakhage's approach to the ques-tion of the relation between private utterance and public audience is exactly Emerson's.

In looking to Emerson to illuminate Brakhage, one has the double reward of discovering a source for some of Brakhage's assertions (a traditional source for assertions often criticized as brazen and obscure) and of finding a cohesion to ideas that, because of Brakhage's sporadic writing, hitherto have seemed only loosely related. In Emerson's essay, "The American Scholar," personal expression, childhood, and dailiness are all brought into line with the work of the "scholar."

First, Emerson discusses the memory of childhood as a lesson in the origin of thought itself:

> The actions and events of our childhood and youth are now matters of calmest observation. They lie like fair pictures in the air. . . . So is there no fact, no event in our private history which shall not, sooner or later, lose its adhesive, inert form, and astonish us by soaring from our body into the empyrean. Cradle and infancy, school and playground, the fear of boys, and dogs, and ferules, the love of little maids and berries, and many another fact that once filled the whole sky, are gone already; friend and relative, profes-sion and party, town and country, nation and world, must also soar and sing.[5]

For Emerson, the memory of childhood is a fecund one, able to gener-ate great thoughts. By its importance it serves as a model for experience. It is a sign of the fate of the present, since today, too, will one day transcend its "adhesive, inert form," just as childhood did. He finds that childhood itself is no more important than any other time of life as it is lived, but is privileged in its position in the chronology. That it comes first in life determines its usefulness as a model. All other developments of memory, and the ideas generated from it, originate in one's initial encounter with the memory of childhood. This is very much the spirit of Brakhage's emphasis on the "re-membering" of childhood.

Coincident with Brakhage's reevaluation of childhood in light of his own children as an appropriate subject for his films, Brakhage finalized his movement away from the "dramatic" to the "personal" film. The use of his life, his environment, his family, and his perception of it all signals a radical break from his previous filmmaking and is, perhaps, Brakhage's greatest contribution to film history. His own sense of it was as "growth":

> I would say I grew very quickly as a film artist once I got rid of drama as a prime source of inspiration. I began to feel that all history, all life, all that I would have as material with which to work, would have to come from the inside of me out rather than as some form imposed from the outside in. I had the concept of everything radiating out of me, and that the more personal or egocentric I would become, the deeper I would reach and the more I could touch those universal concerns which would involve all man.[6]

While this idea of going deep into oneself to reach all man was carried out by Brakhage in a manner new to cinema, the idea itself can be traced directly to Emerson's "American Scholar":

> The poet, in utter solitude remembering his spontaneous thoughts and re-cording them, is found to have recorded that which men in crowded cities find true for them also. The orator distrusts at first the fitness of his frank confessions, his want of knowledge of the persons he addresses, until he finds that he is the complement of his hearers;—that they drink his words because he fulfills for them their own nature; the deeper he dives into his privatest, secretest presentiment, to his wonder he finds this is the most acceptable, most public, and universally true. The people delight in it; the better part of every man feels, This is my music; this is myself.[7]

There have been many filmmakers who have sought to bring to the public imagery and structures that tend toward a psychic universality. Surrealist cinema was to some degree, such an attempt. Abstract film, in general, can be seen as a kind of universalization of an ideal vision. In the case of Brakhage, his inclusion of the details of domestic life and childhood, closer to home movies than any filmmaker heretofore had presented as art, differentiates him from his poet/filmmaker precursors, and again, draws him into line with an Emersonian sense of the "American scholar." Not only does he concentrate on his personal vision, but in so doing, he raises the value of the minutiae of his life, the subject of his vision.

> Instead of the sublime and beautiful, the near, the low, the common, was explored and poeticized. . . . The literature of the poor, *the feelings of the child*, the philosophy of the street, the meaning of household life are the topics of the time . . . I embrace the common, I explore and sit at the feet of the familiar, the low. Give me insight into today, and you may have the antique and future worlds. What would we really know the meaning of? . . . Show me the sublime presence of the highest spiritual cause lurking, as

always it does lurk, in these suburbs and extremities of nature; let me see every trifle bristling with the polarity that ranges it instantly on an eternal law; and the shop, the plough, and the ledger referred to the like cause by which light undulates and poets sing;—and the world lies no longer a dull miscellany and lumber-room but has form and order; there is no trifle, there is no puzzle, but one design unites and animates the farthest pinnacle and the lowest trench.[8]

Brakhage's notion of "dailiness" is coincident with Emerson's "familiar." They both include the child as aesthetic material.

Both Charles Olson and Gertrude Stein carry aspects of the Emersonian vision. They do so in different ways, both of which Brakhage found useful. Olson reevaluated his personal history in light of universal history. His poems are filled with geological, archaeological, anthropological, mythological, and historical references in an attempt to locate his origin and his present. In his major work, *The Maximus Poems,* he uses his home town of Gloucester, Massachusetts, as a point in space and present time to fix himself in relation to the world, its history, and its dynamic. Along with this all-embracing sense of subject, Olson proclaimed an immediacy of form that permitted the act of writing and speaking poetry to assume equal status with the content. Olson calls it "proprioception,"[9] Brakhage calls it "the dance."[10]

The unity of form and content through the subject of dailiness and personal history was underscored for Brakhage in his reading of Stein. Her formal structures are far more rigorous than Olson's, and Brakhage seems to have responded to that aspect of her literary theory and practice. She treats history in a much more unassuming fashion than Olson but places herself in the world with equal intensity. In *The Making of Americans,* for example, she presents the ordinary routines of a household as if they were major social forces. Through repetitive but small changes in word order, the novel progresses to include not only generations but American social history. It will be shown that this play of myth and heroics in daily life sustains Brakhage during the writing of *Metaphors on Vision.* Brakhage's *Film Biographies* are written on the same assumptions as Stein's *Four in America,* her personalized biographies of Ulysses S. Grant, George Washington, Henry James, and the Wright brothers. Both books conflate subject and object, and inject myth and nominalist etymology as if they were facts.

Even Stein's poetics were generated from observation of her own life. In "Portraits and Repetition," she describes her aunts as giving her the clue to successful structuring of language: that when someone is listening, when there is an audience, there is never repetition, only insistence. The issue of audience is important when the private utterance is made public. Stein was conscious of the difference between private and public utterance and made an issue of it in her book of lectures, *Narration.* Brakhage makes the distinction when he forms home movies into works of art, using repetition like Stein's insistence.

Brakhage's reading of Stein gave him the freedom to base his aesthetics on his own life and to make use of the power of highly structured imagery, repeated as the motifs in music[11] and children's games are. Furthermore and perhaps most importantly, Stein pointed to these solutions of aesthetic questions as essentially cinematic:

> In *The Making of Americans,* I was doing what the cinema was doing, I was making a continuous succession of the statement of what that person was until I had not many things but one thing. As I read you some of the portraits of that period you will see what I mean.
>
> I of course did not think of it in terms of the cinema, in fact I doubt whether at that time I had ever seen a cinema but, and I cannot repeat this too often any one is of one's period and this our period was undoubtedly the period of the cinema and series production. And each of us in our own way are bound to express what the world in which we are living is doing.[12]

In Stein, Brakhage found a link with Emerson that could permit him to accept the tenets of that older American as modern artist and filmmaker.[13]

Brakhage as Writer

With periodic pauses, Brakhage has almost continually written about film while remaining the most prolific American avant-garde filmmaker. He has four books—*Metaphors on Vision, The Moving Picture Giving and Taking Book, Film Biographies,* and *The Seen. Metaphors on Vision* and *Film Biographies* are the most relevant here. In addition, he has made numerous contributions to poetry and film journals and has written sheaves of letters. Although most of the letters are not meant for immediate publication, he copied and sent them to filmmakers, writers, poets, and others when their subject matter seems to be of interest to more than just the addressee. Those which are available to the public are, by and large, those sent as carbon copies to Jonas Mekas, who preserves them at Anthology Film Archives. The letters, like some of the films, are about the family life of the Brakhages, in intimate detail. There is often a discussion of the children—their accomplishments, difficulties, and presence in Brakhage's life. Of more interest here, there is some analysis of childhood in general and in relation to filmic representation. He writes of how one represents the children and makes meaning out of the report of their lives.

Metaphors on Vision pronounces the importance of raw perception as crucial and childlike. Furthermore, it places the home as central subject for Brakhage's filmmaking and transforms daily activity into heroics. *Metaphors on Vision* was written during the time between *Anticipation of the Night* (1958) and *The Songs* (completed in 1965), when Brakhage had just established a family. The lessons an adult artist can learn from a child are much on his mind. The notions of childhood presented in it will be exemplified in his films.

The book opens with the valorization of a prelinguistic, "untutored" form of perceiving the world—that of an infant.

Imagine an eye unruled by man-made laws of perspective, an eye unprejudiced by compositional logic, an eye which does not respond to the name of everything but which must know each object encountered in life through an adventure of perception. How many colors are there in a field of grass to the crawling baby unaware of "Green"? How many rainbows can light create for the untutored eye? How aware of variations in heat waves can that eye be? Imagine a world alive with incomprehensible objects and shimmering with an endless variety of movement and innumerable gradations of color. Imagine a world before the "beginning was the word."

To see is to retain—to behold. Elimination of all fear is in sight—which must be aimed for. Once vision may have been given—that which seems inherent in the infant's eye, an eye which reflects the loss of innocence more eloquently than any other human feature, an eye which soon learns to classify sights, an eye which mirrors the movement of the individual toward death by its increasing inability to see.[14]

There are a number of issues here. Brakhage makes many presuppositions about infants's vision and perception. According to Brakhage, young children see without perspective; the world is incomprehensible to them; they see more because they are not bound by language, and consequently, they grow to see less and less as they learn language. None of these observations is unique to Brakhage. Since the Enlightenment notion of "innocence" in childhood, higher powers of perception have been ascribed to children before civilization (here, language) revises their mode of being.[15] What is of import is Brakhage's concentration of perception and "in sight" in a visual model. The child's supposed superiority is in the breadth and range of his vision. When Brakhage proposes the "adventure of perception," he is simultaneously describing the infant and his own filmmaking to come, the nonnarrative, silent, rendering of "each object encountered in life." Simply put, the infant is a metaphor for the filmmaker at his best moments.

In this passage, Brakhage unites the discussion of innocence with fear. When he proposes that the "elimination of all fear" is what "must be aimed for," he means to say that that is the goal for the individual *and* the filmmaker. The individual cannot sustain that mission. As the child grows, he loses his powers in his "increasing inability to see." But the filmmaker does not. He struggles against the limitations of language by the image-gathering and -structuring process that is filmmaking. In positing this one opportunity to thwart the "movement of the individual toward death," Brakhage claims a prolongation of earliest infancy for filmmakers, or at least offers the possibility of a retrogressive movement toward a higher form of vision.[16] This idea of vision as the transcendence of fear will become important later, as it is the subject of some of his films.

Metaphors on Vision also stresses the importance of the observation of and engagement with children as necessary for good parenting *and* as inspiration and education for the artist. For Brakhage, the two go hand in hand. Unlike many other artists and writers, particularly women, Brakhage finds no distinction between art making and child rearing. He has no guilt about putting the priorities of art above those of the children or about using the children to objectify the concerns of the artist. He sees his work as filmmaker and parent as being continuous. When he asks, "How many of us even struggle to deeply perceive our own children?"[17] he asks as much for his sake as filmmaker as for the benefit such perception will afford the children. Similarly, in his "additional note for parents and teachers," he is interested in the nonintervention of adults in children's activities, not just for the liberating benefits the children will gain by being left to their own devices, but for what he can observe and relate to as filmmaker in what they intuitively create.

> Please don't force your militantly Prussian or goblin Cobalt or any other kind of crayon bluing into the drawing of yellow sky happy children, respect those young ones who use any and all of the wax spectrum, and marvel at those who remain still representationally dissatisfied.[18]

He finds colleagues among children. They see and render color complexly, and they "remain . . . dissatisfied." He does not admit that those drawings may be the result of ineptitude or laziness, nor does he admit the desire of the children to assimilate themselves into conventional society.

Another issue Brakhage raises in the book is the use of "pretending." "To pretend is to act upon actual tendency before it itself is in motion, emotional. That is why it is foremost a child's game, evokes and is evoked by the child in us—thus seen by adults as a hood for hiding."[19] He uses a loose etymology to arrive at a definition. He describes the child's ability to act before thinking or repressing the desire to act. By "actual tendency," he seems to mean both an unconscious desire and a mature decision that involves the ability to carry out an action and understand its consequences. He is also using the term *act* in a dual sense of "doing something" and theatrically "acting." It is a child's game insofar as it is prerational. However unstated, he also means that it is good; that, like the first passage in *Metaphors on Vision*, it is not based on language and is more in tune with the real interior reality. The pun on *hood* proposes that adults pervert the true use of pretense because they have and need language. Pretending becomes feigning. An adult pretending is falsely representing himself. That pretending "evokes and is evoked by the child in us" makes it a kind of conduit between these two states of being. That there is a "child in us" makes an unbroken chain that can be drawn in either direction from childhood to adulthood and back again. The passage on pretending occurs within a discussion of his relationship to Jane, his wife. While they are arguing and acting childishly toward each other, they discover that their pretending allows them to resolve their differences. There is not an unqualified pejorative sense of the word when applied to adults; insofar as pretending can reaffirm the connection to childhood, it is redemptive.

The concept of the child is thoroughly interwoven in the language and intention of Brakhage's first theoretical work. One finds childhood being called upon to account for his own anger at not having enough money to make films, when he describes his financial insecurity, "which dates back to the cradle."[20] The very nature of the book is expressed in terms of pregnancy when Brakhage berates himself for writing rather than making a film. He says: "All contained within this book has died in the womb. I abort it to save the living organism."[21]

It is in his project for the unmade "Dailiness Film" that one can see most clearly how artistic incarnation and inspiration are motivated by the presence of children. In thinking about making the film, Brakhage studies the form of his baby and finds a continuity of its shape and his filmmaking: "Our child sleeps in the shape of the egg, can become the breaking of the egg (in a lens turn from extreme soft-focus over-exposure, rounding and whitening her image, to sharp focused correct exposure) with awakening movement."[22] Even the Romantic ecstasy necessary to filmmaking is induced by children who can "transform forests into the fairylands which they originally inspired."[23] In the same passage, he goes on to point to the Romantic source for his metaphor: "I am reminded of Novalis': 'Where is the stream?' cried he, with tears. 'Seest thou not its blue waves above us?' He looked up, and lo! the blue stream was flowing gently above their heads."[24] And most importantly, the child makes him aware of hidden forces that will become the subject of filmmaking. The pattern and rhythm of home life bind Brakhage, Jane, and the children inextricably together.

> As she sews, my wife may find the two other fated aspects of herself flashing about her, weaving and cutting may subtly surround her, and the weave of her pattern may (subliminally superimposed) affect the movements of our child in play. And I will be working on the very film in the making, the statement that this is a work of art being integral with the work itself, and in so doing will be directing the movements of wife and child and will be directed by their movements, with all our actions integrated until we return to the chaos of sleep out of which we are born each day and to which we inevitably return.[25]

The lack of distinction between his role as a father and his role as a filmmaker is crucial. It is a central issue in *The Weir-Falcon Saga.*

Beyond finding the phenomenological equivalent to the art-making process, Brakhage has also found specific imagery to connect filmmaking powerfully with childhood. In *Metaphors on Vision,* he describes one such image.

> I had as a child always one predominant vision of my future life: I was, with all my friends, backed into caves of a mountain and attacked by an enemy (most often the police, sometimes Germans, later Russians, etc.). I was always the leader, most distinguished by the possession of the only machine-gun. We were always hopelessly outnumbered but always confident of eventual success. I had usually worn, in my imagination, a cartridge belt (patterned after those of FOR WHOM THE BELL TOLLS, etc.). Three years ago Jane fashioned a leather belt, to my specifications, with pockets for carrying film, light meters, inst. books, and bags (including an actual bulls-balls, given us) for carrying lenses, prisms, filters, etc.; and when I saw it completed, hooked over my shoulder as intended, I recognized the whole transference pattern into my contemporary living.[26]

The machine gun as metaphor for movie camera has been part of the cinema since Marey's prototype for a sequential camera. When Brakhage uses the image of a child with a gun (as he does in *The Weir-Falcon Saga*), it is a signal that the film in which that image occurs is self-conscious. Brakhage is remembering his own childhood; he is evaluating what is before him with the careful eye of a filmmaker.

Although Brakhage makes reference to the womb in *Metaphors on Vision* to get himself out of an inward spiral of language, the image and issue will be taken up vigorously several years later in his *Film Biographies.* The book focuses on one issue with regard to childhood—the birth trauma. In the cases of a few of the filmmakers whose lives he draws, he speculates on their childhood experience. Most notably, with F. W. Murnau, he postulates a primal-scene experience. But by and large, he reiterates his sense of life in the womb and the birth experience as formative of the artists' beings. With each filmmaker, the important event is the same. The crucial experience is described as horrible or terrifying, thereby reaffirming his sense of the importance of fear in the art-making process.

A number of the invented accounts of the early lives of filmmakers can be grouped together to illustrate the point. Of Méliès:

> Your George then—already defeated by some-such creatures as we can begin to imagine on the barren planet of his foetal mind . . . completely overwhelmed, torn to pieces before what-we-would-call his "birth"—begins as a child to invent a spirit-of-himself which will revenge him.[27]

Of Dreyer:

> Some men are caught before their birth by some monstrousness which tears

them to pieces of horrible imagination ever after . . . Some men are stopped in all previous tracks by a quick of event which picks up every foetal and cultural trick-in-the-bag of their pre-birth trauma—an occurrence which acts as a snag in the fabric of their thought . . . an image even, in their experience—usually very early in their life—which creates a symbol of their birth neurosis and supersedes any either natural or national symbolism . . . and it can be something as simple as a picture or picture book.[28]

Of Eisenstein:

> . . . because he was an artist: and an art leaves a record of just exactly this— and very little else—just exactly this process of traumatization before, during, and very shortly after being born . . .

> Something alien as an animal had ravaged personal being in the womb: at his birth, the mouth of The World had opened to swallow him: the teeth and claws of air, then, had raked his body warmth: he was born out of a broken bag of streaming water.

> . . . let us see him as "child of his Times" then—already trapped at birth by codes of behavior in every one around him, begun in each womb;

> . . . the primordial urgencies previous to intellect . . . the primitive King any child is in the womb and for many years after being born—[29]

Of Chaplin:

> I take this trouble—to lament this unknown child's death—because Spencer [Chaplin] was a natural artist . . . the only kind of artist there ever is, born-to-it-artist, then.[30]

(Regarding *The Gold Rush*):

> Charlie emerges from this shuffle, as naked here in his city clothes as every babe in his skin and as "out of place" in this enormous alien space, as obviously cold.[31]

Although there are passages on the childhoods of some of the filmmakers (Jean Vigo and Buster Keaton, most notably), the origins of the artists are almost always "discovered" in prenatal experience. That life in the womb is nonverbal seems to be important to Brakhage because he has consistently maintained language's destructive potential vis-à-vis visual art. That fetal life is also undocumented reaffirms the "fictional" in these biographies. The book hangs in a kind of balance between true biography (that is, nonfiction) and fiction. The disclaimer at the opening of the book, reminiscent of the openings of both Cocteau's *Paris Album* and Stein's *Four in America*, is often lost in the individual essays: "Let me then present . . . an historical novel so to speak—whereat I, as demonstrator, lie to you . . . tell a tale, as it's called

... in order to get to the truth."[32] It is in his calling on life in the womb that we are reminded that this is Brakhage's version of the lives of filmmakers. As such, they are as much about Brakhage as about his ostensible subjects.

He recognizes the issue once in the book: "My 'guess' is conditioned by some similar pre-birth ghostliness, social disordering, and eventual snag-of-thought in myself, some chain of events perhaps utterly different from those I imagine for Sergei."[33] That is, he finds an affinity with the pantheon he puts forward. It is an ephemeral parallel. He finds himself able to guess at the origins of others' artistic beings because of some semblance, however elusive, with his sense of his own incarnation. It is not Everyman who can make this discovery or risk this speculation. It is someone of similar origin and equal stature. Brakhage places himself within the pantheon by applying the same criteria (however different the "chain of events") to himself as he does to the artists about whom he writes.

This is, however, a key metaphor in the book that points away from the book's subjects and toward its author as a passive autobiographer. Brakhage, in his account of Chaplin's childhood, inadvertently equates it with his own. He does so through the metaphor of Moses. "Charlie was born, as surely as basketed Moses, then!—little poor boy up from hell . . . innocent betrayer of his origins—Boss Man to come."[34] In Metaphors on Vision, Brakhage had described himself as a possible Moses.

The natural mystery of my own origins, as I was adopted, had kept both the father and mother images nebulous enough that childhood imaginings (his majesty in exile, bastard son of an international whore, found floating in a basket among the barges on the Mississippi River, creature of another planet, etc.) could project themselves into the immediate present and continue a' sending. I always tend to identify with the father of TOTEM AND TABOO, especially when his stature became fully developed in MOSES AND MONOTHEISM.[35]

Brakhage recognizes his own tendency to identify with Moses. Further, a few paragraphs later, he alludes to Otto Rank, a psychoanalyst involved in the analysis of identifications of this type. Rank's work, The Myth of the Birth of the Hero, elucidates the individual's need to find parallels in the childhoods of mythological and historical figures in order to validate one's own life history. Brakhage briefly refers to Rank's discussion of the "double." Rank's example is the saga of Cyrus, who, like Moses, would have been killed had he not been raised by foster parents. Brakhage's identification is at once conscious and obscure. While making oblique references to his own past history and parallels to the lives of other artists, he does not recognize the importance of the Moses identification in one of the central issues of his aesthetics. In the Bible, Moses was a conduit between God and man. The Ten Commandments were given to Moses to pass on to the Israelites. The mediation ascribed to Moses is exactly what Brakhage claims for himself as filmmaker. Substituting "the Muse" or "Inner Vision" for God, he says his films are "given to" him to make, thus making a Romantic version of a prophetic tradition. As Moses' role was to speak and ultimately write (that is, give form to) the commandments, so Brakhage claims: "I BECOME INSTRUMENT FOR THE PASSAGE OF INNER VISION, THRU ALL MY SENSIBILITIES, INTO ITS EXTERNAL FORM."[36] In one respect, it coincides with the Emersonian sense of the poet as being "representative of man, by virtue of being the largest power to receive and to impart."[37]

There is an inevitable relationship between Brakhage's film and his children—both "given to" him. The Moses connection becomes even more apparent when one considers his attitude with regard to his children. By disavowing ownership, by not creating them but receiving them, he puts them in exactly his own position as a child. As he was given to his foster parents, so his children were given to him. In his system, however, this is not a wholly negative occurrence. The rejection by the natural parents and the peril of being a parentless child are compensated for by identification with the biblical figure who became the conduit of God with just such an infancy. Moses, rejected out of fear for his own life, became the adopted son of Pharaoh's daughter, and later, leader of the Jews.

There is, however, a negative aspect of the Moses identification, which will become clear in light of *The Weir-Falcon Saga*. By concentrating his energies on the receipt and transmission of vision, Brakhage is sometimes forced to disengage himself from life itself. "The dance" is not always appropriate to the situation in which Brakhage as filmmaker and father will find himself. Sometimes his children will demand to be touched or helped, for example, rather than watched, and this will throw Brakhage into a crisis. Whenever the basic formula of family life (Jane "weaving," the "child at play," and Brakhage "working on the very film in the making*") is disrupted by one of its elements, Brakhage is forced to question his own role. In *The Weir-Falcon Saga*, Brakhage's son makes a physical appeal to him that Brakhage only watches. The boy is then taken away. Brakhage's inability to *see* his subject is the central dilemma of the film. Both his unwillingness to do more than see and his exclusion from the boy's image are expressed as parts of the frustration of vision. As the single sense, it does not always transcend experience.

Brakhage recognized the dangers of his attraction to the Moses figure and explored his ambivalence in film. *Blue Moses* (1962) is Brakhage's only didactic film about the nature of the cinematic experience.[38] The film centers on a performance by Robert Benson that ranges from high theatricality to nonsense to mime to direct address. Throughout his performance, a number of other images appear. Their function is to force the dramatic situation into an experiential one. He refers to the other shots in the film. He includes himself and the audience as the subject of the film, by taking off his makeup while conversationally confessing that he is an actor and "this whole film is about us." In all, the film forces to our awareness the nontheatrical in cinema, that "there's a film-maker behind every scene."

Brakhage plays the filmmaker in *Blue Moses*, not the prophet himself. This is significant in a number of ways. *Blue Moses* is a meditation on a transitional phase in Brakhage's filmmaking. There is a sense in which one can see Benton's role in the film as a stand-in for Brakhage, who plays God—the "film-maker behind every scene." The notion of the source of cinematic power is changing at this time in Brakhage's career. He had been making lyrical films for several years, not the dramatic films with which he began. There is a conflict between the sense of film as prophetic and visionary and the more traditional (and very appealing) notion of the film director as God, who creates his own world on film. For Brakhage to *act in* the film would be the antithesis of his blossoming aesthetic of the filmmaker-as-vehicle. Nevertheless, it was important to include the prophetic figure, to point to the correct version of the *idea* of the filmmaker.

While the filmmaker can delude himself that he is God, he cannot present himself as a prophet. Brakhage felt that the dramatic film directors whom he emulated in his early career were "false prophets." He wanted to be a prophet, but an audience would have to declare him one; and he made films for which, at the same time, there was no natural audience. He was alienated from the people to whom he would prophesy. Unlike Moses to the Jews, he was no natural leader to a natural audience.

Instead, Brakhage divided the character of Moses into a receiver and a transmitter of revelation. He makes the receipt of revelation more important than prophecy or the transportation of messages. Not that Brakhage denies any audience at all (being too good a Steinian for that), but he opts to concentrate on the aspect of Moses as revealed-to rather than as prophet and leader of his people. In *Blue Moses*, Brakhage offers his audience access to the same mechanism of revelation to which he is privileged, not claiming that only he has a right to it. In so doing, Brakhage frees himself from the responsibility of transporting messages and permits himself to concentrate on the observation of his own life, sharing it as if it were universal.

In terms of Brakhage's treatment of childhood, this is important in two ways. First, in becoming an observer of the world and an analyst of the process of revelation, Brakhage focuses his attention on what is perceptible, what is seen. He deals with ideas only insofar as they can be constructed or gleaned from the visible world. Daily observation becomes necessary. Second, he posits that self-understanding can only come about through insight into what is before him. If he cannot see it or find it in the world, then it does not exist. The burden for him as a filmmaker is to keep on seeing the patterns of his own life repeated in the lives of his children.

The Films

Anticipation of the Night

The first major example in the visionary period of Brakhage's filmmaking of his use of childhood is *Anticipation of the Night*. In it he united a clearly worked-out formal strategy based on shape, movement, and color with powerfully evocative imagery of children at play and asleep. The film is framed within a moment of suicide and seems to represent the intensity of thought and memory of a man about to die by his own hand. The children within the film perform three acts. A baby crawls in the grass, virtually illustrating the opening of *Metaphors on Vision*. A group of children play with abandon on a revolving carnival ride, and they sleep. Except for the animals, the hanging shadow man, and a few frames of a riot at an Elvis Presley film screening, they are the only living beings in the film. Characteristically, they represent a vibrancy of life that is counterposed through editing to the artist's death wish. Both the energy of their play and the vividness of their dreams are manifestations of a rich present and inner life seemingly lost to the protagonist. They are idealized and separated from the hanging man, Brakhage, in a way that children will never be again, once he contemplates the lives of his own children in his cinema.

Scenes from under Childhood

Brakhage's chief work on the theme of childhood is *Scenes from under Childhood* (1967–70). It has been written about extensively. Marie Nesthus,[39] P. Adams Sitney,[40] Fred Camper,[41] and Phoebe Cohen[42] have elucidated the film for us. What is of concern here about *Scenes from under Childhood* is the theoretical groundwork Brakhage lays out for the film, and the ideas that spin off from it, in both his writing and his filmmaking. It was a work that, in its conception and making catalyzed a great deal of thought and much more work. The film stems directly from *The Art of Vision*, as a further exploration of the origin of sight and meaning through vision, and permits the evolution of filmmaking through *The Weir-Falcon Saga* to *Murder Psalm*.

Brakhage wrote a great deal about *Scenes from under Childhood* during and after the period of its making. Some of the concerns he touched on in *Metaphors on Vision* are elaborated during the period of the making of this film. Unarticulated, perspectiveless sight; enriched color sense; fear as a function of vision; and the continuity of existence among family members are all developed as themes in *Scenes from under Childhood.* Making the film seems to have inspired new thoughts about the similarities of children and artists for Brakhage. The film is not only an observation of childhood, but an effort to remember what childhood was like.

In an essay prepared as a lecture on the filmmaker Ken Jacobs, three years after completing *Scenes from under Childhood,* Brakhage analyzes several aspects of the film. It is in the context of a discussion of Jacobs's own notions of innocence, child rearing, and filmmaking. A number of the concerns that Brakhage reiterates throughout his career are present here. They all are relevant to films that will come after *Scenes from under Childhood.*

> The impulses that went into making *Scenes from under Childhood* among others, were specifically those that recognize the difficulties of childhood. In this case I am photographing the children given to me to care for; I avoid calling them *my* children because I do not want to possess them. They were born to Jane and me to care for; and I really found myself coming to understand the intense and terrible struggle of growing up . . . I mean, for a child, just trying to distinguish where the table leg leaves off and the floor begins is agony, where the hand leaves off and the table leg and floor begin; how they detach their hands from table. legs, breasts, each other is painful, especially the experience of picking up a ball. Children do not understand gravity as we have persuaded ourselves to understand it. They pick up a ball and it comes loose from the floor, but not quite. It is still attached to the floor. There is a weight to it. Children do not know where gravity leaves off and material begins. We do not know either, whether gravity could be called matter or not. The child knows it does not know and in that sense is smarter than adults, but more terrified continually. We begin with this film, which uses myself as an emotional metaphor to consider childhood, when even by conventional standards it is lived "happily" as they say.[43]

What comes to mind immediately upon reading Brakhage on children is how similar it is to Brakhage on filmmaking. The children are "given to" him to care for. This disclaimer of possession is exactly parallel to his of his own films; he speaks of them as "given to" him to make. There is something to be said for the ephemerality of revelation in the art-making process and, in filmmaking in particular, the distance or difference of what is seen through the camera and what appears on the film after developing or printing edited rolls. And, too, childbirth—in which sexual pleasure produces an embryo that develops, sheathed, for nine months, to be born as a child—seems a miracle out of the control or ownership of the parents. Yet, neither films nor children are dispossessed; they are authored. And while they grow to stand on their own, they are at first physically attached and legally owned by their parent/ author. Brakhage's disclaimer seems to be the result of having been given up for adoption. The parents of whose bodies he was made dispossessed him. They gave him to others to care for. In rejecting ownership of his own creations, Brakhage reenacts the fundamental drama of his own life.

In an autobiographical statement in 1975, Brakhage rationalized the normative aspect of his own childhood, by disparaging the facts of his and everyone's origins as unknowable.

> I tell you I was born in 1933, January 14th. One would have reason to believe it but, the truth is that I don't know, because I was adopted shortly after my birth and my birth certificate was filled with lies that were to make gentle the fact that I was an adopted child, filled in a whole hypocritical background, giving fake names for my original parents. I don't know when I was born. In fact, who does, who was watching the calendar when they were born?[44]

For Brakhage, since the documentary evidence of his birth was tampered with in some respects, it is invalid in all respects. He posits the absurd standard that the only real knowledge would come from a newborn, conscious of calendrical time. The distrust of any but his own sensory experience is pervasive throughout his filmmaking. It is the central issue for many films. It is the basis for a dialectic with "conventionality" in which the natural and the culturally conditioned are opposites. The depiction of his sensory experience is the mission of his works on childhood—to relive with a mind conscious of the implications of what is seen, the spectrum of his life to now. Sitney sees Brakhage's comments on *Scenes from under Childhood* in relation to Proustian autobiography. In this light, Sitney writes, "the children form a synchronous order of the stages of the father's diachrony."[45] He sees it as a much-used strategy of the autobiographer. But the collapsing of his children's lives into his own raises larger issues than the structure of autobiography. *Scenes from under Childhood* can only loosely be called autobiographical. One understands Brakhage to be as much concerned with filmmaking as with child rearing when he asks in *Metaphors on Vision*, "How many of us even struggle to deeply perceive our own children?" By claiming he is "given to" make both children and films, he cannot separate them. Not satisfied to have once grown up himself, he renews himself through his children and his filmmaking. It is crucial to maintain their separate existence from himself in order that they not be contaminated by his experience, so that they can be made into true documents as his birth certificate was not.[46]

The center of the quotation in the Ken Jacobs letter deals with the sensory difficulty of the young child in finding its way in the world. It could just as well be about the filmmaker who, having given up on cinema-as-story seeks to find meaning outside of narrative. Brakhage's emphasis on the "agony" of exploration of the physical world is only a partial truth. There is much evidence to say that children find pleasure in their early forays and experiences.[47] Brakhage had acknowledged earlier both the pleasure (or interest) in the world of the child and the metaphor for the artist, in a letter to Jerome Hill in 1970, just after completing *Scenes from under Childhood.*

> I recently was prompted to new-Brakhage definition of Artist by a question from Ken Jacobs' students in Binghamton: 'He is child in non-competative [*sic*] play, previous to simply attempting to exhaust the possibilities of out-growth just as the 1-or-2-year-old child exhausts the movement possibilities of bending of knuckles, drumming of tips, etc. often complicatedly symmetrical but with all symmetry usually hidden in complex movements of fingers yet steadily oriented to the accomplishment of the movement in every conceivable way until the hand has been exhausted: or, to put it simply, *the making of an Art is simply pre-sport child's play.*[48]

To ground the origin of his kind of filmmaking ("Art"), Brakhage returned to earliest childhood for an equivalent. He set out to film the minutiae of life. He chose the subjects of his films from the slightest movements or spots of illumination and the most ordinary activities. Without prejudice for so-called worthy content, he proposed filmmaking as a kind of intensified life. He used it "to exhaust the possibilities of out-growth."

Song IV

The four minutes of *Song IV* are some of the most fertile in Brakhage's early film work. The three identically dressed girls playing with a ball are among the first of a long series of children-and-ball imagery that extends from *Song IV* to Brakhage's work in the 1980s. The film is gemlike in its purity and simplicity, yet it opens the door to an exploration of extended meaning that is perhaps equal only in its breadth to Brakhage's preoccupation with his wife, Jane, throughout his work.

Song IV begins with a shot of one girl in a dress with a red top and white patterned skirt. The camera zooms out to show the frame of a window, out of which the girl has been watched. The film is painted and scratched. A shot of a house and street, from the same material out of which *Song III* (1964) had been made is shown, giving the girl a context. The freedom of her gestures occurs within the confines of a very ordinary yard. Only after situating the one girl do we see the others, identically dressed, playing with a red ball. As the camera frames two of them at a time, they bounce and hold the ball, running and bending in

Song 4. Children and the ball. *(Courtesy Anthology Film Archives and Stan Brakhage.)*

slow motion. The largest stands with her mouth open, a look of wonder extended by the ritardando. As the camera pans down her body, gestures are isolated, including a joyful laugh. The ball is picked up by one of the girls, and the film cuts to a pure orange field, accenting the color of the ball and the girls's dresses. When the film cuts back to them, their running is buoyant, as if their dresses, by their color, unified them with the floating ball and the orange "air." Their feet tread heavily on the ground but they rise in nearly weightless ascension. They follow one another in a circle, chasing the ball, but equally occupied with the pleasure of running through space. The film cuts to green, again referring back to *Song III*, but here also, green as grass. The girl bends toward the grass and prepares to throw the ball. The film cuts again to orange. With this cut one senses the possibility that the orange is the ball, thrown forward to fill the frame with its color. The film ends with a shot of one of the girls sitting with the ball, and the full orange screen.

The private relationship of the children to the ball, the intensity of their play, seems to make the sight of them attractive to Brakhage. They are oblivious to all else in their study of an object that is a metaphor for the world. Over the course of Brakhage's oeuvre, the child-ball relationship will become less simple. Children will cry in the presence of the ball, and ultimately, in *Murder Psalm* the ball will be used as a weapon against the child. Here, however, is its origin. A colored sphere with which the children play, a metaphor for their being in the world, and an ideal form that they imitate in their circular movement.

The loss of the normative sense of movement, speed, and gravity is an issue that is important to Brakhage's whole notion of childhood. In his comments on *Scenes from under Childhood,* he raises the question of the relationship of gravity to matter and poses children's inability to separate the two as their awesome sophistication. Although there is no evidence that Brakhage has read that other meticulous observer of children, Jean Piaget, their conclusions conform. In *The Child's Conception of Physical Causality,* Piaget outlines the development of children's concept of weight and presents evidence to say that children understand weight as "latent force, which is both thrust and resistance, and can be used in the service of each and every end."[49] In early stages, gravity is thoroughly tied to animism—that is, bodies fall because they want to. Moreover, gravity and weight are perceived inversely. That is, the heavier the object, the more likely it is to remain suspended. Piaget's clinical observations coincide with Brakhage's intuition and repre-

Song 4. Nearly weightless ascension. *(Courtesy Anthology Film Archives and Stan Brakhage.)*

sentation here. To the girls, the ball is animated. It is nearly as large as they are; they watch it with amazement after it leaves their hands, as if it had left on its own power. Brakhage cuts the film to permit the ball to appear from outside of the frame, so the origin of its thrust is unknown—it could be self-propelled. It seems both heavy and light, filmed in slow motion. In Brakhage's presentation of the girls and the ball, he makes the children's world view part of that of the film. He treats his subject as if the principles of the world that children understand were those he represented.

The footage of *Song IV* is some of the earliest of his children at play. It represents a phase of Brakhage's treatment of childhood that is the most idealistic. The euphoria of the girls, their gracefulness, and the delight with which they encounter the world are signs of Brakhage's embodiment of a number of his theories of the relationship of children and artists. In the intensity of their play, Brakhage finds the model for the artist's relation to the physical world. Their ordinary movement is transformed into dance, just as Brakhage describes the ideal relation of filmmaker to subject as "the dance" in *Metaphors on Vision*. The influence of Maya Deren is evident here, as theory becomes the image itself. The three girls are but a variation on the three women in Deren's *Ritual in Transfigured Time* (1946). The combination of observation and structure (through framing, slow motion, and editing) is clear-cut, because the film itself is so simple. His own relationship to the children is untroubled. The camera work, distanced and slowly moving, renders Brakhage unobserved by the children. They have no interest in him, and he can thus engage himself with them on his own terms.

Their independence allows him to project his own vision onto their image without the interference of their self-consciousness. It is an outgrowth of his position of nonownership of his "given" children. In *Song IV,* the representation of such a mutually independent relationship is idealized. It will not remain so, as the Brakhage children grow and he becomes more involved in the drama of their lives. They will intrude more on him, demanding more of him as a father. He will respond as a filmmaker.

Song IX

The primary images of *Song IX* are a wedding ceremony, the moon, a rhinoceros, and naked boys and girls. There is a broad joke, inspiring what Guy Davenport calls "masculine . . . Laughter."[50] The moon as the symbol for woman; the rhinoceros's horn, clearly phallic; the overlay of these images with those of children playing with their sexual parts—all join together to present the marriage ceremony as socially condoned and diluted sex. Children are used to connote the healthy and free attitude to sex that adults lack. They bring out the latent sexual content of social forms.

Song IX begins with the image of a rhinoceros. The subsequent montage includes imagery that will be rhythmically intercut throughout the film with the pacing of the rhinoceros: a building, naked children bouncing on a bed, a door, and the silhouettes of a group performing a marriage ceremony. The dark, flattened image of the wedding is dramatically contrasted with the rich, flesh tones of the children. They are usually shot in close-up, their bodies framed so that they resemble the shape of the rhinoceros. The boy's penis is made equivalent to the rhinoceros's horn by its placement in the frame.

Both the wedding and the children's play are elaborated as the film proceeds. Patches of light on the children and through the window work to create a warm interior scene of home, family, and joyful sexuality. The bed, a child's hand holding a stuffed bear, and naked bodies intertwined are contrasted with the hard-edged silhouettes and moonlight. In a funny and symbolic sequence, a naked child walks toward the camera. The rhinoceros turns, its horn points toward the camera. The child's penis appears in the center of the frame. The wedding participants are shown, with the moon shining in the background. The primitive male and female symbols—the rhinoceros's horn and the moon— are juxtaposed and made ridiculous in the context of the image of the little boy. Immediately after, a woman's hair, perhaps the bride's, blows

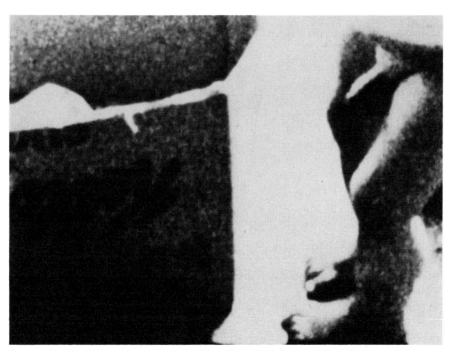

Song 9. A naked boy. (Courtesy Anthology Film Archives and Stan Brakhage.)

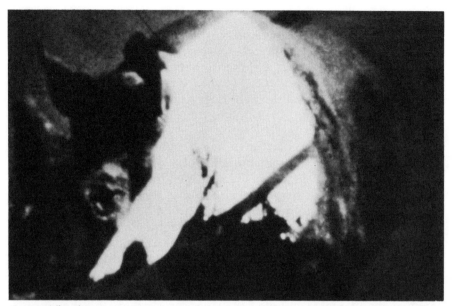

Song 9. The rhinoceros turns toward the camera. *(Courtesy Anthology Film Archives and Stan Brakhage.)*

in the wind and makes a shape like the animal's horn. A little girl with a doll is shown. The constant symbolization and playacting afforded by the images of the animal and the children poke fun at the ceremony.

The rest of the film continues the repetition of the same imagery, concentrating more and more on the moon lighting the wedding and on the window's light on the children's bed. After the couple kisses, sealing their vows, the film reverts to its earliest two elements. The children jump on the bed, and the rhinoceros paces. The last shot is of a square of light falling on the animal.

By and large, children's sexuality in Brakhage's films is placed in a metaphorical context. He does not seem to be interested in the real relationships children have to their own bodies or to one another, but in what their sexual behavior says about the sexual and social behavior of adults.[51] In *Song IX*, the evident pleasure of the children's use of the bed seems much richer than that which the silhouetted adults will ever find there. They bounce on it, lie on it, play with themselves, and watch one another. Their sexuality forms the opposite pole of the representation of the sexual through the image of children in *Murder Psalm*, and coincides with the general idealistic projection of Brakhage's own attitude as a young man onto the image of children.

Throughout *Scenes from under Childhood* and a number of the *Songs*, as he films children more often and as they grow more and more accustomed to being before a camera, they lose their status as pure projections (as the children in *Anticipation of the Night* were). By their interaction with him and his recognition of the increasing complexity of the father/filmmaker-to-child relationship, Brakhage will recognize the quandary of his self-projection.

The Weir-Falcon Saga

The Weir-Falcon Saga is the crucial film of the middle period of Brakhage's treatment of childhood. It is the first part of a trilogy also called *The Weir-Falcon Saga,* which includes *The Machine of Eden* (1970) and *The Animals of Eden and After* (1970). The title suggests a number of interpretations. Brakhage, who claims to have literally dreamed up the title, points to Basil Bunting's poem "The Spoils" as the source of the "falcon."

> Have you seen a falcon stoop
> accurate, unforseen
> and absolute, between
> wind-ripples over harvest? Dread
> of what's to be, is and has been—
> were we not better dead?
> His wings churn air
> to flight.
> Feathers alight
> with sun, he rises where
> dazzle rebuts our stare,
> wonder our fright.[52]

In the poem, the bird is an index of fear. A weir-falcon could be one that rises from a bog. Or if one traces the etymology of *weir* to another of its sources, a weir-falcon could be the ornithological version of a werewolf, a bird/human who changes with the onset of the full moon. It goes well with the theme of fear Brakhage points to in "The Spoils." Each part of the trilogy ends with an image of the moon. A saga is a Norse narrative of a legend. The elements of the title overlay a vast puzzle on the film, as they seem to bear little relationship to its imagery or structure. "Dread" and "wonder" from the poem seem much more closely related to the film than the arcane title. In the loosest sense, it seems a manifestation of Brakhage's private mythology. (He had referred to the composer Phillip Lamantia's "Weir" in *Metaphors on Vision*.)[53] One senses that this is a "Brakhage saga" in much the way one can recognize, by its elements, a Grimm fairy tale.

The film begins as a kind of continuation of *Scenes from under Childhood,* opening with an image of the floor that was so meticulously explored in the earlier film. Unlike *Scenes from under Childhood,* the opening perspective of the film is that of an adult. While in the previous film, a great deal of the imagery seems to be from a child's point of view, here the camera is more distant and often high up. Certainly the way in which images are framed and joined suggests an adult trying to "deeply perceive" his children. Although that perspective will change over the course of the film, the adult view generally prevails.

It is often the case in Brakhage's films that there is no fixed point of view. One sees the child and alternately sees as the child might. This early shifting of perspective will form the central dichotomy of the film: the encounter with the hospital. What at first is an indecipherable mixture of viewpoints later becomes a distinguishable solo point of view. The dramatic intensity of the evolution from several to one point of view is heightened by the extremity of the transformation. The opening scenes, which begin from an adult's point of view, but quickly shift to include the children's eye view, stand in stark contrast to the individual version at the end of the film.

The structure of the film's opening persists throughout most of the film. Visual rhymes create relationships between things that are sometimes proximate but often spatially removed from one another. It is an editing technique Brakhage had begun to use in *Anticipation of the Night;* it is very like that of Joseph Cornell's in the Brakhage collaboration, *Centuries of June,* where a child "becomes" a butterfly by its

The Weir-Falcon Saga. **The circle dance.** *(Courtesy Anthology Film Archives and Stan Brakhage.)*

The Weir-Falcon Saga. **The boy fallen with a gun.** *(Courtesy Anthology Film Archives and Stan Brakhage.)*

position in the frame. In *The Weir-Falcon Saga,* Brakhage extends that technique to many more sequences than Cornell ever did. (Two years later, in *Riddle of Lumen* (1972), Brakhage achieves his most comprehensive exploration of visual rhyme.) After the opening of *The Weir-Falcon Saga,* green-tinged images of the children are paralleled to green trees. A fire flares up, and Jane and the trees echo the fire as their images yellow and bleach out because of a cinematic flare.[54] The children are then included in the fire imagery, as they dance in a circle, like the ring of fire, and the girls's hair breaks the surface of the image like the negative space between individual flames.

If one looks at *The Weir-Falcon Saga* trilogy as a meditation on illness and recovery, then the structure of the editing gains a context. It is certainly plausible to claim that the three films are centered on the fevered child: The Weir-Falcon Saga shows the sick boy; *The Machine of Eden* is referred to as the "dream of Eden" by Brakhage in his note on the film and could be the deepest fevered dream of the child; and *The Animals of Eden and After* shows the boy's recovery. If in Brakhage's attempt to deal with illness in the child, he is endeavoring to represent the visual attributes of fevered hallucination, then the editing structure falls into a pattern. Visual relationships are no longer random and superficial, but primary and replete with meaning unobtainable in rational (or linguistic) relationships.

The film's opening elements form a loose whole if one looks at them as parts of a meditation on fever; staring into the fire while the children dance and play, free-floating associations are made of fire, dance, film flare, and red and golden colored objects and their green and blue afterimage counterparts. Suddenly, a boy falls. He has a machine gun and lurches forward, grimacing as if in terrible pain, acting the part of a wounded soldier. A smaller boy plays with the gun. Several shots later, this smaller boy is seen fallen, panting, ill. While possible linguistic and metaphorical connections have been made between play and illness,[55] and fire and fever, Brakhage establishes the unity through a series of images. The children at play and the fire merge. The fire metaphorically enters him and strikes the boy down. At the same time, Brakhage himself becomes subject of the film, casting his son in the role he himself played as a child—the embattled soldier with machine gun.

The Weir-Falcon Saga is not the first film in which Brakhage has used the image of a child with a gun to signal his own childhood and the natural violence of children. The most elaborate use of this image is in *23rd Psalm Branch* in which men at war are intercut among children playing with guns, and the war of his childhood—World War II—is intercut with the (then) contemporary Vietnam War. Brakhage posits the concept of natural violence in very much the same way as he insists on children's sexuality. His reading of Freud and his general interest in the causes of children's behavior led him to conclude that children learn neither sex nor violence but manifest both urges from a very early age. While there is a degree of mimicry in their behavior, they use the given forms of society and culture (for example, fairy tales and war movies) to act out more profound desires. From the passage quoted earlier from *Metaphors on Vision* on Brakhage's own childhood war games, one can surmise that he makes a continuum from children's acting out of deep-seated desires to his own filmmaking. This is true of *The Weir-Falcon Saga.*

The next series of shots of some trees; Jane, nude from the waist up; a flapping sheet in front of a window; water drops on pine needles have no specific "point of view." They represent shared experiences of the family and are presented very much in the spirit of Brakhage's comments in *Metaphors on Vision* on the interweaving of family life with filmmaking. The connections between images are made on the basis of shape or color or size or movement. They are perceived relationships shared by all members of the family, not restricted to Brakhage's subjectivity.

The first separation of visual perspective occurs when we see the panting boy lying on the bed. Overall, the image is blue. In three shots, the camera distances itself, showing the stark isolation of the small figure. The boy is seen from overhead. The sequence is interrupted by a series of exterior views. A barking dog runs toward the camera, and the

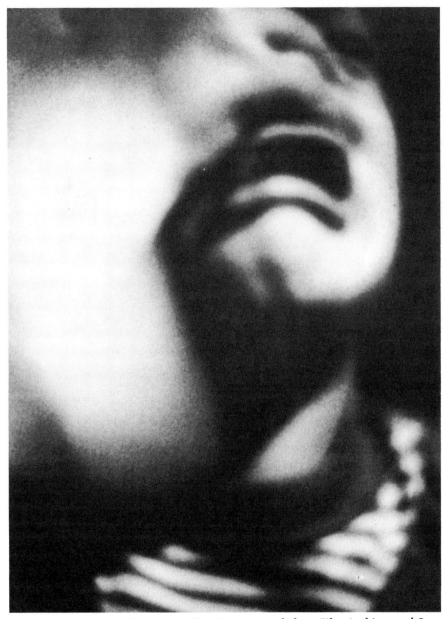

The Weir-Falcon Saga. The sick child. *(Courtesy Anthology Film Archives and Stan Brakhage.)*

camera retreats from it. Although the insertion of this shot here is puzzling, it foreshadows a later sequence in which the boy appeals to the camera. The next shot of a blue ball calls up the image of the boy

The Weir-Falcon Saga. A moving appeal to the heavens. *(Courtesy Anthology Film Archives and Stan Brakhage.)*

again, seen subsequently bathed in blue light. The ball foreshadows the exterior shots of children on the swings. The sick boy is the pivot on which the film turns. His image is the center of the film's duality. Brakhage looks at him through the camera—a worried and rather helpless father. Throughout the rest of the film he investigates his fear and impotence in a frustrating attempt to represent the abstractions of *fever* and *cure.*

The sequence of the children on the swing is made up of a series of luminous, slow-motion, positive and negative shots. It is an image with both a history and a future in Brakhage films. Both *Song IV* and *Murder Psalm* (as well as a number of other films) contain versions of it. Shots of the swings are interspersed with shots of the car and the boy being carried to this car. The quality of light and motion is altered in such a way that one can conclude that it represents the halfwaking perception of the sick boy. The floating figures of the girls on the swing seem antigravitational, as does the ball tossed in slow motion and made the negative-stock image of itself. Unlike *Song IV,* here Brakhage uses imagery that poses the representation of weight and movement in the context of the fevered perception of a child. Slow motion is a quality of the child's altered state of mind.

The color changes also point to a fevered state of perception.

Brakhage's concern with hypnagogic and closed-eye vision is well known.[56] Both sorts of sight are formed in part on the perception of negatives of light and color—that is, darkness and complementary colors. In presenting negative-stock shots of considerable length, Brakhage redoubles the insistent theme of fever. He reinforces the sense of a blinking or half-awake vision of the world, in which the boy's sight is relaxed enough to hold for quite a long time the negative afterimage of what he sees. Also, Brakhage unifies the color scheme of the film by balancing colors with their opposites, and by matching the colors of clothing or objects in the complementary colors of other objects. The dominant relationships are between red and green, and orange and blue. The harmony of color is posited as a function of the heightened perceptual state of fever.

The swing sequence ends with a dramatic gesture on the part of one of the girls, Myrenna, Brakhage's oldest daughter. She throws the ball up, and her arms are stretched as if in supplication, worship, prayer, or abandon. This prolonged gesture is interrupted by a shot of the boy's head illuminated by flashing light as he rides in the car. The ball drops. The boy is seen again, this time staring into the camera with tear-filled eyes that he occasionally shields from the light and the gaze of the camera. The shots of the girl and boy are the two most emotionally charged in the film. The girl's playful gesture with the ball is transformed by slow motion and a cut into a moving appeal to the heavens.

The perspective of the film seems, at this point, to have shifted away from that of the boy back to Brakhage, who finds in the behavior of his daughter an analogue to his state of mind. This shift becomes pronounced with the image of the boy's stare. He appeals to the filmmaker. He looks ill and miserable, in need of loving attention. Brakhage seems coldhearted to keep filming in the face of such a heart-wrenching look. At this moment in the film there is a breakdown in the Brakhage family order as it was described in *Metaphors on Vision*. No longer does it seem enough for the children to play, for Jane to "weave" and act the mother, and for Brakhage to make films. The child's evident need for human comfort and aid from his father is unambiguous, yet Brakhage keeps filming. Brakhage tests the limits of his father/filmmaker role and finds himself insufficient. Filmmaking will not cure the child or even comfort him. But Brakhage can do nothing else.[57]

The issue of the role of the filmmaker as a participant in the events he films is not limited to Brakhage or even to avant-garde film. Certainly the aesthetics of documentary film (and cinema verité, in particular) have focused on the presence of the filmmaker as a factor in every shooting situation.

But in *The Weir-Falcon Saga,* Brakhage's presence behind the camera has two important aspects that go beyond the basic recognition that "there's a filmmaker behind every scene." First of all, this shot dramatically highlights Brakhage's presence in the film since it is so evidently from his point of view. Jane is driving the car, and the boy is seen from the high angle natural to his father. They are very close together. All of the other shots in the film *may* have been from Brakhage's point of view; this shot is unquestionably so. It is striking for the reason that the first-person assumption of the film is made explicit. Secondly, there is an emotional contradiction in the shot. One wishes to help the child and wishes that Brakhage would put down the camera and succor him. It is the same kind of contradiction as in Luis Buñuel's *Las Hurdes (Land without Bread)* (1932), in which a cameraman approaches a sick child. In that film, however, the narration ironically alludes to the inherent contradiction. The tension in *The Weir-Falcon Saga* arises because of the failure of the father/filmmaker model. The role of father is simply not the same as that of a filmmaker. By including this shot, Brakhage seems to recognize the inadequacy of his art to transcend the child's physical and emotional reality. One must, then, read the film as an elucidation of his dilemma and crisis.

As Jane and the boy enter the hospital, the quality of the image undergoes a change that indicates a change in the quality of experience. Fluorescent lighting replaces the rich reddish yellow sunlight of the car trip. Brakhage is excluded from the examining room. He can no longer see his family. He seems to flee downstairs, through a door into the basement. We are presented with imagery of the substructure of the hospital, stripped of its public veneer. A bare lightbulb, open plumbing, wiring, and latticework locked stalls form a sinister ambience. A shot of the boy naked on the examining table reminds us that his illness has

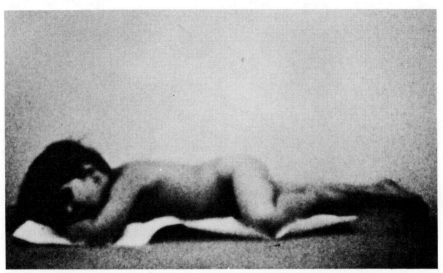

The Weir-Falcon Saga. **The boy lies naked on the table.** *(Courtesy Anthology Film Archives and Stan Brakhage.)*

The Weir-Falcon Saga. The boy stares at the filmmaker. *(Courtesy Anthology Film Archives and Stan Brakhage.)*

brought Brakhage to this place. The film returns to the image of wet pipes. Brakhage makes a metaphor for experience in the metonymy of his environment. He shows the inner structure of the building since he can neither see nor show the inner structure of his son.

The film moves back and forth between the basement and the examining room several times. With each alternation, the gesture becomes more coherent. At one point, the naked boy lies on the table, light and shade beautifully shaping his body. Jane looks toward the camera with tear-filled eyes and a half-hearted smile. The scene is presented tenderly. The doctor is depicted as a parody of Brakhage himself. He shines a flashlight onto the boy. It recalls the image of the flashing light in the car. But now it is the doctor, not Brakhage, in charge.

Each human encounter is matched by a frenetic retreat to the basement, where the image of the locked stalls seems to literalize Brakhage's inability to take control over the scenes above. Constantly drawn to the examining room and his family's suffering, he cannot bear to look and cannot bear not to look. He is locked out of the experience, condemned by filmmaking to analytical distance.

The crisis in the film passes when Jane (and Brakhage filming her) looks out of the window. The dark recesses and dimly lit corridors of the building are replaced by a return to natural light and landscape.

Though he had searched the basement like a maintenance man searching for the cause of some dysfunction, Brakhage seems to come to terms with his role in this family drama, but only after they leave the hospital. In contrast to the shots in the basement and the alienating institutional environment, the camera work and simultaneous-editing associations are smoother. There is a release of the tension built up in the clinic.

As the trio drives again, the earlier imagery of the fire and fever is countered now, with that of water, and by association, cure. Water, introduced with the sweating plumbing in the hospital, takes on special prominence in the image of the lake.

On the return trip, the boy compulsively rubs his hair. Again, the camera passively oversees him. This sequence, however, has little of the pathos of the earlier encounter of the child and the camera. Here, he seems still weak, but less needy. The repetitive movement of his hand on his forehead is equivalent to Brakhage's compulsive filmmaking. There is a series of visual rhymes that continue as we see the boy back in bed. Porch arches are mimicked by compositions within the frame of a lamp (always an indicator of "home" in Brakhage's films), or the boy lying down. The doorjamb divides the frame as does the bedstead in the next shot. Small patches of light recur in interior and exterior images: light falls on the bed, small lights make star patterns in darkness, and light glitters from the aspen trees.

The sense of home is reestablished at the end of the film. Glittering water emphasizes the healing process. The dog, close-ups of the child's skin, and the texture of cloth and blanket affirm an intimacy that had disappeared after the film's opening. The quality of the imagery recalls the beginning of the film, but its subject has been transformed from fire to water. The final image is of the moon behind the clouds.

The Weir-Falcon Saga presents a crisis of representation. As was described earlier, Brakhage's mode of filmmaking is revelatory and dependent on sight. To come to grips with any subject, Brakhage must be able to explore it visually. Here, he is closed out of the visual field, both by the institution and the limits of vision itself. He cannot *see* what is wrong with his son. He uses the metonymy of the hospital basement, but ultimately it is unsatisfactory as a metaphor for his son's body. It comes to represent Brakhage's panic and frustration.

The panic extends in two directions, both outward and inward. There is the very real struggle at the moment of filming, to do what one can for the child. Since Brakhage finds himself most effective as a seer, his response to the boy's need is predictable. He studies the look of illness and its surroundings. Jane carries the boy, drives the car, and leads him to the doctor. Brakhage films—knowing, showing, all the while that he is inadequate. But the inward difficulty, at the time of editing, is fully directed toward himself and at seeing what aspect of his experience is manifested in his son's own. By and large, this is the issue of all of

Brakhage's films made of his children while they are growing up. He casts his son in the role of himself as a child, as we have seen in the machine-gun scene. While he can study him, Brakhage has a way of transferring the memory and fantasy of his own illnesses (of which there have been many) onto the image of his son. But during the examination, when the doctor supersedes the filmmaker as examiner, Brakhage is left without the ground for his own history. He is closed out of the examining room, with the doctor as his surrogate vis-à-vis his son. In the course of the film, the boy begins to recover as the filmmaker recovers the image and context for himself.

The Machine of Eden and *The Animals of Eden and After* extend the boy's recovery. The family is metaphorically rewoven by the image of the loom—that machine at which Jane sat in the idyllic family scene Brakhage describes in *Metaphors on Vision*. The landscape is the metaphorical pattern of the cloth of the film. In *The Animals of Eden and After*, the Brakhage version of childhood first seen in *Anticipation of the Night* reappears, and the full force of his imagination and projection is again asserted over the image of his children. The final segment of *The Weir-Falcon Saga* trilogy is one of the most Romantic of Brakhage's family portraits. The family order that had been disrupted by one child's illness is established with renewed intensity. In one of the last scenes, Brakhage films Jane leading the children through a meadow. They look like a troupe of nomads or gypsies. The freedom of their dress and their ease in traversing the countryside make them seem timeless and joyful. Their lives, the lives of animals, and the landscape combine to represent Brakhage's ideal.

Murder Psalm

Brakhage describes the impulse to make the *Murder Psalm* as coming from a nightmare he had of murdering his mother.[58] The film is made largely from found footage. Like Cornell, Brakhage gives the original material new meanings by juxtaposition.[59] The film is silent. Brakhage treated the found footage in ways reminiscent of his own films of the 1960s. He bleached, patterned, and otherwise gave the photographic imagery a painterly overlay. The texture ranges from a thick pattern that recalls *Oh Life—A Woe Story—The A Test News* (1963), to a thin tint, like some of the early *Songs*. He also uses negative, solarized-looking footage. In combination, the texture of the film is rich and very varied.

Many kinds of material are repeated throughout *Murder Psalm*. The different footage, for the most part, is very rapidly cut. The most striking imagery comes from an educational film on epilepsy, and Brakhage's film is structured around that preexisting narrative. There is a girl seen in various settings: in a yard gazing into a birdbath into which a bright red ball is thrown; as a rider in a car; as the subject of a medical examination; and as a figure contemplating herself before a mirror and, through a cinematic dissolve, growing into a mature version of herself. Also included in this film is a doctor who seems to explain the cerebral dysfunction that causes her epilepsy.

In a narrative parallel to the saga of the modern girl being treated for epilepsy is the flight of a small, hooded girl through a forest. She is also epileptic. The footage of the forest is in a lightly tinted black and white, and at first it appears to be from a totally different film. The girl looks like Little Red Riding Hood, running to her grandmother (and the wolf). Since Brakhage is an avid and sophisticated reader of fairy tales, the implications of the image would not be lost on him, and the significance of Red Riding Hood as a cautionary tale would surely have inflected his use of this footage.

Besides the medical film in *Murder Psalm*, old movies of pioneers moving in covered wagons, Civil War battles, and national heroes (Lincoln, in particular) are used, often in negative and bleached or painted. Some of the material may have been refilmed from television. A cartoon of a mouse running furiously forward, swinging his nightstick, alternately avoiding and having collisions, is intercut throughout the film. And footage of an autopsy, from the material out of which *The Act of Seeing with One's Own Eyes* (1971) was made, is also included. There are other shots in the film, but these make up the central image sources.

Within the first few minutes, *Murder Psalm* lays out the themes that will be developed and restated as the film progresses. The rich orange followed by a thick, colorful abstraction establishes the film material (celluloid and emulsion) as a fundamental prerequisite to the image. Within the scope of Brakhage's work, the color orange is a sign of a cinematic flare, light directly striking the film emulsion at the beginning and end of a roll.[60] While sometimes related to fire imagery, orange normally affirms the film's filmicality. The mold or paint that follows seems very much in the spirit of *23rd Psalm Branch* (1967), in which Brakhage found it necessary to point out that the most moving wartime imagery was presented through the media of film and television. By reaffirming the filmic surface, Brakhage forces the acknowledgment of representation as (at least) once removed from reality, a product as much of the medium as the image source. This distance will be increased by degrees as the film moves into black and white, and negative, and with the use of imagery from earlier Brakhage films. Shots of a man on horseback looking off frame and then a body being carried on a stretcher form a sequence that introduces the theme of death and the watchers over death that will reappear in many ways. A circle, hand scratched into the emulsion is both another reminder of filmicality (it is the mark of the end of a reel, made for the convenience of projectionists), and the impression of the round shape that will dominate the film. It is followed by the first shot of a large, bright red ball.

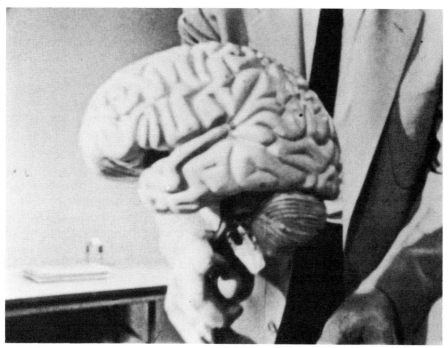

Murder Psalm. The hemispherical brain. *(Courtesy Anthology Film Archives and Stan Brakhage.)*

The girl in the film is consistently linked with the image of the ball. While the girl herself appears in many situations throughout the film, the crucial events occur when she comes into contact with this ball. She has a fit. Moreover, the subject of the film becomes more and more motivated as hemispherical imagery makes historical, political, and biological connections between different film material. Brakhage makes visual relationships between the ball, water in the birdbath, the girl's hand, a scale model of the brain, a half of a wagon wheel, a covered wagon, and a semicircular tunnel. Circular imagery is cut in half by the frame to make semicircles or hemispheres. The film material about epilepsy is transformed into a meditation on the social and cultural circumstances of childhood trauma via a visual string of semicircular imagery. By substituting one image for another—for example, the model of the brain for the covered wagon—Brakhage links their meanings and implications. The girl's seizure is made part of the social organism through visual rhyme. Within Brakhage's system, all of the semicircular imagery can be said to "cause" her traumatic response.

Travel is one motif in *Murder Psalm.* The hooded girl wanders through the forest. The covered wagons move, presumably, westward. Sometimes they form a circle for protection. A car travels down a main street in a town. At times we catch glimpses of the girl in the front seat. She passes store windows. As the car slowly passes, the words in the windows offer clues to the film's meaning. They are significant despite the fact that they have been randomly encountered. "Life" becomes "If" as the camera frames the word obliquely. "Maternity" becomes "Mater" and then "Mate." It is as if traveling through life, the girl encounters sexuality in the form of pregnancy ("Maternity"), motherhood ("Mater"), and the double entendre of husband ("Mate") or copulation ("Mate!"). Immediately after this shot, images of an open skull and a cartoon explosion occur. The reference to sex is thus linked with death.

This is not a new equation for Brakhage, who had pointed out the phallic nature of war in the making of *23rd Psalm Branch,* but it is interesting to see it at this point in Brakhage's career, in that it includes childhood in the equation. He recognizes the Freudian position that in the mind of the child, sex and death are bound together because of children's interpretation of sexual acts as violent assaults.[61]

Brakhage has used found words before, in *Oh Life—A Woe Story— The A Test News.* "A Woe Story" came from the title of a television movie, "A Woman's Story." The film, very much in the spirit of *23rd Psalm Branch,* is a form of castigation of the medium's representation of reality, in that case, womanhood. The dot-patterned, painted overlay of images of a fashionable woman in a melodrama almost obliterates the image. The dots mimic the snow of a badly tuned television. The melodrama is joined with hand-painted television imagery of an atomic bomb test. Brakhage's film changes the meaning of the original imagery, including the titles, by patterning the surface and juxtaposing the two kinds of footage.

The highly mediated footage in *Murder Psalm*—historical drama, instructional-medical film—takes on the burden of psychological reality when placed next to the documentary footage of a charred or dissected body. The central figure of the child makes these cinematic juxtapositions seem horrific. The girl is often seen near water, and shots of her are often intercut with fire imagery. Both water and fire imagery are interrupted by explosions. The bursts are like punctuation in the film, drawing our attention to the theme of trauma. The birdbath is the central image of water. The stream to which the Red Riding Hood figure walks is another powerful image. With explosions, including the sudden burst when the red ball is thrown into the water, there are often very brief images of fire or orange flarelike imagery. But the most shocking form this fire imagery takes is by implication in a shot of a charred body—a child perhaps—intercut with the two different girls who fall when in epileptic shock. The images of seizure seem extremely violent in this context. In one case, the seizure is "caused" by the red ball thrown at the girl. In the other, it is "caused" by a bolt of lightning. The water is inextricably linked with the fire. One recognizes that this film favors violent relationships between imagery.

The course of *Murder Psalm* is loosely narrative. Its story climaxes with each girl's seizure. But consistent with Brakhage's world view, this is not a simple story; rather, a speculative union of sociocultural, natural, and biological phenomena is made to cause the child's catharsis. And other visual events seem to be caused by it. If each one is looked at thematically, a pattern can be discerned with which Brakhage makes his case—a case very similar to that made in *23rd Psalm Branch.*

The historical material centers around American social mythology. Pioneers, fathers of the country, cowboys, and foot soldiers are shown. Some of the imagery comes from movies; some is taken from television. To anyone familiar with Brakhage's work, this immediately makes the material suspect, since Brakhage consistently rails against commercial film (and his own participation in it as a young man as a maker of "commercials."). There is a repeated linkage of all of the dramatic material to images of death. From the opening sequence of a cowboy looking off screen and a body being carried on a stretcher, one can sense that for Brakhage the American heritage is ultimately tied to war and death. The historical interrelation among wars had been established in *23rd Psalm Branch* by Brakhage's inability to conceive of the Vietnam War in terms other than the war of his childhood, World War II. Here, the issue is traced even further, linking notions of American patriotism and history with the death they spread. Representing recent political life is Hubert Humphrey; the past, Washington and Lincoln. Because of the negative stock and patterned overlay, even the covered wagons (those vehicles traditionally carrying heroic settlers west to populate the United States) look like tombstones. A television image of Christ is followed by one of Abraham Lincoln. That sequence makes clear some of the larger relationships in the film. We see Christ, dressed in a robe; then we see the hooded girl walking through the woods. There is a shot of Lincoln looking out of the frame and then one of a woman at a desk, perhaps the girl grown up. Finally, there is a shot of a battle, which looks like recent war footage filmed from television. The line of thought that links the Christ figure with the girl because of their dress, and also with Lincoln, a "savior" of the United States, is critical of what has been done in the name of both God and country. The girl is the witness and the victim.

Historical meditation becomes social comment in *Murder Psalm.* A cartoon of a mouse-as-policeman careening forward is integrated into the rest of the film material in a number of ways. The mouse's club is shaped like a penis and at one point, placed like the penis of the cadaver in the autopsy footage. Again, Brakhage is pointing out the phallic nature of violence in general. The city that the mouse runs through recedes in a fashion very much like that which the girl is driven through. Perspective is maintained and buildings are slowly passed. But no landscape is merely itself in *Murder Psalm.* By giving the cartoon and the

Murder Psalm. **The mouse and club.** *(Courtesy Anthology Film Archives and Stan Brakhage.)*

filmed city similar characteristics, Brakhage makes the city and the car threatening and ominous. The mouse is "killed" many times, and so the girl might be. Negative images of car headlights—black dots on white light—reinforce the threat. Yet the natural landscape is also troubling. The hooded girl runs through the woods, often immediately preceded or followed by the mouse running through the city. As we watch her flee, we see soldiers burrow through a jungle. Both the city and the country portend danger. Those who travel through them bring trouble and suffer from it. Early in the film there is a cartoon image of a truck pulling a house and, absurdly, the land with it. Brakhage points to many ways in which we carry our own difficulties with us. Just as the westward migration of settlers created as many problems as it solved, so the cartoon man carries his ridiculous burden with him. The natural and man-made landscape are equally part of the burden of social man.

Travel through space is only one of the kinds of change Brakhage explores in *Murder Psalm.* Time—specifically, growth—is also a concern. Brakhage leaves in this film dissolves from the original film on epilepsy, showing the young girl's transformation into a young woman. But the implicitly optimistic content of the dissolve is not maintained. One has the sense that in the original, the dissolve meant that while in

Murder Psalm. **Drops of sweat.** *(Courtesy Anthology Film Archives and Stan Brakhage.)*

the past an epileptic child would be isolated and abandoned to suffer the consequences of a seizure, in the present, with enlightened medical practices, a child could grow up to be an attractive, well-integrated adult. Brakhage, however, subverts this optimism by cutting to the image of a charred baby immediately after the dissolve. Further, he presents the same girl's face looking into the pool of water as if in contemplation; and then a shot of combat soldiers and, ironically, a couple, out of focus, kissing. As with the sign written "Maternity-Mate," the future here, indicated by the adult version of the girl and the embrace, seems violent because of the war footage. The life of this person is contextualized in an ominous forward-looking image.

Brakhage's editing frequently implies the inherent violence of sexuality. He makes the same case for play. Again, he uses footage of war to make his point. A boy throws the red ball at the girl by the birdbath. The water splashes her. He laughs. She grimaces, making an expression full of an ambiguity that Ray L. Birdwhistell, a Brakhage source, describes in "There Are Smiles . . ." In that essay, he outlines the varieties of smiles that range from pure joy to teeth bared in anger.[62] Brakhage does not leave us to meditate on the meaning of this cruelty or on her response. He cuts to a battle scene and then again to the girl, who falls

Murder Psalm. **The hooded girl.** *(Courtesy Anthology Film Archives and Stan Brakhage.)*

backward, as if wounded. The childish cruelty of the boy is equated with that of his grown counterparts, with all of the horror reflected back on him.

Hemispherical shapes like the wagon wheel and covered wagons are continually rhymed with the scale model of the brain. But the shape and texture of the brain is also rhymed with the cloud formations—in cartoons and in the other, more realistic, footage. Brakhage is not content just to make a social context for the child. The natural and biological are given equal weight as determinants, and the particular social history of America is expanded to include both internal biological functions and larger forces. A cartoon figure of a man is shown sweating profusely, drops of sweat appearing from his head. The next shot is of the stream to which the hooded girl runs. The evident relationship is one of cause: The drops of sweat (from the head, site of the brain that we have seen to be the "cause" of epilepsy) created the stream. And reverse relationships are also made: When the hooded girl runs through raindrops, and a flash of light causes her to fall in a fit, Brakhage cuts in a shot of the cartoon mouse charred black and then the horrible image of the charred body. The potential destructive power of light is hyperbolized.

The biological metaphor is expanded through the gestures Brakhage

Murder Psalm. The girl recoils from sparklers. *(Courtesy Anthology Film Archives and Stan Brakhage.)*

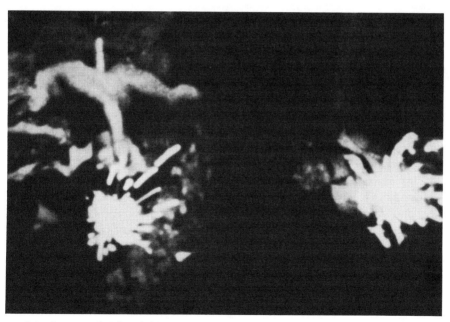

23rd Psalm Branch. The children play with sparklers. *(Courtesy Anthology Film Archives and Stan Brakhage.)*

has used in his films for more than twenty years. The pattern of the ball, negative-stock image of the headlights, water patterns reflected on the girl's face—all are equated through juxtaposition with film grain. The surface of what we see becomes the surface through which we see in this film about, among other things, our moving-picture heritage.

The girl reminds us of the children in Brakhage's other films—his own children. The Red Riding Hood figure brings to mind the Brakhage children dressed in capes in *Scenes from under Childhood* and *The Animals of Eden and After.* In the first film, they are costumed deliberately, as though in a fairy tale. In the second, they are only loosely in costume, out for a walk with their mother. The girl by the birdbath at one point recoils from sparklers, just as the children at the end of *23rd Psalm Branch* reenact war through their play with sparklers.[63] But it is in the image of the red ball that *Murder Psalm* draws its closest parallels to the rest of the Brakhage canon. In *Song IV,* child's play with the ball signals an inherent relationship to the world—to space, gravity, shape, and to time. In many of his early films, the ball had been an object of play and discovery, and a metaphor. Through the image of the ball, Brakhage as filmmaker, could "play" with the measures of experience as a child would: cutting the film when the ball left the frame to make it disappear. He made a metaphor of the ball, as astral body or atom (*Dog Star Man,* 1961–64). In *Song IV* he filled the screen with the ball to present its surface as the equivalent of film grain and luminescence, and he made it weightless in reference to the edge of the frame. In all, Brakhage could equate himself with the child in his manipulation of the ball. In *Murder Psalm,* however, the ball carries menacing overtones. It is not only an object of contemplation and play, but now a weapon. In making this point, Brakhage develops a theme that had begun to appear in earlier films—that child's play at war games is both the cause and the effect of war. In Brakhage's earlier film, boys and guns had been used to make this point. Here, the lives of children, color, and gesture are inherently violent. Personal violence is equated with major sociohistorical violence as the child is swept up into the culture.

The epileptic child in *Murder Psalm* is the only figure with a modicum of sensitivity to the horror around her. When the doctor waves his arm and, immediately after, soldiers fire rifles, she goes into shock. She falls repeatedly, responding to the natural, social, historical, and biological world, while others (like the perpetually resurrected mouse) continue unabated. She reveals her sensibility through shock.

Epilepsy is a subject that has engaged Brakhage at least since the writing of *Metaphors on Vision.* There he wrote of it as one of a string of disorders allied to the one that plagued his childhood, asthma:

Asthma, Hay-Fever, Para-Hay-Fevers, Acne, Migrain, Epilepsy, etc., all scientified by Dr. Freeman (a natural pun) as Toxic Ideopathies . . . He [the disease] is (note as the lungs begin to whistle, the head to ring) the Prince of Wants. He is (mark the familiar and recurring shape as the spot begins to spread blood color across the whole swelling area of the skin) the burn of desire. He will (well record it in all chronically as you learn how the tendencies of these diseases are inherited) the god of fury, revenger-protector of "the sins of the fathers."[64]

Brakhage's dense prose may be difficult to comprehend. He is describing the psychological and social catalysts for diseases like asthma. Economic need ("the Prince of Wants"), sexual desire, and anger can trigger an attack.

That Brakhage finds in physical disease a sociopsychological root is no surprise. Brakhage considers his childhood disorders to have contributed to his becoming an artist by isolating him, keeping him inactive, forcing him to read and think in solitude. Also, both asthma and epilepsy have been identified as "possession" in many cultures, a concept intriguing to Brakhage who very early in his artistic career associated his own notions of revelation with Maya Deren's of possession. Deren's *Divine Horsemen* and footage of Haitian ritual possession were extremely interesting to Brakhage. Further, he drew parallels between possession and epilepsy based on their physical appearance. The film

Murder Psalm. The ball lands in the birdbath. *(Courtesy Anthology Film Archives and Stan Brakhage.)*

Murder Psalm. **The girl reacts . . .** *(Courtesy Anthology Film Archives and Stan Brakhage.)*

documents of epileptic seizure in the Library of Congress, shown to Brakhage by Hollis Frampton in the early 1970s, fascinated him. He saw in them evidence, not of the clinical symptoms that they were made to illustrate, but a kind of demonism and rage.[65] In this analysis of *Murder Psalm*, the notion of rage is particularly important.

The "psalm" in the title recalls Brakhage's earlier *Songs*. The *Songs* bear a very loose relationship to the biblical psalms. Their lyricism and, in *23rd Psalm Branch*, historical meditation, are similar. The notion of prayer and supplication in the form of a song (or written poem) appealed to Brakhage's sense of one of the uses of poetic film. *Murder Psalm* comes more than fifteen years after the making of the *Songs;* while maintaining the sense of personal "singing out" of a theme, it is much less lyrical and much more a meditation on a particular psalm. The most violent, most threatening of the psalms—Psalm 137—ends in contemplation of murderous revenge. A number of images in the film are more easily understood in its context. Significantly, it is the murder of children that the psalm invokes.

> By the waters of Babylon, there we sat down, yea, we wept, when we
> remembered Zion.
> We hanged our harps upon the willows in the midst thereof.

Murder Psalm. . . . and falls in epileptic shock. (Courtesy Anthology Film Archives and Stan Brakhage.)

For there they that carried us away captive required of us a song; and they
  that wasted us required of us mirth, saying, Sing us one of the songs of
  Zion.
How shall we sing the LORD's song in a strange land?
If I forget thee, O Jerusalem, let my right hand forget her cunning.
If I do not remember thee, let my tongue cleave to the roof of my mouth;
  if I prefer not Jerusalem above my chief joy.
Remember, O LORD, the children of Edom in the day of Jerusalem; who
  said, Rase it, rase it, even to the foundation thereof.
O daughter of Babylon, who are to be destroyed; happy shall he be, that
  rewardeth thee as thou hast served us.
Happy shall he be, that taketh and dasheth thy little ones against the
  stones.

Murder Psalm bears a number of very direct relations to Psalm 137.
The image of the river as the site of meditation and lamentation informs
the film's image of the girl by the stream. Flight, travel, captivity, and
the "strange land" are all depicted in the incessant movement of the
film. The image of people carrying their possessions in covered wagons,
driving, fleeing through the forest—all coincide with the themes of the
psalm. The film maintains the angry spirit of the psalm, but is directed
at our own history and present.

The figure of the child is the vehicle for the violence against one's own heritage. The child suffers from history, playacts it, and will repeat it as an adult. The continuity of life, from child to adult, country to city, and nature to artifice insures that those who would "dasheth thy little ones against the stones" are only manifestations of the "little ones" themselves. Society insures the continuity by formulating patterns that are mimicked from nature and the human body. History ensures it equally. The pessimism of the psalm is doubled in the film, which depicts a culture that dashes its own little ones against the stones, or teaches them to dash themselves. Brakhage offers no alternative. Instead he poses this as a cosmic truth, revealed through film documents of our culture. In combination with Psalm 137, the Red Riding Hood story reinforces the looming violence of the film and points to an undercurrent that is sexual in nature. Bruno Bettelheim's *Uses of Enchantment* is useful in interpreting the fairy tale. *Murder Psalm* emphasizes some of the same issues that Bettelheim discusses. Bettelheim's work is helpful in deciphering the figure of the hooded girl in the film.

Bettelheim interprets Red Riding Hood as wanting her grandmother's destruction. By giving the wolf explicit directions to grandmother's house, she gets out of an anxiety-provoking situation herself and endangers her grandmother. Bettelheim sees the release of the child's tension and the violence toward the elder as important in the tale. It is a psychological truth that children do sometimes actively seek to destroy their parents (or here, grandparents). By giving the wolf directions to grandmother's, she must encounter the anxiety-provoking figure of the wolf again. According to Bettelheim, he is made up of equal parts of sex and death. He is in bed, she joins him and he wants to eat her up. She is tricked by the wolf just as her grandmother had been before her.[66]

The relevant part of Bettelheim's analysis for *Murder Psalm* is the equation of sex and death and the death wish toward one's parents since both *are* aspects of Brakhage's film.

By using the psalms for his title, and by publicly announcing the origin of the film as a nightmare of murdering his mother, Brakhage directs our inquiry into the film in specific ways. *Murder Psalm* is a film made when most of his children were grown. By the time of *Murder Psalm*, Brakhage's interest in child observation had waned. No longer does he have their presence before him, to carry the burden of his self-discovery through his observation of their own. He can now see the result of his own child rearing. His children were raised according to an ethos radically different from that under which he grew up. They are now grown. The rage of the film seems to be an outgrowth of his inability as a parent to break the cycle of sociocultural heritage and convention. The rage is directed against his mother who taught him the conventions he despises.

In the psalms, the song of Zion is substantially different from the song of Babylon, because it is the song of a people exiled, living in alienation. Brakhage is not concerned with literal, physical distance. Instead, Brakhage is preoccupied with the distance between art and society. His alienation is that of an artist. The issue is how one can "sing . . . the songs of Zion" with the tools of commercial film, the found footage with which he works. By drawing on all of his skill as a filmmaker—using painting, solarizing, and complex editing techniques to heighten our attention to the deliberate flow of images—Brakhage transforms the conventional found footage. He recontextualizes it on *his* terms. Even the fairy tale is stripped of its mystery, its latent content revealed.

Murder Psalm reflects a crisis in Brakhage's filmmaking. His interest in the notion of seizure, his thoroughgoing disparagement of American history as a continual drive toward death, and his equal disdain for the products of the film and television industries are the culmination of a number of strains of Brakhage's filmmaking since *Anticipation of the Night*. But the key elements of rage and matricide are new to his endeavor. By 1980, Brakhage is witness to the maturity and integration into the culture of his own children. He has lost their physical presence to the society he wrestled with over his entire career as a filmmaker. He is forced to use images of children from commercial film. The contemplation of images other than his own family's is problematic for Brakhage, a filmmaker who perpetually sees himself in the people he films. The rage evinced by *Murder Psalm* is partly an outgrowth of his new, familyless situation.

That the film and its rage are directed against his mother is understandable from the point of view of an adopted child. It is possible that Brakhage regarded her as having saved him from complete abandonment as a boy. On the other hand, it is equally possible (and psychologically documented in Freud's analysis of the "family romance")[67] that he felt she stole him from his real parents. Psalm 137 tells of the Jews in Babylon "carried away captive" from their homeland. Their rage is against their captors. Brakhage's is against his captor, his mother.

The basic issue becomes clearer in light of this reading of *Murder Psalm*. One of the ways in which an adopted child can come to grips with the world is to separate "nature" from "nurture," since the separation is a fundamental condition of his life. His concept of self can remain distinct from the concept of society. The continuity of parent/self and society is broken, since his natural parents did not raise him. His adopted parents are complicit with the social order, since they introduced him to it and instilled its values in him. In *Murder Psalm*, his desire to kill his mother is hinted at in the use of the Red Riding Hood figure, but is expressed in the violence of the edited found footage.

Simultaneously, the film reinvents a relationship between "nature" and "nurture" based on filmic principles. The intercutting of internal body parts, with images of the child and all of the other found footage creates a continuity that is Brakhage's own. Nevertheless, it remains highly alienated from the values of the social order the film depicts. Brakhage's antithetical stance to the original film material results in his alienating picture.

*   *   *   *

There are many other Brakhage films in which children take roles. Sometimes, very brief or abstracted appearances by children are part of the films. In *Dog Star Man,* a baby's face, its mouth open, is collaged to make a universe appear to be coming through its cry. Brakhage describes the function of the child in part 2 of that film as a metaphor for spring and the vehicle for the filmmaker (the "Dog Star Man") to become engaged autobiographically with his own childhood.[68] The child's physiognomy and metaphorical potential intrigue him. Both aspects of the child mesh with the greater purpose of the film to forge a continuity of the micro- to the macrocosmic, the human organism to the seasons, and the sexual to the spiritual. The child is one major stage of the flow of meaning.

In other films, children are the catalyst for filmmaking. They inspire Brakhage to shoot the original footage, in particular birth films— *Window Water Baby Moving* (1959), *Blue White* (1965), and *Song V* (1964). In these films, the idea of the child is crucial, and the child's place within the family is stressed. While Brakhage explores the cinematic equivalents to the violence of birth, the focus of these types of films is usually either Jane or both Brakhage and Jane. The child is their product and sometimes their witness. The moment of the child's birth is mimicked in the intensive camera work and later editing structure. In those films, the birth of the child is made parallel to the birth of the film.

There are many other films in which children are integrated into the flow of events. In *Foxfire Childwatch* (1971), the filmmaker Ken Jacobs, his wife, and daughter appear. The subject of the film is the parents' tracking of their child, who wanders off in an airport. In *Trip to Door* (1971), the Brakhage family rides in a car. The children as well as Jane are the subject of flashing light and Brakhage's camera framing and movement. They are on their way to something we never see, and they are depicted as a unit. In *Sincerity (Reel 3)* (1978), we see a grammar-school play. By and large, the film is as much about the audience as about the play. One assumes a Brakhage child is on stage. The American flag, the tacky costumes, and the institutional atmosphere serve to contextualize the family. Except for rare individual portraits (for example, "Crystal" in *15 Song Traits,* 1965), in most of the short films, children are part of the family unit, inseparable from one another and from their parents.

As part of the living landscape of Brakhage's life, he has recorded the lives of children copiously. His representation of them changed over the years of his filmmaking and the growth of his family. But it is important to stress that it is in the family that Brakhage finds the most satisfactory role for the child, and one can read its function as one reflection of the filmmaker's intervention in his own films. The children are aspects of Brakhage himself, the family a perpetuation of his own traits. One can analyze Brakhage's film style as a series of techniques to highlight *his* perception and representation of the world. By and large, the children are included for the same purpose. Despite his changing stance toward the issue of childhood, the function of it in his films has remained the same. Filmmaking is the means by which, and the family is the context in which, Brakhage can best explore himself.

4
CONVERGENCES

The Backdrop of Romanticism

Looking to the image of the child in Romantic literature, one can see a tradition for the attraction of filmmakers.[1] Rousseau's Emile is perhaps the most coherent figure to discuss here. He is the tabula rasa for the teaching of Jean Jacques, his tutor. His naive awe at the physical world, his general interest in the causes of phenomena, his native spirituality, and his untutored antisociability are all characteristics for which one could find equivalents in the idealism of avant-garde filmmakers. Rousseau, like Brakhage, exhorts us to "begin, then, by studying your pupils better. For most assuredly you do not know them at all."[2] The corruption of literary language is denied Emile until he has developed a sensory relationship to the world. Jean Jacques and Brakhage have approximated the same evaluation of the dangers of language. Moreover, Emile's relationship to the world is based on a calculated presexual misunderstanding of his own motivations—Jean Jacques, unlike his filmmaking heirs, extols sexual sublimination as a useful pedagogical tool.

Avant-garde filmmakers, like their precursors in Romantic poetry and fiction, provide variations on Rousseau's Emile. The child, by and large, is the young artist, appreciating and being formed by the world. Each filmmaker found different particulars that sealed their bond with Romantic culture. For Cocteau, the Nervalian death wish, Novalis's *Hymns to the Night,* and Carroll's subtly sexualized child photographs all contained aspects of the child obsession. Cornell's fixation on androgynous females points to Goethe and Nerval as precursors, as well as to Carroll. Cornell's poetic equations of children with other small things is very like that of Novalis.[3] Certainly, the sexuality that attracted him to child imagery can be found in the figures created by his Romantic influences. For Brakhage, the model of the artist is the child, as it was for Rousseau. The innocent who marvels at the world in both of the above-mentioned authors' works is recalled in the opening to *Metaphors on Vision*. Brakhage quotes Novalis's *Henry von Ofterdingen* in that context, and one finds later in the novel a philosophical passage on the nature of childhood like Brakhage's own.[4] Within the Romantic tradition, Brakhage found voices appealing to his other major concerns, too. When Coleridge writes, "I regard truth as a divine ventriloquist,"[5] it is very much in the spirit of Brakhage's "film given to me to make."

Avant-garde film history rests within the specifically Baudelairean tradition of the treatment of childhood as an icon for the artist. The social function of the child is nonexistent, or predominantly operates as antisociability. The notion of the child and the convalescent as models for the artist[6] are at the root of the work of the filmmakers under discussion. It is through the major reinterpretation of the usefulness of Baudelaire's equation of child and artist that Brakhage ultimately distinguishes himself from his precursor Cocteau. For Cocteau, "childhood recovered at will" was a metaphor for the artistic act. Cocteau's theoretical writings on art and film are based on the Baudelairean model of the child genius. And further, the "ecstatic gaze" that Baudelaire calls forth as exemplary of the child genius permeated Cocteau's films and occasionally forms their substructure.

For Brakhage, the Baudelairean model becomes literal. While one can see in the early films (particularly *Anticipation of the Night*) some parallel to Cocteau's metaphorical reading of Baudelaire, in *The Weir-Falcon Saga*, Brakhage makes a film showing what Baudelaire describes. The child *is* the convalescent. The "brightly coloured impressions," seen "in a state of newness," the "child confronted with something new, whatever it be, whether a face or a landscape, gliding colors, shimmering stuffs," describes scenes from the film. Brakhage moves the application of Baudelaire from the general to the particular. He collapses the visual perspicacity of the convalescent, the child, and the artistic genius into one. And while *The Weir-Falcon Saga* is illustrative of the "Painter of Modern Life," Brakhage's mature work as a whole takes off from the Baudelairean approach of seeing "everything in a state of newness." Inclusive of the image of childhood, the visual world is presented in Brakhage's films with an insistence unparalleled in the history of cinema.

From Cocteau to Cornell to Brakhage

While it is difficult to ascertain how important Cocteau was to Joseph Cornell, the similarity of some of their iconography and artistic structures offers evidence that Cocteau was admired by Cornell. There are some obvious reasons that Cornell would have been drawn to Cocteau's films, and more importantly, some similarities in imagery, structure, and intent that allow us to draw them together.

Cornell loved France and modern French art. He studied French performing arts and literature. As an artist, he identified with the French surrealist movement. In other words, he imaginatively aspired to the milieu of which Cocteau was a part. As a voracious moviegoer, of both low and high film culture, it is very likely that Cornell saw *Blood of a Poet* at the Museum of Modern Art or at one of the art-film clubs or theaters he frequented during the 1930s, perhaps while he was at work on *The Children's Party* trilogy.

Cornell was also fascinated by the female lead of *Blood of a Poet*. Among his movie-star memorabilia, Cornell kept a photograph of Lee Miller as the statue/woman.[7] Later, in 1940 or 1941, Cornell made a collage using a double image of Lee Miller.[8] In the upper background of the collage, she is dressed as a man; in the lower front, as a woman. The same image of her face is collaged on the two different costumes. It is likely that both her status as an objet d'art in the film and her androgynous appearance were attractive to Cornell.

Besides Cornell's direct interest in Cocteau's films, the two filmmakers converge when one analyzes the imagery that obsessed them. Both filmmakers used constellations, and both shared an interest in hotels. Cornell's boxes and collages are filled with star imagery; constellations play an important part. The star patterns unify the schematics of the collages with their subjects. Very often the stars outline human features, just as they do in Cocteau's drawings.[9] And, as in *Blood of a Poet*, the hotel as an image of imaginative space is frequently used by Cornell as the pretext for his boxes. Very often the stars are also included with images of movie stars or other cultural luminaries. Cocteau and Cornell shared the love of puns. Cocteau's *"étoiles"* were as often his friends and those he admired as they were stars in the sky.

In addition, one finds a similar image and structural device at work in the use of mirror imagery and backward motion. Cocteau was interested in the image of the mirror itself, while Cornell's films make more use of the reverses it offers. The look of their films is very different, yet they both were drawn obsessively to this image. One might look to Lewis Carroll's "Jabberwocky" as a possible mutual source. It, too, was written to be read in a mirror. In the same vein, both filmmakers are intrigued by spatial and temporal reversals. The mirror affords the possibility of tension between surface and depth. With a mirror one confronts both glass and image simultaneously. The temporal equivalent is backward motion, which cancels the illusion of movement and depth by recalling it. Reflection, particularly in the form of mirror writing is directly related to dream structure, and permits a bivalent approach to

Joseph Cornell. *Untitled (Portrait of Lee Miller)* c. 1948–49. Collage, 9¼ × 11″. *(Collection and courtesy Vivian Horan.)*

any given image. In "On the Antithetical Sense of Primal Words," Freud proposes that in dreams, opposites are representations of similars— most notably that *no* means *yes* in another form. In Cocteau's work, one sees this applied in the representation of death as yet another life; in Cornell, with "The End" written backward at the beginning of *The Children's Party*. In the case of both filmmakers, their approach to reality as presented via mirror imagery and structures runs parallel to that which they present in their treatment of childhood.

Both men found the ludic metaphor appropriate to the art-making process. Cocteau presented his character's lives as games. The game of cards and snowball fight are allegories for experience in *Blood of a Poet*. The notions of art as play and life as a game sustained his aesthetic. Cornell fostered this same myth of art and play. He fashioned box after box as toys for children and adults. The "Soap Bubble" sets are taken from children's toys. The imaginative act inscribed in play is seen by both filmmakers as similar to that of the artist and his audience. Both made work addressed to children or the child within the adult.

Peering through keyholes, grates, and windows and as we have seen in *Orpheus*, a hierarchy of seeing are all issues for Cocteau and are all in a direct relationship to accounts of his childhood. For Cornell, the importance of vision is less evident. One does know, however, that looking into windows and directional gazing are constituent images throughout Cornell's films. He cuts his films when someone turns to look; he holds on the screen images of children staring at the audience. This happens most often in *The Children's Party* trilogy. In his system, looking was part of childhood.

Cocteau was a role model for Stan Brakhage, especially because of his economic relation to the commercial cinema (that is, his nonrelation in the making of *Blood of a Poet*). When Cocteau praised the new generation of filmmakers in America for using 16-mm film equipment as freely as poets use pens,[10] he could not have predicted how appropriate his comments were to the young filmmaker Brakhage. He uses Cocteau in the same manner that Cocteau had used Méliès—as the wellspring of creativity in film. Brakhage describes his experience of seeing *Orpheus* as the single experience that most convinced him that film could be an art form.[11]

Brakhage makes a great deal of Cocteau as the progenitor of his filmmaking. They shared notions of the importance of lying. Cocteau's "true lie" ("I am the lie that always tells the truth") begins Brakhage's lecture on him and the *Film Biographies*. Brakhage points to the figure of Cocteau as the source of the problem Brakhage felt plagued with as a young filmmaker—that to be an artist one must be homosexual. And Brakhage calls on lessons from *Blood of a Poet* to support his argument against sound, particularly synchronous sound, in film:

> Jean Cocteau's poetic film plays, for all their dramatic limitations, had demonstrated beautifully to me that only non-descriptive language could co-exist with moving image (in any but a poor operatic sense), that words, whether

spoken or printed could only finally relate to visuals in motion thru a necessity of means and or an integrity as severally visually as that demonstrated by the masterpieces of collage.[12]

Moreover, Brakhage is most attracted by Cocteau's presentation of the experiences of the child in film. He describes *Beauty and the Beast* as "the only example of the child's world of fantasy" in film.[13] In his 1972 lecture, Brakhage compared Cocteau and Méliès by their treatment of the child. He showed *The Bobkick* with *Blood of a Poet* and lectured on the image of the "bobkick" as an adult man acting as a child. He traces the image to the Victorian notion of children as little adults. He describes the Méliès film as a dream of hubris, the childish man who attacks the father. In light of his identification with Cocteau, it is interesting to notice that he discusses *Blood of a Poet* in autobiographical terms, centering on the "Flying Lesson" sequence. He describes it as "one of the most terrifying explications of the training of the child in art . . . the whole story of my life, that scene. Finally crawling beyond the mantlepiece where my mother and my teachers wished to put me, thumbing my nose at them, sticking my tongue out and inhabiting the ceiling, upside down, defying gravity from that point on and thereby horrifying everybody."[14] The "Flying Lesson" is an image stemming from Cocteau's life. Here Brakhage appropriates it in his own life. This is a poignant story in light of the later film *Murder Psalm*, where Brakhage goes "beyond" his mother once again, "horrifying everybody."

Brakhage echoes Cocteau in his discussion of film "given to" him to make. Cocteau also described himself as a medium: "Unless I happen to become the vehicle of an unknown force, which I then clumsily help to take shape, I cannot read, or write, or even think."[15] Their difference is that Cocteau draws on the Greek tradition of Orpheus, Brakhage on the Hebraic tradition of Moses. Because Cocteau's reputation was made long enough in the past and because Cocteau was of an older generation, Brakhage could look to him as a cinematic role model and ancestor, and could find the ways in which their efforts converged. As he found necessary to do in the invention of his children as ideal precursors to the artist in him, so with Cocteau, Brakhage found an ideal progenitor of his own filmmaking.

In Joseph Cornell, Brakhage found not only a role model but a collaborator. In his lecture on Cornell, Brakhage unknowingly points to one of the structural similarities between Cornell and Cocteau. In describing his encounter with Cornell while making *The Wonder Ring/ Gnir Rednow*, Brakhage talks about the principle that generated the film:

When I did go out to him with the footage of "The Wonder Ring" he was delighted. I do not have a print with me of the film I made out of it; but I can show you the film he made out of my film. My film is called "The Wonder Ring" and his is to be called "The Wonder Ring" as you would say it if seen spelled in a mirror. The film is made so that it runs backwards and forwards. It can run in four versions, from side to side this way, and that way; or backwards or forwards, or backwards or forwards emulsion side to the gate, or base side to the gate.[16]

The emphasis on the inversion of the image is one that Brakhage periodically would assert as a quality of great filmmaking—that any film should be able to be seen end to beginning or verso and maintain the standard of a work of art. In a proposal to the Guggenheim Foundation, he described a project based on this principle: "Very recently I have begun working toward a filmic realization which will retain its integral form (considering the structure of the work of art as integral with all its emotional and intellectual statements) even when run backwards."[17] He made several other attempts at such films himself during his early career. He struggled with the idea of "turning" around the experience of a film in *Blue Moses*. When the protagonist insists "there's a cameraman behind every scene" and "you *see* . . . *you* see my back; but if I really turn myself around and SEE—," Brakhage is not only speaking about the phenomenological experience of movie watching, but of the movie machinery and material itself. For the cameraman to turn his back is to change the scene of the film; for the audience to turn is to encounter the projector beam; for the actor to do so is to tear through the illusion of the image projected on the screen. It is interesting to find in Freud's "Dream Work"[18] a discussion of "turning one's back on something." He mentions it in the context of his earlier article on "The Antithetical Sense of Primal Words." It forms part of the discussion of various reversals, applicable to any discussion of both Cocteau and Cornell's use of mirrors and reversals.

The unifying vision created via the noncontradictory use of opposites or mirror imagery brings us to the more direct line of influence from Cornell to Brakhage: the substitution of one image for another in a sequence of shots to equate the two. Cornell worked with the techniques of substitution in all of the films discussed here, and Brakhage even more than Cornell finds the strategy useful. To belie the contradiction of two images that are clearly not alike, substituting one for the other in the visual field, makes their meaning interdependent. Cornell had used this technique extensively in *The Children's Party* trilogy. Brakhage first encountered it in Cornell's work in his collaboration, *Centuries of June*. The image that is so transformed is that of a child. It is not unusual that Brakhage would seize on the technique and the image of the child simultaneously, as he did in *Song IV*. His theory of the unity of form and content would necessitate the treatment of the image of the child in a manner appropriate to it. Equivalency by substitution is not only the work of dreams but the play of children.

In Brakhage's discussion of the shooting of *Centuries of June,* he describes Cornell's approach to a subject and the "lesson" he took from it. The description points to some of the ways in which Brakhage really was a student of Cornell:

We took a walk through the town; we wandered here and there. And *there* was a beautiful old house being torn down, and suddenly tears came to Joseph's eyes. He asked me to take some pictures of it. I began taking pictures and he began pointing things out to me: "You see that?"—"You see this?" Never more than that. Never did he direct me in any overt sense, but he cast a whole magic aura over this old house and the demolition that was going on next door and would soon engulf it. Then some neighborhood children were coming home from school, and he began pointing to them. Then he gave them some candies and asked them to stand there to be photographed—all in a way that would seem to produce the most completely corny film in the world. But his subtleties and nuances completely dominated this occasion; and out came something that I can only compare to one of the most intensive poems of Emily Dickinson. In fact, Joseph thought of calling it after "Bolts of Melody" for some time. OK—let's take a look at "Portrait of June [*sic*]." FILM Everything in "Portrait of June" takes on the most unbearable intensity if you have opened yourself to watch for it. The slightest shake of the camera becomes significant in relationship to every occurrence. The old white house itself is made up of trees at times. There are images within its branches, and I can't imagine how they got into the film. How did the smoke, for instance, illuminate the slats of those buildings in the back of it? One could say it is light reflected off the smoke back onto the building which increased the illumination, but that does not explain the incredibleness of that image. There are fire flies in the film—something I have never been able to photograph again. I can't imagine how they made an imprint on the grossness of Kodachrome. I did do a shot I thought was not quite smooth enough for what Joseph wanted so I told him I was going to retake it. The pan down the building and across the steps was too jerky. I set up and started to do it again and Joseph moved two boys to sit on the steps while I was busy panning down that tower. He put them in place and stepped aside and when I panned to there the camera pauses because now, instead of the empty steps, there are two boys sitting there. The girl assumes a metaphorical relationship to the house. Joseph was almost immediately in love with this girl, you might say. The boys walk down the sidewalk rather stogidly [*sic*] and grossly and looking very much like the workmen who are tearing up the lot next door. In the next image the girl runs down the street in the direction of the boys. This would seem a sad loss to Joseph's sense of things; but one does not have to know his way of looking at things to feel the absolute cohesion of emotion in this film; the butterfly that cannot quite be caught, for instance. Everything takes on that quality of obsession. He taught Ken Jacobs, Larry Jordan, and myself, to name three of the filmmakers who worked under him, that if the occasion is right, if the occasion is magic, then practically everything is usable. Practically everything that happens will be intrinsic to that occasion and will make its own form. By being true to itself, that occasion, or the obsession, or the magic (the word Joseph would use) will create the form.[19]

Many other filmmakers within the venue of the avant-garde have recognized childhood as subject matter and metaphor. Maya Deren planned to make a film using children's games as its structure and subject. She was also a major influence on Brakhage, and it is possible to draw specific inferences about the nature of her influence on his films that deal with children. But it is in the figures of Sidney Peterson and James Broughton that one can see the true origin of the child orientation of the American avant-garde. Peterson is the filmmaker most closely allied to the French surrealists and Cocteau. The definition of the artist as a child at play can be deduced from his filmmaking enterprise.

Peterson's *Petrified Dog* (1948) uses the image of a girl dressed as Tenniel's illustrations for *Alice in Wonderland* placed among the oddly behaving adults. She follows their actions. Her eye is anamorphically enlarged and distorted. Even though she is depicted in as distorted a fashion as the other people in the film, she observes them as we might. Her lack of comprehension stands for that of the audience. Peterson's film is the first among many American avant-garde films in which the child is the protagonist and mediator. (It is interesting to note, too, that in his recent film, *Man in a Bubble* (1981), Peterson brackets the events with an image of a girl blowing bubbles, thereby positing the film as a child's world view.)

It was to study with Sidney Peterson that Brakhage went to San Francisco as a young filmmaker, and Brakhage still claims Peterson as a vital precursor. But it is through James Broughton that some of the most explicit aspects of the child orientation of the avant-garde are manifested. The circle around Broughton was a direct influence on Brakhage. Robert Duncan, in particular, was vitally important for Brakhage. One of the areas to which he introduced Brakhage was the serious consideration of nursery rhymes and fairy tales. Broughton was among Duncan's fellow poets who took up the structure of children's poetry and prose. He used it not only in his writing but in his films as well.

Broughton's *Mother's Day* (1948) depicts a group of adults as if they were children. Even "Mother" and "Father" in that film behave childishly. The "children" in the film are men and women who have never grown apart from their mother. She, in turn, is not a model of maturity. They play with toys, ride cycles, and scribble on walls. The writing style and language posit the film as a family album, the moving images as snapshots.

The child orientation of *Mother's Day* is taken up in other of Broughton's films. For the most part, the sound tracks of the later films are spoken in a singsong voice, as if the films were stories being told to children. Broughton uses sound to simplify and make naive serious, esoteric, and even sexual imagery and content. Broughton's poetry is childlike, and is often used as the sound track to his films. *This Is It* (1971) is one film in which he combines the rhyming sound track with the image of a child. In *Testament* (1974), we find the autobiographical source of imagery he had used since *Mother's Day*, and hear the continuity of his poetic "voice" from childhood through his childlike maturity.

Of a slightly younger generation, Kenneth Anger has made much more specific use of the image of the child in several of his films. Like Peterson and Broughton, Anger comes from the West Coast, having grown up in southern California. He claims he appeared in Max Reinhardt's *A Midsummer Night's Dream* as the "Changeling" when he was a small boy. Anger does not make autobiographical films, nor does he often use children, but he has recreated his own (fantasized or real) image as a child movie star twice in his films. In *Invocation of My Demon Brother* (1969), a small turbaned figure is pixilated and quickly descends a staircase. He carries a sign: "Zap. You're pregnant. That's witchcraft." While the film is about Anger's "magickal" powers, the turbaned figure recalls his childhood. Similarly, in *Rabbit's Moon* (1970), the Pierrot figure is comforted by two boys, costumed like Reinhardt's "Changeling." One carries a mirror, the other a lute. In *Rabbit's Moon,* they represent the options of narcissism or Orphism, both of which are rejected by the hero, Pierrot. It is as though Anger could find no better image of simple goodness than his own self-image as a child star.

In order fully to trace the image and idea of the child in avant-garde film, one has to consider film diarists and filmmakers who use home movies. Recently, Jonas Mekas began to incorporate his daughter in his film diaries. *Paradise Not Yet Lost (Oona's Third Year)* (1980) uses his child as the raison d'être of the film. Mekas's premise is not only to make a record of Oona's third year, but to interpret the world with the idealism he hopes she has and will be able to maintain as she grows. Mekas is the foremost of the film diarists, but there are many others who, in the course of their daily film records incorporate children as part of their world, and a few who structure their film around a child's world view. The personal film has been one major outlet for the image of the child, since it democratizes subject matter and is conducive to the presentation of family life. Brakhage, certainly, has based his film aesthetic on similar premises.

The two most committed child-oriented filmmakers of Brakhage's generation are Larry Jordan and Ken Jacobs. Larry Jordan uses collaged imagery taken from eighteenth- and nineteenth-century etchings. Very often children are included in his invented landscapes. In addition, Jordan made a feature film in the form of a fairy tale, *Huldur and the Magician* (1969). The simplicity of his film, the gentle and naive compilation of sound and image, is similar to Broughton's. Jordan's films are often complex and serious in subject matter. Nevertheless, the fanciful relationships between things would appeal to children as well as adults. Joseph Cornell was his mentor, not only as a collagist himself, but as a man who addressed his artwork and films to children.

Ken Jacobs was also an assistant to Cornell and has been continually involved in notions of innocence, naiveté, and childhood in his films. There are two distinct strains of the theme, divided between his early and later films. In his work with Jack Smith and Bob Fleischner on *Blonde Cobra* (1963) and in *Little Stabs at Happiness* (1963), Jacobs presents the artist as a playful, infantile figure. In *Blonde Cobra*, Jack Smith tells the story of "his" childhood, when he was left alone, always waiting for his mother. We see him dismembering a doll, and playing with other objects in a childlike way in *Little Stabs at Happiness*. Smith survives in the depressing environments of Jacobs's films by being a naïf. Very much in the tradition of Cocteau, Jacobs valorizes childhood as it is manifested in the lives and work of artists. Later, however, Jacobs had his own family and used his child as the subject for a film. *Nisan Ariana Window* (1969) is the name of both his daughter and the film. There, the camera studies the crawling baby, as though a parent were looking down to the floor. The blank stare of the baby, intercut with her mother and a cat, make a family portrait in which the child is the center and the most fulfilled part. Brakhage later filmed the same family in *Foxfire Childwatch* (1971).

All of the filmmakers discussed in this conclusion serve to reinforce the notion that childhood is a major theme in American avant-garde film. There have been and will continue to be many variations on the theme. Cocteau, Cornell, and Brakhage are the pivotal figures, however, representing a major current in avant-garde film history. For reasons partially or wholly hidden to the filmmakers themselves, they incorporated the image and the idea of the child in their films to reinvent themselves as artists. They were attracted to the use of childhood in their predecessors work, including the literature that immediately preceded the cinema. Each filmmaker found his own form for his own predilections, thereby transforming the theme of childhood *and* the course of avant-garde film history simultaneously.

NOTES

Introduction

1. Stan Brakhage, *Film Biographies* (Berkeley, Calif.: Turtle Island Press, 1977), p. 130; elisions in text.

Chapter 1. Jean Cocteau

1. Stuart Liebman has pointed out to me some rich variations on *carte blanche* lost in translation to "white paper." *Carte blanche* means not only a manifesto (as Cocteau intended) but also implies "free rein" and "tabula rasa." The implications of the title are important to Cocteau's confessions of an adventuresome young homosexual.

2. Cocteau distinguished between childhood *(enfance)* and youth *(jeunesse)*. Although he made no severe categories, *childhood* is the term most consistently associated with presexual life. *Youth* is invested with a sense of blossoming sexuality (here, homosexuality), adventure, and a poetic sensibility. In Cocteau's vocabulary, *enfance* is a much richer term, used often and to varied metaphorical ends. While I do not deny the importance of the concept of youth for Cocteau, it is in childhood that the root of his aesthetic can be found.

3. Jean Cocteau, *Paris Album, 1900–1914*, trans. Margaret Crosland (London: W. H. Allen, 1956), dedication.

4. Francis Steegmuller, *Cocteau: A Biography* (Boston: Little, Brown,. and Co., 1970), p. 6.

5. Cocteau, *Professional Secrets*, ed. Robert Phelps (New York: Farrar, Straus, and Giroux, 1970), p. 11.

6. Cocteau, *Paris Album*, p. 86.

7. Ibid., pp. 22–23. In *Professional Secrets*, the same passage is translated by Richard Howard, who substitutes "region" for "zone." For the purposes of this dissertation, it is crucial to retain the original "zone."

8. Cocteau, *Paris Album*, pp. 23–24.

9. Ibid., p. 30.

10. Cocteau, *Opium: Diary of a Cure*, trans. Margaret Crosland and Sinclair Rond (New York: Grove Press, 1958), p. 143.

11. Cocteau, *Paris Album*, pp. 31–32.

12. Eisenstein, Arnheim, Braudy, Burch, Cavell, and others have postulated the cinema's likeness to the world seen through a frame. Film theory has found the metaphor to be a useful one

in describing the phenomenological and metaphorical bases of film technique and film viewing.

13. Cocteau, *Paris Album*, p. 36.

14. Cocteau, *Professional Secrets*, p. 12.

15. Ibid., p. 10.

16. Ibid., p. 11.

17. Ibid., p. 20.

18. Ibid., p. 23.

19. Ibid., p. 24.

20. Steegmuller, *Cocteau*, p. 427.

21. Cocteau, *Professional Secrets*, p. 24.

22. Ibid., p. 23.

23. Ibid., p. 25.

24. Ibid.

25. Cocteau, *Paris Album*, pp. 83–85.

26. Plays and films sometimes raise the same issues. Insofar as they are media that involve large numbers of people—drama, the manipulation of an established reality through stage or cinematic trickery, and an audience—they are grouped in Cocteau's generalization about art. Lydia Crowson and Neal Oxenhandler have made detailed studies of the plays in order to ascertain their aesthetic structures and significance. I consider the plays as texts, noting, however, that much of what Cocteau says about film audiences applies as well to those of theater. The ways in which Cocteau directed actors in films, the kind of drama, and the inventive use of cinematic devices are significantly different from his interaction with the theater and warrant this distinction.

27. There are a few exceptions to this rule. *The Potomak* (1919) was begun as a story to entertain a child: "Jacques-Emile Blanche had a young nephew or cousin whom I used to keep amused—scaring him sometimes, for children dearly love to be scared. And I had found this word 'Potamak,' to stand for a kind of formless monster. And gradually this formless monster took on a certain importance for me" (Steegmuller, *Cocteau*, p. 91). It is interesting to note that this "formless monster" becomes strikingly like a cinematic apparatus. Accordidng to Frederick Brown, it looks like a projector. Cocteau also wrote and drew an album for children called *Drôle de ménage* (1948), which included whimsical drawings and descriptions. Its elegant frontispiece is reproduced in *Album Cocteau*, ed. Pierre Chanel (Paris: Tchou, 1970). On two occasions he titled brief pieces as if for children: in 1913, for the *Revue Hebdomadaire*, he wrote an article on his experiences as a young man in Venice, "Venice vue par un enfant"; and in 1963, the preface to a cookbook, *La cuisine est un jeu d'enfants* by Michel Oliver (Paris: Plon, 1963).

28. Philippe Ariès, *Centuries of Childhood: A Social History of Family Life*, trans. Robert Baldick (New York: Random House, 1962), p. 110–27.

29. Gerard de Nerval, *"Aurélia" et "Les filles de feu"* (Paris: Gallimard, 1972), p. 294.

30. "Je me perdis plusieurs fois dans les longs corridors, et, en traversant une des galeries centrales, je fus frappé d'un spectacle étrange. Un être d'une grandeur demésurée—homme ou femme, je ne sais—voltigeait péniblement au-dessus de l'espace et semblait se débattre parmi des nauges épais" (ibid).

31. Jean Piaget, *Play, Dreams and Imitation in Childhood*, trans. C. Gattegno and F. M. Hodgson (New York: W. W. Norton, 1962), pp. 167–68.

32. Cocteau, *Opium*, p. 69.

33. Ibid.

34. Cocteau, *The Holy Terrors*, trans. Rosamond Lehmann (New York: New Directions, 1957), p. 50.

35. Ibid., p. 24.

36. Ibid., p. 58.

37. Stephen Koch, "Cocteau," *Midway* 2 (Winter 1968): 124.

38. Cocteau, *Thomas the Imposter*, trans. Dorothy Williams (London: Peter Owen, 1957), p. 23.

39. Ibid.

40. Cocteau, *Opium*, p. 71.

41. Cocteau, *Du cinématographe*, André Bernard and Claude Gautier (Paris: Pierre Belfond Publishers, 1973), p. 17; translated by Ellen Burt.

42. Cocteau, *Journals of Jean Cocteau*, trans. and ed. Wallace Fowlie (Bloomington: Indiana University Press, 1956), p. 107.

43. Ibid., p. 101.

44. See Cocteau, *My Contemporaries*, pp. 101–2.

45. Ibid., p. 38.

46. Cocteau, *Journals*, p. 93.

47. Ibid., p. 94.

48. Cocteau, *The Hand of a Stranger*, trans. Alec Brown (London: Elek Books, 1956), p. 20.

49. Jacques Brosse, *Cocteau* (Paris: Gallimard, 1970), pp. 133–34; my translation.

50. This is not the only example of Baudelaire's interest in children. See his discussion of the analytic violence of children toward their toys in "La morale de joujou," *Oeuvres Complètes*, ed. Y.-G. Le Dantec (Paris: Editions Gallimard, 1961), pp. 523–29. In English "The Philosophy of Toys," in *The Painter of Modern Life and Other Essays* trans. and ed. Jonathan Mayne (Greenwich, Conn.: New York Graphic Society, 1965), pp. 197–203.

51. Charles Baudelaire, *The Painter of Modern Life*, trans. Jonathan Menpre (London: Phaidon, n.d.), pp. 7–8.

52. In a marvelously terse article on the painter Balthus, Guy Davenport finds the child-genius simile particularly French, and the separation of childhood from adulthood as an American debasement:

> Modern French writing has been interested in childhood and adolescence in a way that American and English writing has not. The French see not an innocent but an experienced mind in the child. Montherlant treats children as an endangered species needing protection from parents.
>
> Gide's understanding runs parallel, except that he makes allowance for the transformation to maturity. The child in Alain-Fournier, Proust, Colette, Cocteau inhabits a realm imaginatively animated with a genius very like that of the artist. Children live in their minds.
>
> Baudelaire saw genius as childhood sustained and perfected. There is a sense among the French that adulthood is a falling away from the intelligence of children. We in the United States contrast child and adult as we contrast ignorance and knowledge, innocence and experience. (Guy Davenport, "Balthus," *Antaeus* 39 [Autumn 1980]: 83)

Davenport is a critic who has occasionally written on the films of Stan Brakhage. Although he does not mention his work in this connection, he points to the European roots of Brakhage's treatment of childhood. See chapter 3.

53. Baudelaire, *Painter of Modern Life*, p. 6.

54. Cocteau, *Paris Album*, p. 54.

55. Roger Philandin, *Jean Cocteau tourne son dernier film* (Paris: La Table Ronde, 1960), p. 169. I wish to thank Ellen Burt for the translation.)

56. Cocteau, *Paris Album*, p. 79.

57. Letter in *France-Soir*, January 1952.

58. Cocteau, *Opium*, p. 46.

59. Neal Oxenhandler, *Scandal and Parade* (New Brunswick, N.J.: Rutgers University Press, 1957), p. 44.

60. "Leonardo da Vinci: A Psychosexual Study of an Infantile Reminiscence," in *Standard Edition of the Complete Psychological Works of Sigmund Freud*, ed. James Strachey (London: Hogarth Press, 1955), 11:59–137.

61. "Giovanni Segantini: A Psychoanalytical Study," in *Clinical Papers and Essays on Psychoanalysis*, trans. Hilda Abraham (London: Hogarth Press, 1955), pp. 210–61.

62. Ibid.

63. Karl Abraham, "Restrictions and Transformations in Scoptophilia in Psycho-Neurotics; with remarks on Analogous Phenomena in Folk Psychology," in *Selected Papers of Karl Abraham*, trans. Douglas Bryan and Alix Strachey (London: Hogarth Press, 1948), pp. 169–234.

64. Abraham, "Giovanni Segantini," trans. D. T. Carew *Psychoanalytic Quarterly* 6 (1937): 453–512.

65. Though Cocteau was little aware of the extent to which he was fascinated with children for an ulterior motive, he was not unaware of that mechanism in the work of others. In his "Hommage à Lewis Carroll," he shows that he shares a perception of children with Carroll. One understands why Carroll's photographs would appeal to Cocteau. In describing "their artful rags" ("leurs sournoise loques") and the "cruel cortege of motherless heroines" ("cortège cruel d'heroines sans mères"), he is not far from an accurate description of Carroll's representation of girls and completely within his own way of speaking of children. But it is the sexual interpretation he makes of the act of photographing itself that is interesting about the poem. The "virile lens" ("objectif mâle") and the vents that occur under the "black hood" ("capuchon noir")—with the double meaning of the photographer's cloth and the priest's robe—point to Carroll's sexual motivation for his art.

66. In the memoirs of Mme. Singer, Cocteau's cousin, she says: "Jean and I came home from a walk one day and were told that his father was dead. The news made little impression on us at the time—I remember that we were soon laughing and playing as usual. The word 'suicide' was never used in the family, but later I was told that my uncle had shot himself in the head with a pistol, in bed, and was found in a pool of blood. I never heard why he did it" (Steegmuller, *Cocteau*, p. 9).

67. Cocteau, *Opium*, p. 18.

68. Sigmund Freud, "Three Essays on the Theory of Sexuality," in *Standard Edition of the Complete Psychological Works of Sigmund Freud*, ed. James Strachey (London: Hogarth Press, 1955), 12:125–243.

69. Otto Fenichel, *The Psychoanalytic Theory of Neurosis* (New York: W. W. Norton, 1945).

70. Phyllis Greenacre, "The Influence of infantile Patterns," in *Emotional Growth* (New York: International University Press, 1971), pp. 260–99.

71. Jacob Arlow, "The Revenge Motive in the Primal Scene," *Journal of the American Psychoanalytic Association* 28 (1980): 530n.

72. P. Weissman, "Early Development and the Endowment of the Artistic Director," *Journal of the American Psychoanalytic Association* 12:59–79.

73. *Paris Album*, p. 36.

74. Cocteau's *Paris Album* can be read as an elucidation of the "Spectacles et Concerts" column in *Le Figaro* at the turn of the century. It is in that column that the Cinématographe was advertised, as well as other events and places Cocteau describes with enthusiasm. After 1896, films were playing all over Paris: the Grands Magasins Dufayel, the Châtelet, the Cigale, the Musée Oller, and most notably, the Folies Bérgère included films as part of their family entertainment programs. In 1899, the Cigale and the Folies Bérgère featured American Biograph films, which were reviewed with great excitement by the staff of *Le Figaro*. Although the advertisements for films were not large and the reviews infrequent, the overwhelming positive reaction on the part of the critics must have been infectious.

Paracinematic events were occurring simultaneously. Certainly the shows at the Théâtre Robert Houdin were the most noteworthy, but they were not isolated. While Méliès's "Le Pilori" and the "Rêve de Coppelius" were playing on the boulevard des Italiens, at the Châtelet (one of Cocteau's favorite places as a child) the *Seven Chateaux of the Devil*, a kind of show-play theater using moving projections, was featured. *Le Flouroscope* is advertised on 8 May 1896 as a "Vision directe et instantanée de l'Invisible" at the Café Riche. In 1901, on 27 January is advertised and reviewed with excitement "Mlle. Marguerite Lanya et M. Henrys Dahan dans leurs experience de 'Telegraphie humaine' et de Voyage à travers l'impossible." Both of these shows would become Méliès films of 1904. Shadow plays, and visions of saints, moving panoramas of exotic places were featured weekly.

75. *Paris Album*, p. 37.

76. *Paris Album*, p. 40.

77. The "Spectacles et Concerts" column of *Le Figaro* of those years coincides with many of the subjects of Cocteau's cinema. On 29 February 1896, the entire last page of the newspaper is filled with large type: " 'Orphée,' Opéra de Gluck," (then playing at the Opéra-Comique). On 8 January of the same year was advertised "La Belle et la Bête," a ballet at the Folies Bérgère. *Ruy*

Blas plays for years between 1899 and 1902 in several Paris theaters.

78. *Paris Album*, p. 75.

79. Cocteau, *Cocteau on the Film*, ed. André Fraigneau (New York: Dover, 1972), p. 17.

80. Walter Benjamin, "The Storyteller," in *Illuminations*, ed. Hannah Arendt (New York: Schocken Books, 1969), p. 89.

81. Ibid., p. 102.

82. As the smokestack falls, the narrator says, "While the cannons of Fontenoy thundered in the distance, a young man in a modest room . . ." Cocteau here recalls the hero of *Thomas the Impostor*, Guillaume de Fontenoy.

83. Cocteau, *Opéra* (Paris: Stock, 1927), p. 223.

84. Méliès's *Merry Deeds of Satan* (1905) is full of such magical appearances and disappearances. The devil, in the classic exchange of services for a human soul, offers an English engineer all wishes fulfilled. Riches and goods appear as Satan pops in and out of the image.

85. In the later films, disappearing is a sign of anger or desperation. Heurtebise and the Princess in *Orpheus* and Beauty in *Beauty and the Beast* all resort to disappearing as extreme measures.

86. Two recent manifestations in film theory of this metaphor for cinema are in Judith Mayne's "Woman at the Keyhole: Women's Cinema and Feminist Criticism," in *New German Critique* 23 (Spring/Summer 1981): 27–45; and E. Ann Kaplan's *Women and Film: Both Sides of the Camera* (New York: Methuen, 1983), chap. 1.

87. Cocteau, *Professional Secrets*, p. 15.

88. Siegfried Kracauer quotes Hugo von Hofmannsthal's "Ersatz fuer traeume," in which flying is described as a metaphor for film itself: "To sit in moviehouses and watch the screen . . . is like the ride through the air with the devil Asmodi who strips off all roofs, bares all secrets" (*Theory of Film: The Redemption of Physical Reality* [New York: Oxford University Press, 1965], p. 167.

89. Cocteau, *Opium*, p. 122.

90. Cocteau, *Two Screenplays*, trans. Carol Martin-Sperry (New York: Orion Press, 1968), pp. 24–27.

91. Elizabeth Sprigge and Jean-Jacques Kihm, eds., *Jean Cocteau: The Man and the Mirror* (New York: Coward-McCann, 1968), p. 25.

92. Cocteau, *Paris Album*, p. 79.

93. Cocteau, *Two Screenplays*, p. 3.

94. Cocteau, *Opium*, p. 71.

95. See Sigmund Freud, *Interpretation of Dreams*, trans. James Strachey (New York: Avon Books, 1965), pp. 305–7, 405, 428–29; and Paul Federn, "Dreams of Flying," in *The Psychoanalytic Reader*, ed. Robert Fliess (International University Press, 1948).

96. Frederick Brown, *An Impersonation of Angels* (New York: Viking Press, 1968), p. 297.

97. Cocteau, *Two Screenplays*, pp. 43–45.

98. Ibid., pp. 36–39.

99. Cocteau, *Professional Secrets*, p. 147.

100. Neal Oxenhandler interprets the entire scene in the courtyard as symbolical: "Through a flash-back we see the poet's childhood in which he acquires a symbolic wound and dies a symbolic death. . . . The film tells us something about the poet's responsibility to his art (it must be paid for with blood) and his total abnegation before it" ("Poetry in Three Films of Jean Cocteau," *Yale French Studies* 17 [1956]: 16).

101. André Breton, *Manifestoes of Surrealism*, trans. Richard Seaver and Helen R. Lane (Ann Arbor: University of Michigan Press, 1969), p. 3.

102. Breton, "Lettre à une jeune fille américaine," in *La clé des champs* (Paris: Pauvert, 1967), pp. 329–34.

103. For a discussion of the vicissitudes of the Cocteau-Breton relationship, see Steegmuller, *Cocteau*, pp. 225–27 and chap. 6; and Brown, *Impersonation of Angels*, chap. 9.

104. Steegmuller, *Cocteau*, p. 412. Written many years later, the surrealist-follower Jacques Brunius provides a marvelous description of the anti-Cocteau feeling evinced by *Blood of a Poet*:

During the shooting of *L'age d'or* (1930–31), the rumor circulated that when M. Cocteau had heard about Buñuel putting a cow in a bed he ran out and stuck a cow in his own film. . . . The cow of *Blood of a Poet* merely resembled a tasteful mantlepiece in the shop window of an effeminate interior decorator.

Actually, if you're going to expose M. Cocteau's artistic thefts, there are no end to them, not in his literature, not in his films; just take *the mouth in the hand* which comes from two scenes in *Un chien andalou* (the hand with an ant-hole—the hand wiping off the mouth, which gets replaced by pubic hair). A close look would reveal others of ths sort. Unfortunately for M. Cocteau, they are no longer showing Buñuel films. He is stuck copying himself again, which he does shamelessly. Happily he has already made enough films to have a large backlog of inspiration.

The violent impact of *L'age d'or* owes almost nothing to its technique, which is really relatively low budget when you compare it to the rich photographic effects of the excellent camera-man Georges Périnal, his assistant Louis Page and the technical director Michel Arnaud, all of whom lent their talents and their knowledge to the *Menstruations of a Poet*. (Jacques Brunius, *En marge du cinéma français*, Collection "Ombres Blanches" [Paris: Arcanes, 1954], pp. 141–43; translated by Marjorie Keller)

105. Steegmuller writes: " 'L'oiseau chante avec ses doigts . . .' is, according to Cocteau, a line that Apollinaire had once sent him in a letter" (*Cocteau*, p. 482).

106. I have discussed the autobiographical source of the term *zone* from *Paris Album* on page 23. However, it is important to note that the term had a resonance beyond Cocteau's specific usage at the time *Orpheus* was made. Paris had been an occupied "zone" throughout World War II.

107. The same metaphor will be used several years later by Stan Brakhage in *Reflections on Black* (1955). In that film, however, any humor is subsumed under the menacing violence of the scene.

108. This is unlike the most recent films of George Landow (Owen Land) where the disjunctive events are ironically accounted for at the end by the exclamation of a woman startled as she wakes, "Oh, it was a dream!"

109. Cocteau, *Coctea.: on the Film*, p. 62.

110. Stuart Liebman has pointed out to me that this comment is itself a reference to the famous comment by Courbet, "Show me an angel and I'll paint it."

111. Cocteau, *Cocteau on the Film*, p. 63.

112. Lewis Carroll, *Through the Looking Glass*, in *The Annotated Alice* (Clarkson N. Potter), p. 204.

113. I wish to thank Sue Ann Estevez for pointing this out to me.

114. They even share motives for creating such fanciful adventures: They both admitted the relevance of a child's-eye view to adult sensibilities. They both were blind to the sublimation of sexual content.

115. Cocteau, *Journals*, p. 46.

116. Freud, "Leonardo da Vinci."

117. Cocteau, *My Contemporaries*, p. 113.

118. Cocteau was unaware of the very scholarly criticism of Freud's piece on the grounds of mistranslations. Nor does he read the essay as Meyer Shapiro does, to find the superstructure of Freud's own obsessions in his analysis of Leonardo. This issue is taken up at length in Jack Spector, *The Aesthetics of Freud* (New York: Praeger, 1972).

119. Freud, "Leonardo da Vinci," pp. 59–137.

120. Cocteau, *Hand of a Stranger*, pp. 23–24.

121. Oxenhandler, *Scandal and Parade*, p. 27.

122. For an explication of the child's understanding of authority, see Jean Piaget, *The Moral Judgment of the Child*, trans. Marjorie Gabain (New York: Free Press, 1965), pp. 374–76.

123. Cocteau, *Hand of a Stranger*, p. 24.

124. Cocteau, *Paris Album*, p. 69.

125. Cocteau, *Beauty and the Beast*, trans. Robert Hammond (New York: NYU Press, 1970), prologue, p. iv. This volume includes the "Diary of a Film."

126. Cocteau, *Hand of a Stranger*, p. 24.

127. Steegmuller, *Cocteau*, p. 457.

128. Lydia Crowson, *The Esthetic of Jean Cocteau* (Hanover, N.H.: University Press of New England, 1978), pp. 117–18.

129. Piaget, *Play, Dreams and Imitation*, p. 250.

130. Cocteau, "On the Marvels of Cinematography," in *The Difficulty of Being*, trans. Elizabeth Sprigge (New York: Coward-McCann, 1967), p. 50.

131. Cocteau, *Beauty and the Beast*, p. 424.

132. Jean Epstein, "De quelques conditions de la photogénie," in *Ecrits sur le cinéma* (Paris: Seghers, 1974), 1:137–42; and other essays.

133. Cocteau, *Paris Album*, p. 52.

134. Ibid., p. 75.

135. Baudelaire, *Painter of Modern Life*, p. 2.

136. Brosse, *Cocteau*, p. 39.

137. Jonathan Cott, "Notes on Fairy Faith and the Idea of Childhood," in *Beyond the Looking Glass* (New York: Stonehill Publishing Co., 1973), p. xlvii.

138. Benjamin, *Illuminations*, pp. 108–9.

Chapter 2. Joseph Cornell

1. By "like Brakhage" I mean such lyrical, nonnarrative filmmakers as Marie Menken, Ken Jacobs, Jack Smith, Bruce Baillie, and many, many others.

2. *Vaudeville DeLuxe* was neither presented nor distributed in Cornell's lifetime. Because of its imagistic and structural relationship to *The Children's Party* trilogy, however, it will be discussed here.

3. I quote it here because I find it applicable to more than the study of *Rose Hobart*. It is useful in many respects when considering his other films as well:

1. The affirmative use of the frame
2. The use of found materials
3. Their assemblage or montage as the organizing principle
4. The play with, variation on, scale
5. The implication of temporal flow and its arrest
6. Narrative tension
7. Rhythmic use of compositional elements
8. Repetition and variation
9. The use of color, and of blue in particular, to make an ambiance of space
10. The use of other artworks as material
11. The interest in reverse sides and angles
12. The female portrait as a privileged genre.

(Annette Michelson, "Rose Hobart and Monsieur Phot: Early Films from Utopia Parkway," in *Artforum* 10 [June 1973]: 54)

4. See Cornell's collection of letters and papers, on microfilm at the Archives of American Art, Smithsonian Institution, Washington, D.C. (Uncataloged).

5. "La femme réelle révoltait notre ingénuité; il fallait qu'elle apparût reine ou déesse, et surtout n'en pas approcher."

6. Kynaston McShine, ed., *Joseph Cornell* (New York: Museum of Modern Art, 1980), pls. 48, 236.

7. Johann Wolfgang von Goethe, *Wilhelm Meister's Apprenticeship and Travels*, trans. Thomas Carlyle (London: Chapman and Hall, 1824), pp. 104–5.

8. William Empson, *Some Versions of Pastoral* (London: Chatto and Windus, 1935), pp. 253–54.

9. Ibid., p. 260. This is the same kind of photograph that Cocteau described in his "Hommage à Lewis Carroll."

248 THE UNTUTORED EYE

10. Ibid., pp. 268–69, 273.

11. It is possible to interpret the conflation as a manifestation of homosexuality. In the cases of Carroll and Cornell, however, there is no evidence with which to even begin to make such a claim.

12. Among his books is an issue of *Yale French Studies* (vol. 13) subheaded *Romanticism Revisited.* That issue contains an article on Balzac's *Seraphita,* a novel about a girl perceived as a boy and a girl by two lovers of the opposite sex. The novel is described in the article with Cornellian flair: "une histoire vraiment céleste."

13. Howard Hussey pointed this out to me in conversation in the spring of 1981.

14. Joseph Cornell, "Enchanted Wanderer—Excerpt from a Journey Album for Hedy Lamarr," *View* 9/10 (December 1941/January 1942): 3.

15. Jean Piaget, *The Language and Thought of the Child,* trans. Marjorie Gabain (New York: New American Library, 1974), p. 28.

16. This notion, filtered through the writing of Emerson, is a central tenet of Brakhage's aesthetic. See chapter 4.

17. As a bookmark between pages 122 and 123, Cornell used an obituary. The man eulogized is Alvin G. Lustig, a graphic designer who continued to work after he lost his sight. The peculiarity of such a story, told so economically as the account of the life of a man, would have appealed to Cornell. A man who made his living as Cornell had, as a commercial artist, whose talent or fortitude was so great that he would not be defeated by a major handicap to his profession, is a poignant, nearly impossible story. To be a blind visual artist is to surpass the physical limits of any medium and enter the realm of a purely spiritual relationship to one's tools. Though applied to graphic and industrial design, this transcendence must have seemed fabulous to Cornell, who felt his own work to be mere "tokens and traces" of a more ephemeral reality. Moreover, Cornell was committed to the work of his brother Robert, another severely handicapped person, who produced artwork Cornell admired.

18. Piaget, *Language and Thought,* pp. 122–23.

19. For a more detailed discussion of *Rose Hobart,* see Michelson, "Rose Hobart and Monsieur Phot," pp. 47–57; and P. Adams Sitney, "The Cinematic Gaze of Joseph Cornell," in *Joseph Cornell,* ed. Kynaston McShine, MOMA, pp. 74–78.

20. Carter Ratcliff, in the MOMA catalog, is particularly prone to this kind of titillation.

21. Otto Fenichel, "The Symbolic Equation: Girl = Phallus," in *Collected Essays,* vol. 2 (New York: W. W. Norton, 1954).

22. Ibid., p. 4.

23. I have not read this article, which appears in the German psychoanalytic journal *Imago* 19 (1933).

24. Fenichel, "Symbolic Equation," pp. 10–11.

25. *Joseph Cornell,* ed. Kynaston McShine, MOMA, pl. 100.

26. Lynda Roscoe Hartigan, "Joseph Cornell: A Biography," in *Joseph Cornell,* ed. Kynaston McShine, MOMA, p. 112.

27. *Joseph Cornell,* ed. Kynaston McShine, MOMA, pl. 260.

28. Fenichel, "Symbolic Equation," p. 13.

29. Ibid., p. 8.

30. Conference on "Working with Cornell," 26 March 1976, Anthology Film Archives, New York.

31. Stan Brakhage lecture, School of the Art Institute of Chicago, Spring 1972.

32. *Bookstalls,* a Cornell film not discussed here, contains the counterpoint of both aspects of travel within its parenthetical structure. Ostensibly about travel and other cultures, the film is bounded by the subjective experience of a boy wandering through the bookstalls along the Seine as he leafs through books. It begins and ends with his reading, making the people represented in the travelogue the objects of his imagination.

33. It is interesting to note the difference between Cornell's use of the footage for *A Legend* and Rudy Burckhardt's for *What Mozart Saw on Mulberry Street* (1965). By using the Mozart bust as the mediating figure in the film, and intercutting the bust in the way that Cornell intercuts the Lorca poem, Burckhardt extols the passive nonintervention of the statue in the street life. The play

of the children and the birds becomes limited to its own lyricism instead of being replete with possible meaning.

34. *Joseph Cornell,* ed. Kynaston McShine, MOMA, p. 8.

35. The name that Cornell gave to his house has a special history. Clearly he named it thus because of its tower; however, there is another Tower House, now commemorated with a large sign on its front porch, on Broadway in Nyack, New York, down the street from where Cornell grew up.

36. Stan Brakhage lecture, School of the Art Institute of Chicago, undated recording.

37. Cornell kept a book called *Poetry and Children* in his library. There is a passage in the chapter "Poetry and Films" that is germane in the context of Cornell's use of Dickinson's poem: "Several keen amateur photographers have found delight in trying to make films to match particular poems. They take hundreds of shots and then select and arrange them to reflect as sensitively and artistically as possible the imagery and changing mood of the poem" (Committee of Yorkshire Teachers, foreword by Bonamy Dobrée, *Poetry and Children* [London: Methuen and Co., 1956], p. 72).

38. Norman Talbot, "The Child, the Actress, and Miss Emily Dickinson," *Southern Review* (June 1972): 108–9.

39. Sitney, in "The Cinematic Gaze of Joseph Cornell," does not consider *The Aviary* among the films with mediators. He ignores the woman who appears, albeit briefly, in the beginning of the film.

40. This statue will set the scene for the adventures of the photographer in Cornell's scenario, *Monsieur Phot.* In the illustration that accompanies the scenario reproduced in, P. Adams Sitney, ed., *The Avant-Garde Film: A Reader of Theory and Criticism* (New York: NYU Press, 1978), the raised statue is used as the background to the "urchins" who pose for the photograph. Cornell whimsically proposes, later, a snowstorm so great that the horse would appear to be running over the snow.

41. Kynaston McShire, ed., *Joseph Cornell,* pl 34.

42. Whitman edition of collected poems in the Joseph Cornell Study Center, Washington, D.C. Here I am thinking particularly of Whitman's "To You" from "Birds of Passage."

43. I have discussed this in view of the "Flying Lesson" sequence of Cocteau's *Blood of a Poet.*

44. Freud, *Interpretation of Dreams,* pp. 428–29.

45. Ariès, *Centuries of Childhood,* p. 124.

46. Lynda Hartigan, of the Joseph Cornell Study Center, has discovered an illuminating set of illustrations, which Cornell had cut or prepared to cut out, presumably for use in collages. They are from Oscar Wilde, *The Young King and Other Fairy Tales* (New York: Macmillan and Co., 1962), with drawings from an Italian edition. The story of "The Happy Prince" is illustrated with a series of drawings of a swallow who, sent by the Prince, performs good deeds. Cornell singled out those areas of the image in which the bird is seen in its immediate context: visiting a sick boy, perched on the shoulder of the Prince, and flying amid the rigging of a ship. They are powerful Cornellian images, ready-made. Within the fantasy, the bird represents the kind soul of the Prince.

47. In her talk at Anthology Film Archives, Thomas said that Cornell had told her she was a young girl returning home from a ball. While looking up at the trees, she forgets her parasol (Conference on "Working with Cornell," 26 March 1976, Anthology Film Archives, New York).

48. Sitney, "Cinematic Gaze," p. 85.

49. This shot is used again in *Angel,* as the next to the last shot. It is difficult to ascertain which fountain it comes from.

50. "Working with Cornell."

51. *Dance Index* 9 (September 1945): 155–59.

52. There is a letter from Cornell to Jay Leyda on the occasion of the editing of *The Children's Party.* It is dated 15 November 1938. "Dear Jay, I have just completed a rough (very rough, in fact) draft of the children's party film—you've probably since forgotten that I have ever started one. I was wondering if I could come over to the museum and run it off, with you on the sidelines to throw in a little encouragement—if it deserves it. Could we view it alone, do you think, some night this week around five? Would appreciate your giving me a ring at Col. 5-2090 if it is convenient for

you. I'm very anxious to get somewhere with it. Also have a new Newsreel, all my own this time, that I haven't seen projected yet. Best regards, Joe Cornell." Cornell file compiled by Sean Licka, Anthology Film Archives, New York.

53. Though the films seem whimsically structured and repetitive, if studied with an eye to the overabundance of meaning within each shot and between shots, their interpretation becomes unique and rich. Cornell was hesitant to show his films, these in particular. This forms a major obstacle in trying to make a detailed analysis of any of his films except for *Rose Hobart*. Biographical reports and documentary evidence show that Cornell released his films reluctantly to the public and was never completely at ease with their final versions. It is a particularly tricky problem since there are many very short shots that may have been at the end or the beginning of a desired shot. They may have been left only to assure enough footage for splicing the final version. It is impossible to know the source of Cornell's uneasiness. If he was concerned that he had not spent enough time or did not have the expertise to make a really satisfying film, then one may dismiss any number of shots in the films as mistakes or, at least, loose ends. If, however, Cornell's concern was that his filmic vision was too complex, too strange to be understood by his viewers, or that it would cause an uproar like Dali's after the first screening of *Rose Hobart* (an event of such naked envy as to traumatize Cornell, according to Julian Levy's *Memoir of an Art Gallery*), then it is likely that the many puzzling single-frame images and brief titles were purposefully inserted by Cornell, to act as subliminal visuals or secret "signs," known only to himself or select viewers. For the purpose of this dissertation, I have taken this second view. Cornell was a meticulous artist and filled his boxes and collages with a superabundance of detail. Like the intricacies of his boxes, some frames of the films are invisible to the casual viewer. (Here I am thinking of the *Untitled* [Paul and Virginia] construction in particular, which is hinged, containing many small compartments within it, and collaged on the back.) There is no reason to believe he would not do the same in his films, hiding images by cutting them short. There is as yet no description, and certainly no analysis, of those brief images, to ascertain if they have any place in the overall scheme of a given film. I find that, except for a small number of arcane images for which I can find no source, most shots do fit into the broader structure and theme of the films as if they were meant to be there.

54. Lest there be any confusion, although the editing of the trilogy is ascribed to Larry Jordan, Jordan claims to have only cement-spliced shots that were already taped together by Cornell. In addition, he supervised the making of freeze frames where, and for the duration that, Cornell indicated.

55. There is some confusion about which film belongs to which title. P. Adams Sitney, in his essay "The Cinematic Gaze of Joseph Cornell," has called the film that begins "The End" (upside down and backward) *The Midnight Party*. Anthology Film Archives and the Canyon Cinema Cooperative call that film *The Children's Party*. Because of the nature of the imagery and subject, I hold that the Anthology and Canyon titles are the correct ones and will write about the films accordingly.

56. There is a third possible aspect that Sitney points out in his discussion of Duchamp and Cornell ("Cinematic Gaze," p. 81): that the inverted image comes from Christian Science. The point does not seem relevant here.

57. He had requested of Stan Brakhage that he film from inside the Third Avenue Elevated in Manhattan. Brakhage, misunderstanding that Cornell wished him to film from the inside of the train *out*, into the windows and apartments visible from the El, shot a film that remained almost entirely inside the cars of the train. Light, reflections in metal and glass, and swaying movement form Brakhage's film titled *as* a Brakhage film, *Wonder Ring*. Cornell, dissatisfied with the interiorization of what he saw as a highly voyeuristic experience, found another use for the footage. He turned the footage of the Third Avenue El, shot by Stan Brakhage, upside down and backward. It became graphically "flattened" and abstracted. He attached an end title to the film, "The End Is the Beginning."

58. Freud, Sigmund, *On Creativity and the Unconscious*, ed. Benjamin Nelson (New York: Harper and Row, 1958).

59. Ibid., p. 61.

60. This insight I owe to Rebecca Sky Sitney. As a ten-year-old, she was able to see an oddity in

the shot that I passed over repeatedly. Her perception of transvestism in the trilogy reconfirmed for me the fact that Cornell was presenting imagery of such a type and in such a way that children were often better equipped to perceive than adults.

61. Cornell, file compiled by Sean Licka, Anthology Film Archives, New York.

62. This information was obtained in a conversation with Cornell's sister, Elizabeth Benton, Autumn 1976.

63. Carter Ratcliff, "Joseph Cornell: Mechanic of the Ineffable," in *Joseph Cornell*, ed. Kynaston McShine, MOMA.

64. Sitney, "Cinematic Gaze," p. 81.

65. Ibid., p. 75.

66. "Mickey's Circus" is one of the films Cornell left, as part of his collection, to Anthology Film Archives.

67. *The Poems of Emily Dickinson*, ed. Thomas Johnson (Cambridge: Harvard University Press, 1955), pp. 55–56.

68. A film was also made from the book, which Cornell has among his collection, now at Anthology Film Archives.

69. This phrase is elucidated by Sitney in "Cinematic Gaze," p. 74.

70. Minstrel shows were part of the vaudeville circuit in Cornell's childhood. He surely saw many of them, although I can find record of only one in Nyack—14, 15, and 16 October 1912 at the Lyceum Theater: "A Real Big Colored Show 'The Florida Troubadours' . . . featuring their Mastodon Minstrel First Part High Class Vaudeville, concluding with a funny afterpiece."

Chapter 3. Stan Brakhage

1. In *Stan Brakhage: A Guide to References and Resources* (Boston: G. K. Hall, 1983), Gerald Barrett and Wendy Brabner record an early story by Brakhage, "3 Deaths and the Child," which was published in *Bittersweet Stories and Poems from Scholastic Writing Awards*, edited by Jerome Brondfield (New York: Scholastic Book Services, n.d.), pp. 231–42. "This short story, written in 1951 by high school student 'Stanley' Brakhage, leads off a section devoted to the best student writings from the fifties. The story pre-figures many Brakhage motifs: death, trees, cats, dogs, children, autobiography, and, to some degree, *Unglassed Windows Cast a Terrible Reflection*, made two years later" (Barrett and Brabner, *Stan Brakhage: A Guide*, p. 271).

2. *The Extraordinary Child* is a film that Brakhage made in 1954. It was withdrawn from circulation after it was released. The only material available about it is in Barrett and Brabner, *Stan Brakhage: A Guide*, in which Brakhage is quoted: "Attempting to make a slapstick film was the biggest mistake in film I ever made" (p. 11).

In *Flesh of Morning* (1956), Brakhage looks out of the window to see children playing below. They are a metaphor for innocence in counterpoint to Brakhage's lurid self-portrait. They are, however, relatively unimportant in the scope of the film. A hundred-foot roll of film closely resembling that of the children in *Flesh of Morning* was sent by Brakhage to Joseph Cornell. It was recently discovered at Anthology Film Archives with Cornell's other film material. In it, children play on the street, seen from above, behind grillwork and plants. The camera follows the lines of the grillwork and the movement of the children. Sometimes the children look at the camera. I take this roll of film to be but one more indication of the shared interest of Brakhage and Cornell in childhood.

3. The phrase "make it new" has functioned as an inspiration for American poets for most of this century. Of interest here is the fact that it turns up in poets's autobiographical writings in the same manner as Diaghilev's command to Cocteau, "Astonish me." For Robert Duncan, certainly, it functioned as the catalyst to his poetic career.

4. See, for example, Gertrude Stein, *Tender Buttons* (New York: Haskell House 1970).

5. Ralph Waldo Emerson, "The American Scholar," in *The Works of Ralph Waldo Emerson* (New York: Walter J. Black, n.d.), pp. 560–61.

6. Stan Brakhage, *Metaphors on Vision* (New York: Film Culture, 1963), (p. 19). The pages of

this book are not numbered. My system begins on the first page of the interview, after the introduction.

7. Emerson, "American Scholar," p. 563.

8. Ibid., p. 566; emphasis mine. Brakhage might argue with Emerson's conclusion, insofar as the riddle—Emerson's "puzzle"—is a significant form for Brakhage.

9. Charles Olson, "Proprioception," in *Additional Prose*, ed. George Butterick (Bolinas, Calif.: Four Seasons Foundation, 1974), pp. 14–35.

10. Brakhage, *Metaphors on Vision*, p. 69.

11. For a discussion of Brakhage's musical influences see Brakhage, "Letter to Ronna Page (On Music)," in *The Avant-Garde Film: A Reader of Theory and Criticism*, ed. P. Adams Sitney (New York: NYU Press, 1978), pp. 134–38.

12. Gertrude Stein, *Writings and Lectures, 1909–1945*, ed. Patricia Meyerowitz (New York: Penguin, 1967), p. 106.

13. Brakhage connects Stein's notion of "daily life" with children's language explicitly in the volume of letters by his children, *Letters From/On "HI!"* The frontispiece reads:

> Letters From/On "HI!"
> —by the Brakhage Children
> Dedicated
> (by one—Stan Brakhage)
> to
> Gertrude Stein
> (who would be nowise
> surprised by them,
> confirming as they do
> her ear's hearing of
> the roots of language)

(Photocopy in Brakhage file, Anthology Film Archives, New York)

14. Brakhage, *Metaphors on Vision*, p. 21.

15. Ariès, *Centuries of Childhood*, p. 110.

16. Brakhage, *Metaphors on Vision*, p. 21.

17. Ibid.

18. Ibid., p. 26.

19. Ibid., p. 31.

20. Ibid., p. 44.

21. Ibid., p. 30.

22. Ibid., p. 44.

23. Scenario submitted to and rejected by a foundation for grants to artists, 1960, in ibid., p. 45.

24. Brakhage is quoting from Novalis, *Henry von Ofterdingen*, trans. Palmer Hilty (New York: Frederick Ungar, 1964), p. 106. The passage is from a dream of Henry's. The other speaker is Mathilda, his first love and alter ego in the novel.

25. Brakhage, *Metaphors on Vision*, p. 45.

26. Ibid., p. 75.

27. Brakhage, *Film Biographies*, p. 7.

28. Ibid., p. 83.

29. Ibid., pp. 84, 86, 92, 107.

30. Ibid., p. 119.

31. Ibid., p. 135.

32. Ibid., p. 17.

33. Ibid., p. 84.

34. Ibid., p. 119.

35. Brakhage, *Metaphors on Vision*, p. 64.

36. Ibid., p. 73.

37. Emerson, "The Poet," in *The Works of Ralph Waldo Emerson*, p. 210.

38. Unlike *The Art of Vision* or *The Text of Light*, which are filmic illustrations of some varieties of visual experience.

39. Marie Nesthus, "The Influences of Olivier Messian on the Visual Art of Stan Brakhage," *Film Culture* 63–64 (1977): pp. 39–51, 179–81.

40. P. Adams Sitney, *Visionary Film: The American Avant-Garde, 1943–79* (New York: Oxford University Press, 1979).

41. Fred Camper, "Seminar on Stan Brakhage Taught by P. Adams Sitney," unpublished manuscript (New York University, Spring 1974).

42. Phoebe Cohen, " 'Scenes from under Childhood,' " *Artforum* 5 (January 1973): 51–55.

43. Letter to Ken Jacobs, ca. 1973, Brakhage file, Anthology Film Archives, New York.

44. Lecture at New York University, 23 June 1975, transcribed by Gloria Forster, Brakhage file, Anthology Film Archives, New York, p. 6.

45. Sitney, *Visionary Film*, p. 422.

46. Brakhage reputedly has an equally negative attitude toward documentary film. See Richard Grossinger, ed., "Interview with Stan Brakhage," in *Earth Geography/Io* 3 (Summer 1972): 354.

47. Piaget, *Play, Dreams and Imitation*, chap. 4 and passim.

48. Letter to Jerome Hill, 9 December 1970, Brakhage file, Anthology Film Archives, New York.

49. Piaget, *The Child's Conception of Physical Causality*, trans. M. Gabain (Totowa, N.J.: Littlefield, Adams and Co., 1966), p. 113.

50. Guy Davenport, "Two Essays on Brakhage and His *Songs*," *Film Culture* 40 (Spring 1966): 12.

51. This is most vibrantly true in *Films by Stan Brakhage: An Avant-Garde Home Movie*.

52. Filmmakers' Cooperative Catalogue No. 6, (New York, 1975), p. 30.

53. Brakhage, *Metaphors on Vision*, p. 68.

54. A light leak normally at the beginning and end of a roll of film.

55. As Baudelaire does; see p. 34.

56. For one example; see Richard Whitehall, "Brakhage Sees the World Hypnogogically," *Los Angeles Free Press* (February 1967).

57. As later, in *Duplicity I*, he will be unable to break his own mesmerized stare at his daughter crying.

58. Brakhage, Millennium Lecture, New York, 27 March 1981.

59. This film was made after the release of Cornell's collage film, *By Night with Torch and Spear*, and bears a number of similar traits. I do not know if Brakhage made *Murder Psalm* before having seen the Cornell film. It is certain, however, that he was thoroughly familiar with the earlier collages.

60. In many of the *Songs*, and innummerable later films, Brakhage cuts from orange-colored imagery to flares, or vice versa.

61. Arlow, "Revenge Motive," pp. 519–42. Arlow points to Freud's writings of 1900, 1905, 1917, 1918, 1925 and 1939 to substantiate his claim.

62. Ray L. Birdwhistell, *Kinesis and Context* (Philadelphia: University of Pennsylvania Press, 1970), pp. 29–39.

63. There is disagreement about the meaning of this image in *23rd Psalm Branch*. See Sitney, *Visionary Film*, pp. 450–51, n. 24.

64. Brakhage, *Metaphors on Vision*, p. 64.

65. His interest in these matters became evident to me as a student of Brakhage's at the School of the Art Institute of Chicago, 1971–73. It was conveyed in screenings, lectures, and reading assignments.

66. Bruno Bettelheim, *The Uses of Enchantment* (New York: Alfred A. Knopf, 1977), pp. 166–83.

67. Sigmund Freud, "Family Romances," in *Standard Edition*, 9:237–41.

68. Sitney, *Visionary Film*, p. 175.

Chapter 4. Convergences

1. In *Visionary Film*, Sitney persuasively stated the case for European romanticism as the primary influence on American avant-garde film.

2. Jean Jacques Rousseau, *Emile*, trans. Allan Bloom (New York: Basic Books, 1979), preface, p. 34. This is very like Brakhage's exhortation to "deeply perceive one's own children" in *Metaphors on Vision*, p. 21.

3. For example, see Novalis, *Henry von Ofterdingen*, p. 163.

4. Ibid., p. 161.

5. Samuel Taylor Coleridge, *Biographia Literaria,* ed. J. Shawcross (London: Oxford University Press, 1907), p. 97.

6. See p. 34.

7. This is now at the Joseph Cornell Study Center in Washington, D.C. I wish to thank Lynda Hartigan for finding it for me.

8. McShine, ed., *Joseph Cornell*, pl. 269.

9. See "Untitled (Andromeda; Grand Hôtel de l'Observatoire; Grand Hôtel de l'Universe)," in ibid., pl. 211; and Cocteau's drawing for the opening logo of *Orpheus.*

10. Cocteau, *Cocteau on the Film,* pp. 40–41.

11. Stan Brakhage, School of the Art Institute of Chicago lecture, 8 January 1973.

12. Brakhage, "Letter to Ronna Page," pp. 134–38.

13. Brakhage, School of the Art Institute of Chicago lecture, undated recording.

14. Ibid.

15. Cocteau, *Cocteau on the Film,* pp. 22–23.

16. Brakhage, School of the Art Institute of Chicago lecture, undated recording.

17. Brakhage, *Metaphors on Vision,* p. 44.

18. Sigmund Freud, "The Dream Work," in *Interpretation of Dreams,* pp. 353–74.

19. Brakhage, School of the Art Institute of Chicago lecture, Spring 1972.

BIBLIOGRAPHY

General Bibliography of Psychological, Literary, and Other Sources

Abraham, Karl. "Giovanni Segantini: A Psychoanalytical Study." In *Clinical Papers and Essays on Psychoanalysis,* translated by Hilda Abraham, pp. 210–61. London: Hogarth Press, 1955.

———. "Restrictions and Transformations of Scoptophilia in Psycho-Neurotics: With Remarks on Analogous Phenomena in Folk Psychology." In *Selected Papers of Karl Abraham,* translated by Douglas Bryan and Alix Strachey, pp. 169–234. London: Hogarth Press, 1948.

Aiken, H. D. "The Aesthetic Relevance of Artists' Intentions." *Journal of Philosophy* 52 (24 November 1955): 724–53.

Ariès, Philippe. *Centuries of Childhood: A Social History of Family Life.* Translated by Robert Baldick. New York: Random House, 1962.

Arlow, Jacob. "The Revenge Motive in the Primal Scene." *Journal of the American Psychoanalytic Association* 28 (1980): 519–42.

Balzac, Honoré de. *Seraphita and Other Stories.* Translated by Clara Bell. Philadelphia: Gerbie Publishing Co., 1898.

Baudelaire, Charles. *The Painter of Modern Life.* Translated by Jonathan Menpre. London: Phaidon Books, n.d.

Benjamin, Walter. *Illuminations.* Edited by Hannah Arendt. New York: Schocken Books, 1969.

Bettelheim, Bruno. *The Uses of Enchantment.* New York: Alfred A. Knopf, 1977.

Birdwhistell, Ray L. *Kinesis and Context.* Philadelphia: University of Pennsylvania Press, 1970.

Breton, André. *La clé des champs.* Paris: Pauvert, 1967.

———. *Manifestoes of Surrealism.* Translated by Richard Seaver and Helen R. Lane. Ann Arbor: University of Michigan Press, 1969.

Carroll, Lewis. *The Complete Works of Lewis Carroll.* New York: Modern Library, n.d.

———. *Lewis Carroll Photographer.* Edited by Helmut Gernsheim. New York: Dover, 1969.

Cioffi, Frank. "Intention and Interpretation in Criticism." *Proceedings of the Aristotelian Society* 64 (1963–64): 85–106.

Cott, Jonathan, ed. *Beyond the Looking Glass.* New York: Stonehill Publishing Co., 1973.

Coleridge, Samuel Taylor. *Biographia Literaria.* Edited by J. Shawcross. London: Oxford University Press, 1907.

Davenport, Guy. "Balthus." *Antaeus* 39 (Autumn, 1980): 80–89.

Dickinson, Emily. *The Poems of Emily Dickinson.* Edited by Thomas Johnson. Cambridge: Harvard University Press, 1955.

Duncan, Robert. *Caesar's Gate.* N.p. Sand Dollar, 1972.

———. *The Opening of the Field.* New York: Evergreen Press, 1960.

Emerson, Ralph Waldo. *The Works of Ralph Waldo Emerson.* New York: Walter J. Black, n.d.

Empson, William. *Some Versions of Pastoral.* London: Chatto and Windus, 1935.

Federn, Paul. "Dreams of Flying." In *The Psychoanalytic Reader,* edited by Robert Fleiss, New York: International University Press, 1948.

Fenichel, Otto. *The Psychoanalytic Theory of Neurosis.* New York: W. W. Norton, 1945.

———. "The Symbolic Equation: Girl = Phallus." In *Collected Essays.* New York: W. W. Norton, 1954.

Freud, Sigmund. "The Antithetical Sense of Primal Words" (1910). In *Collected Papers,* 4:184–91. Translated under supervision of Joan Riviere. London: Hogarth Press, 1953.

———. "Family Romances." In *Standard Edition of the Complete Psychological Works of Sigmund Freud,* edited by James Strachey, 9:237–41. London: Hogarth Press, 1955.

———. *Interpretation of Dreams.* Translated by James Strachey. New York: Avon Books, 1965.

———. "Leonardo da Vinci: A Psychosexual Study of an Infantile Reminiscence." In *Standard Edition of the Complete Psychological Works of Sigmund Freud,* edited by James Strachey, 11:59–137. London: Hogarth Press, 1955.

———. *Moses and Monotheism.* New York: Random House, 1939.

———. *On Creativity and the Unconscious.* Edited by Benjamin Nelson. New York: Harper and Row, 1958.

———. "Three Essays on the Theory of Sexuality." In *Standard Edition of the Complete Psychological Works of Sigmund Freud,* edited by James Strachey, 12:125–243 London: Hogarth Press, 1955.

Goethe, Johann Wolfgang von. *The Sorrows of Young Werther.* Translated by Elizabeth Mayer and Louise Bogan. New York: Vintage, 1971.

———. *Wilhelm Meister's Apprenticeship and Travels.* Translated by Thomas Carlyle. London: Chapman and Hall, 1824.

Greenacre, Phyllis. "The Influence of Infantile Patterns." In *Emotional Growth*, pp. 260–99. New York: International University Press, 1971.

Kingsley, Charles. *The Water Babies.* London: Macmillan and Co., 1924.

Levy, Julian. *Memoir of an Art Gallery.* New York: Putnam, 1977.

Nerval, Gerard de. *"Aurélia" et "Les filles de feu."* Paris: Gallimard, 1972.

Novalis [Friedrich von Hardenberg]. *Henry von Ofterdingen.* Translated by Palmer Hilty. New York: Frederick Ungar, 1964.

———. *Hymns to the Night.* Translated by Dick Higgins. New York: Treacle Press, 1978.

Olson, Charles. *Additional Prose.* Edited by George Butterick. Bolinas, Calif. Four Seasons Foundation, 1974.

———. *Maximus Poems.* New York: Jargon/Corinth Books, 1960.

Piaget, Jean. *The Child's Conception of Movement and Speed.* Translated by G. E. T. Holloway and M. J. Mackenzie. New York: Ballantine Books, 1970.

———. *The Child's Conception of Physical Causality.* Translated by M. Gabain. Totowa, N.J.: Littlefield, Adams and Co., 1966.

———. *The Child's Conception of Space.* Translated by F. J. Langdon and J. L. Junzer. New York: W. W. Norton, 1967.

———. *The Child's Conception of Time.* Translated by A. J. Pomerans. New York: Ballantine Books, 1971.

———. *The Language and Thought of the Child.* Translated by Marjorie Gabain. New York: New American Library, 1974.

———. *The Moral Judgment of the Child.* Translated by Marjorie Gabain. New York: Free Press, 1965.

———. *The Origins of Intelligence in Children.* Translated by Margaret Cook. New York: W. W. Norton, 1963.

———. *Play, Dreams and Imitation in Childhood.* Translated by C. Gattegno and F. M. Hodgson. New York: W. W. Norton, 1962.

———. *Six Psychological Studies.* Translated by Anita Tenzer. New York: Vintage Books, 1968.

Rank, Otto. *The Myth of the Birth of the Hero.* Edited by Phillip Freund. New York: Random House, 1964.

Rousseau, Jean Jacques. *Emile.* Translated by Allan Bloom. New York: Basic Books, 1979.

Spector, Jack. *The Aesthetics of Freud.* New York: Praeger, 1972.

Stein, Gertrude. *Four in America.* Introduction by Thornton Wilder. New Haven: Yale University Press, 1947.

———. *The Making of Americans.* New York: Something Else Press, 1966.

———. *Narration.* Chicago: University of Chicago Press, 1935.

———. *Tender Buttons.* New York: Haskell House, 1970.

————. *Writings and Lectures, 1909–1945*. Edited by Patricia Meyerowitz. New York: Penguin, 1967.

Talbot, Norman. "The Child, the Actress, and Miss Emily Dickinson." *Southern Review* (June 1972): 102–24.

Weissman, P. "Early Development and the Endowment of the Artistic Director." *Journal of the American Psychoanalytic Association* 12:59–79.

Whitman, Walt. *The Complete Poems*. Edited by Francis Murphy. Hammondsworth: Penguin, 1975.

Wimsatt, W. K. *The Verbal Icon*. Lexington: University of Kentucky Press, 1954.

Woolf, Virginia. *Orlando*. New York: Harcourt Brace Jovanovich, 1956.

Wordsworth, William. *Poetical Works*. London: Oxford University Press, 1928.

Yale French Studies: Romanticism Revisited 13 (1954).

General Bibliography of Film History and Theory

Arnheim, Rudolf. *Film as Art*. Berkeley and Los Angeles: University of California Press, 1967.

Balázs, Béla. *Theory of the Film (Character and Growth of a New Art)*. London: Dennis Dobson, 1931.

Bazin, André. *What Is Cinema?* Berkeley and Los Angeles: University of California Press, 1967.

Braudy, Leo. *The World in a Frame*. New York: Anchor/Doubleday, 1977.

Burch, Noël. *Theory of Film Practice*. Princeton: Princeton University Press, 1969.

Cavell, Stanley. *The World Viewed*. Cambridge: Harvard University Press, 1979.

Curtis, David. *Experimental Cinema*. New York: Universe Books, 1971.

Deren, Maya. *Film Culture* 39 (1965). The writings of Maya Deren and Ron Rice.

Eisenstein, Sergei. *Film Essays with a Lecture*. Edited by Jay Leyda. London: Dennis Dobson, 1968.

————. *Film Form: The Film Sense*. Translated and edited by Jay Leyda. New York: Meridian Books, 1957.

Epstein, Jean. *Ecrits sur le cinéma*. Paris: Seghers, 1974.

————. *Esprit du cinéma*. Paris: Les Editions Jeheber, 1955.

Farber, Manny. *Negative Space*. New York: Praeger, 1971.

Kaplan, E. Ann. *Women and Film: Both Sides of the Camera*. New York: Methuen, 1983.

Kracauer, Siegfried. *Theory of Film: The Redemption of Physical Reality*. New York: Oxford University Press, 1965.

Le Grice, Malcolm. *Abstract Film and Beyond*. Cambridge: MIT Press, 1977.

Mayne, Judith. "Woman at the Keyhole: Women's Cinema and Feminist Criticism." *New German Critique* 23 (Spring/Summer 1981): 27–45.

Mekas, Jonas. *Movie Journal.* New York: Collier, 1972.

Renan, Sheldon. *Introduction to the American Underground Film.* New York: Dutton, 1967.

Sitney, P. Adams. *Visionary Film: The American Avant-Garde 1943–79.* New York: Oxford University Press, 1979.

Sitney, P. Adams, ed. *The Avant-Garde Film: A Reader of Theory and Criticism.* New York: NYU Press, 1978.

———. *The Essential Cinema.* New York: Anthology Film Archives and NYU Press, 1975.

———. *Film Culture Reader.* New York: Praeger, 1970.

Tyler, Parker. *The Three Faces of the Film.* New York: Thomas Yoseloff Publishers, 1960.

Vertov, Dziga. *Articles, journaux, projets.* Edited by Christian Bourgeois. Paris: Union Générale d'Editions, 1972.

Cocteau

Armes, Roy. "Jean Cocteau." In *French Film,* chapter 2, "From Avant-Garde to Occupation," pp. 39–44. New York: E. P. Dutton, 1970.

Beylie, Claude. *L'Avant Scène du Cinéma* 56 (February 1966). Special issue on Cocteau.

———. "Cocteau." *L'Avant Scène du Cinéma* (1967): 1–56.

Brosse, Jacques. *Cocteau.* Paris: Gallimard, 1970.

Brown, Frederick. *An Impersonation of Angels.* New York: Viking Press, 1968.

Brunius, Jacques. *En marge du cinéma français.* Collection "Ombres Blanches." Paris: Arcanes, 1954.

Chanel, Pierre, and Jean Denoël, eds. *Cahiers Jean Cocteau* 4. Paris: Gallimard, 1974.

Cocteau, Jean. *Album Cocteau.* Edited by Pierre Chanel. Paris: Tchou, 1970.

———. *Art and Faith: Letters between Jacques Maritain and Jean Cocteau.* Translated by John Coleman. New York: Philosophical Library, 1948.

———. *Beauty and the Beast.* Translated by Robert Hammond. New York: NYU Press, 1970.

———. *La belle et la bête: Journal d'un film.* Paris: Janis, 1946.

———. *The Blood of a Poet.* Translated by Lily Pons. New York: Bodley Press, 1949.

———. *Le Cap de Bonne-Esperance.* Paris: Gallimard, 1967.

———. "Charlie Chaplin." *Charlot.* Le Disque Vert, 2d year, 3d series, nos. 4–5 (Paris, 1924): 48–50.

———. *Cocteau on the Film.* With André Fraigneau. New York: Dover, 1972.

———. *Diary of a Film.* Translated by Ronald Duncan. London: Dobson, 1950.

———. *The Difficulty of Being.* Translated by Elizabeth Sprigge. New York: Coward-McCann, 1967.

———. *Du cinématographe.* Edited by André Bernard and Claude Gautier. Paris: Pierre Belfond Publishers, 1973.

———. *Entretiens autour de cinématographe.* Edited by André Fraigneau. Paris: Editions André Bonée, 1951.

———. "Le Grand Seize." *St. Cinéma des Près* 1 (1949): 7.

———. *The Hand of a Stranger.* Translated by Alec Brown. London: Elek Books, 1956.

———. *The Holy Terrors.* Translated by Rosamond Lehmann. New York: New Directions, 1957.

———. *The Infernal Machine and Other Plays.* Translated by Albert Bermel. New York: New Directions, 1963.

———. "Je crois à l'invasion . . ." In *L'art du cinéma,* edited by Pierre Lherminier, pp. 532–36. Paris: Editions Seghers, 1960.

———. *Journals of Jean Cocteau.* Translated and edited by Wallace Fowlie. Bloomington: Indiana University Press, 1956.

———. "A Letter." *Film Culture* 41 (1966): 38.

———. *My Contemporaries.* Edited by Margaret Crosland. Philadelphia: Chilton Book Co., 1968.

———. "Notes de travail." *La Revue de Cinéma* 7 (Summer 1947): 3–5.

———. *Opéra.* Paris: Stock, 1927.

———. *Opéra, suivi de des mots de mon style.* Paris: Tchou, 1967.

———. *Opium: Diary of a Cure.* Translated by Margaret Crosland and Sinclair Rond. New York: Grove Press, 1958.

———. *Orphée.* Paris: Editions de la Parade, 1950.

———. *Les parents terribles.* Paris: Gallimard, 1938.

———. *Paris Album, 1900–1914.* Translated by Margaret Crosland. London: W. H. Allen, 1956.

———. "Portraits-Souvenirs." *Le Figaro,* 19 January–11 May 1935.

———. Preface to *La cuisine est un jeu d'enfants,* by Michel Oliver. Paris: Plon, 1963.

———. *Professional Secrets.* Edited by Robert Phelps. New York: Farrar, Straus, and Giroux, 1970.

———. *Le sang d'un poète.* Paris: Editions Marin, 1948.

———. "Sur le Cinéma." *St. Cinéma des Près* 2 (1950): 11.

———. *Thomas the Imposter.* Translated by Dorothy Williams. London: Peter Owen, 1957.

———. *Three Screenplays.* Translated by Carol Martin-Sperry. New York: Grossman Publishers, 1972.

———. *Two Screenplays.* Translated by Carol Martin-Sperry. New York: Orion Press, 1968.

———. *The White Paper.* Paris: Paul Morithien, n.d.

Crosland, Margaret. *Cocteau.* New York: Alfred A. Knopf, 1956.

Crowson, Lydia. *The Esthetic of Jean Cocteau.* Hanover, N.H.: University Press of New England, 1978.

De Nitto, Herman. "Beauty and the Beast: Cocteau." In *Film and the Critical Eye,* pp. 203–42. New York: Macmillan Co., 1975.

Denoël, Jean, ed. *Cahiers Jean Cocteau* 1–3. Paris: Gallimard, 1971–73.

Diserens, Jean-Claude. *Orphée.* Fiche Filmographique 95. Paris: Institut des Hautes Études Cinématographiques, 1975.

Domarchi, Jean, and Jean-Louis Langier. "Entretien avec Jean Cocteau." *Cahiers du Cinéma* 109 (July 1960): 1–20.

Evans, Arthur B. *Jean Cocteau and His Films of Orphic Identity.* Philadelphia: Art Alliance Press, 1977.

Fowlie, Wallace. *Jean Cocteau: History of a Poet's Age.* Bloomington: Indiana University Press, 1977.

Gauteur, Claud. "Jean Cocteau et le cinéma." *Image et Son* 262 (June–July 1972): 3–42.

Gilson, René. *Jean Cocteau: An Investigation into His Films and Philosophy.* Translated by Ciba Vaughn. New York: Crown Publishers, 1969.

Hammond, Robert M. "The Mysteries of Cocteau's *Orpheus.*" *Cinema Journal* 2 (Spring 1972): 26–33.

Hanlon, Lindley. "Cocteau, Cauchemar, and the Cinema." Unpublihsed manuscript, Brooklyn College, New York, n.d.

Houston, Penelope. "La belle et la bête." *Sequence* 3 (Spring 1948): 28–30.

Koch, Stephen. "Cocteau." *Midway* (Winter 1968): 120–27.

Lambert, Gavin. "Cocteau and Orpheus." *Sequence* 12 (Autumn 1950): 20–32.

Leprohon, Pierre. "Jean Cocteau." In *Présences contemporaines cinéma,* pp. 388–404. Paris: Nouvelles Éditions Debresse, 1957.

Marker, Chris. "L'avant-garde française: *Entr'acte, Un chien andalou, Le sang d'un poète.*" In *Regards neufs sur le cinéma,* edited by Jacques Chevallier, pp. 249–55. Paris: Éditions du Seuil, 1953.

Oxenhandler, Neal. "Poetry in Three Films of Jean Cocteau." *Yale French Studies* 17 (1956): 14–20.

———. *Scandal and Parade.* New Brunswick, N.J.: Rutgers University Press, 1957.

Pillandin, Roger. *Jean Cocteau tourne son dernier film.* Paris: La Table Ronde, 1960.

Raynes, Tony. "Unreal Realism: Cyphers of the Poet." *Cinema* 8 (1971): 3–5.

Renand, Tristan. "Jean Cocteau." *Cinéma 73* 182 (December 1973): 24–26.

Sprigge, Elizabeth, and Jean-Jacques Kihm. *Jean Cocteau: The Man and the Mirror.* New York: Coward-McCann, 1968.

Steegmuller, Francis. *Cocteau: A Biography.* Boston: Little, Brown and Co.,

1970.

Stenhouse, Charles. "La rêve du poète." *Close Up* 2 (June 1931): 134–35. Republished by Arno Press, New York, 1971.

Tournier, Jacques. *La belle et la bête.* Fiche Filmographique 6. Paris: Institut des Hautes Etudes Cinématographiques, n.d.

Wallis, Charles Glenn. "Le sang d'un poète." In *Art in Cinema,* edited by Frank Stauffacher, pp. 73–86. San Francisco: San Francisco Museum of Art, 1947.

Cornell

Ashton, Dore. *A Joseph Cornell Album.* New York: Viking Press, 1974.

Ballatone, Sandy. "Joseph Cornell's Collages." *Artweek* 13 (March 1976): 1–16.

Brakhage, Stan. Lecture. School of the Art Institute of Chicago. Spring 1972. On tape.

Joseph Cornell: Collages, 1931–1972. New York: Castelli-Feigen-Corcoran Galleries, 1978.

Cornell, Joseph. "Enchanted Wanderer—Excerpt from a Journey Album for Hedy Lamarr." In *The Shadow and Its Shadow,* edited by Paul Hammond, pp. 129–30. London: British Film Institute, 1978.

———. "Monsieur Phot." In *The Avant-Garde Film: A Reader of Theory and Criticism,* edited by P. Adams Sitney, pp. 51–59. New York: NYU Press, 1978.

———. "The Theater of Hans Christian Andersen." *Dance Index* 9 (September 1945): 139, 155–59. Reprinted in Sandra Leonard Starr, *Joseph Cornell and the Ballet,* pp. 42–44. New York: Castelli-Feigen-Corcoran, 1983.

———. Collection of Letters and Papers. Archives of American Art, Smithsonian Institution, Washington, D.C., and New York. Microfilm.

———. File compiled by Sean Licka. Anthology Film Archives, New York.

Hartigan, Lynda Roscoe. "Joseph Cornell: A Biography." In *Joseph Cornell,* edited by Kynaston McShine, pp. 91–119. New York: Museum of Modern Art, 1980.

Hussy, Howard. "Excerpts from Howard Hussy's Memoirs of Joseph Cornell." *Parenthèse* 3 (1975): 153–62.

———. "Joseph Cornell (Towards a Memoir)." *Prose* 9 (Fall 1974): 73–86.

McShine, Kynaston, ed. *Joseph Cornell.* New York: Museum of Modern Art, 1980. Includes "Joseph Cornell: Mechanic of the Ineffable," by Carter Ratcliff; "The Cinematic Gaze of Joseph Cornell," by P. Adams Sitney; and "Joseph Cornell: A Biography," by Lynda Roscoe Hartigan.

Mekas, Jonas. "Notes on Films of Joseph Cornell." *Joseph Cornell Portfolio.* New York: Castelli-Feigen-Corcoran Galleries, 1976.

Meyers, John. "Cornell's *Erreur d'âme.*" In *Joseph Cornell.* New York: ACA Galleries, 1975.

Michelson, Annette. "Rose Hobart and Monsieur Phot: Early Films from

Utopia Parkway." *Artforum* 10 (June 1973): 47–57.

Ratcliff, Carter. "Joseph Cornell: Mechanic of the Ineffable." In *Joseph Cornell,* edited by Kyneston McShine, pp. 43–67. New York: Museum of Modern Art, 1980.

Sitney, P. Adams. "The Cinematic Gaze of Joseph Cornell." In *Joseph Cornell,* edited by Kynaston McShine, pp. 69–89. New York: Museum of Modern Art, 1980.

Waldman, Diane. *Joseph Cornell.* New York: Solomon R. Guggenheim Foundation, 1967.

———. *Joseph Cornell.* New York: George Braziller Pub., 1977.

Brakhage

Arthur, Paul. "The Brakhage Lectures–A Review." *Film Comment* 1 (January–February 1973): 64–65.

Barrett, Gerald, and Wendy Brabner. *Stan Brakhage: A Guide to References and Resources.* Boston: G. K. Hall, 1983.

Brakhage, Stan. *Film Biographies.* Berkeley Calif.: Turtle Island Press, 1977.

———. "A Letter." *Scenario* 8 (November–December 1961): 17–18.

———. "Letter to Ronna Page (On Music)." In *The Avant-Garde Film: A Reader of Theory and Criticism,* edited by P. Adams Sitney, pp. 134–39. New York: NYU Press, 1978.

———. *Metaphors on Vision.* New York: Film Culture, 1963.

———. "The Silent Sount Sense." *Film Culture* 21 (Summer 1960): 65–67.

———. "Some Remarks." *Take One* 1 (September–October 1971): 6–9.

———. "Stan Brakhage Letters." *Film Culture* 40 (1966): 72–77.

———. "Stan Brakhage Seminar." *Dialogue on Film* 3 (January 1973):2–11.

———. Descriptions of films. *Filmmakers' Cooperative Catalogue No. 6,* pp. 29–33. New York, 1975.

———. File. Anthology Film Archives, New York.

Camper, Fred. "Seminar on Stan Brakhage Taught by P. Adams Sitney." Unpublished manuscript, New York University, Spring 1974.

———. "Stan Brakhage: A Retrospective." Los Angeles: Los Angeles International Film Exposition, 1976.

Cohen, Phoebe. "Scenes from under Childhood." *Artforum* 5 (January 1973): 51–55.

Davenport, Guy. "Two Essays on Brakhage and His *Songs.*" *Film Culture* 40 (Spring 1966): 9–12.

Glassmire, Charles. "Anticipating Brakhage." *Projections* 1 (February 1973): 7–10.

Grossinger, Richard, ed. "Interview with Stan Brakhage." *Earth Geography/Io* 3 (Summer 1972): 353–63. Reprinted in *Brakhage Scrapbook,* edited by Robert Haller, pp. 190–200. New Paltz, N.Y.: Documentext, 1982.

Hill, Jerome. "Brakhage and Rilke." *Film Culture* 37 (1965): 13–14.

Kelman, Ken. "Perspective Reperceived." In *The Essential Cinema*, edited by P. Adams Sitney. New York: Anthology Film Archives and NYU Press, 1975.

Michelson, Annette. "Camera Lucida/Camera Obscura." *Artforum* 5 (January 1973): 30–37.

———. "Camera Obscura: The Cinema of Stan Brakhage." *New Forms in Film* (1974).

Nesthus, Marie. "The Influence of Olivier Messiaen on the Visual Art of Stan Brakhage." *Film Culture* 63–64 (1977): 39–51, 179–81.

Robinson, David. "The Brakhage Lectures: A Review." *Sight and Sound* 4 (Fall 1972): 236.

Sharrett, Christopher. "Brakhage's Dreamscape." *Millennium Film Journal* 6 (Spring 1980): 43–50.

Sitney, P. Adams. "Autobiography in the Avant-Garde Film." In *The Avant-Garde Film: A Reader in Theory and Criticism*, edited by P. Adams Sitney, pp. 199–247. New York: NYU Press, 1978.

———. "Stan Brakhage." In *The American Independent Film*. Boston: Boston Museum of Fine Arts, 1971.

Sutherland, Donald. "A Note on Stan Brakhage." *Film Culture* 24 (1962): 84–85.

Varela, Willie. "Excerpts from a Conversation with Stan Brakhage." *Canyon Cinemanews* 77 (January/February 1977): 4–8.

Whitehall, Richard. "Brakhage Sees the World Hypnogogically." *Los Angeles Free Press* (February 1967).

INDEX